Three Corners

Exploring Marriage and the Self

Stephen R. Marks
University of Maine, Orono

Lexington Books
D.C. Heath and Company/Lexington, Massachusetts/Toronto

Soc
HQ
728
M28
1986

ROBERT MANNING
STROZIE   ?Y.

MAR 12 1986

Tallahassee, Florida

Library of Congress Cataloging-in-Publication Data

Marks, Stephen R.
   Three corners

     Bibliography: p.
     Includes index.
     1. Marriage. 2. Family life surveys—United States. 3. Married people—United
States—Psychology. I. Title.
HQ728.M28   1986   306.8′ 1   85-23077
ISBN 0-669-11769-2 (alk. paper)
ISBN 0-669-11768-4 (pbk. : alk. paper)

Copyright © 1986 by D.C. Heath and Company

All rights reserved. No part of this publication may be reproduced or transmitted in any form
or by any means, electronic or mechanical, including photocopy, recording, or any
information storage or retrieval system, without permission in writing from the publisher.

Published simultaneously in Canada
Printed in the United States of America
Casebound International Standard Book Number: 0-669-11769-2
Paperbound International Standard Book Number: 0-669-11768-4
Library of Congress Catalog Card Number: 85-23077

The paper used in this publication meets the minimum requirements of American National
Standard for Information Sciences—Permanence of Paper for Printed Library Materials,
ANSI Z39.48-1984.

*To Joan Marks, whose three corners mingle
so delicately with mine.*

Contents

Tables and Figures   viii

Preface and Acknowledgments   ix

1. **Introduction**   1

 The Theory of Triangles   2
 Gender Differences in the Shaping of the Inner-Corner   4
 The Plan of the Book   6

Part I   Marital Statics   9

2. **The Forming of the Inner-Corner**   11

 Marital Socialization   11
 Marital Paradigms   13
 First-Corner Issues   17
 Second-Corner Issues   21
 Third-Corner Issues   35

3. **Marriage Agendas**   49

 Avoiding the Demon   50
 Safe Return Home   55
 Religious Calling   58
 Economic Calling   61
 For the Children   65
 Safe Haven   70
 Hedged Bet   76
 Open Agendas   82

vi • *Three Corners*

Part II Marital Dynamics and Development 89

4. Introduction to Marital Dynamics 91

Paradigm Conflict and Paradigm Consensus 92
Agenda Clashes 95
Varieties of Marital Dynamics 98

5. Romantic Fusion 101

A Case Study 101
The Origin of Marital Disturbances and the Demise
  of Romantic Fusion 105

6. Dependency-Distancing 109

Marital Paradigms and the Management of Disturbances 114
Marital Disturbances and the Problem of Fusion 115
Female Fusion and Male Distancing: The Vicious Circle 120

7. Marital Separateness 129

Comfortable Separateness and Development-Free Marriage 136
The Balance between Comfort and Disturbance 147
Joint Triangulation as Separateness 150

Part III The Dynamics of Marital Connection 157

8. Balanced Connection 159

9. Couple-Centered Connection 169

From Separateness to Connection: The Carters 169
Couple-Centered Connection and Marriage Encounter 178

10. Family-Centered Connection 183

The Turners 183
Family-Centeredness as a Duty: The Jacobs 187
Independent Third-Corners in Marital Connection: The Murrays 191
The Inner-Corner in Marital Connection 195

11. Loose Connection 199

The Jordans 200
The Kings 204
Asymmetry in Marital Connection 210

12. Connection Undone 213

The Sampsons 213
Summary of Part III 216

Part IV Processes of Marital Exchange 219

13. Marital Growth and Its Obstacles 221

The Appropriation Process 221
The Myth of the Perfect Companion 224
The Foreclosure Process 225
The Challenge Process 228
Gender and Marital Exchange 229
The Impact of Patriarchy on Marital Exchange 233

14. The Feminist Challenge to Patriarchy 239

Appendix The Respondents, the Interviews, and the History
of the Project 243

Bibliography 253

Index 255

About the Author 261

Tables and Figures

Tables

1. Length of Marriage by Percentage of Couples   244
2. Educational Level of Respondents   244

Figures

1. A Partnership Diagram   99
2. Romantic Fusion   102
3. Dependency-Distancing   111
4. Separateness   130
5. Joint Triangulation As Separateness   154
6. Balanced Connection   166
7. Couple-Centered Connection   177
8. Family-Centered Connection   186
9. Loose Connection   200

Preface and Acknowledgments

What I thought would be a neatly contained little two-year project somehow swelled into a six-year-plus enterprise. I should have known better. I never do anything quickly, and I rarely have much of an idea of what the outcome will be until the work is nearly done. *Three Corners* was no exception. It took over two years alone to interview 129 people, as virtually all the joy and the travail of data collection were my own. I have never understood why researchers would want to farm out open-ended interviewing to anyone else. Perhaps with deductive studies using forced-choice interview schedules, gathering the data is so boring that doing it oneself becomes unbearable. Or perhaps deductive workers feel that objectivity means keeping as much distance as possible between themselves and their "subjects," as in double-blind experiments.

Three Corners is squarely out of the inductive, exploratory tradition of social science. My goal is to teach the reader about intimate partnership in the same way that I learned about it, moving back and forth between preliminary statement of a principle, case illustration, further refinement of the principle, and so forth. I had no specific hypotheses to test, and no fixed notion of the particular focus of each interview. As explained in the appendix, the questions I asked were all geared to one purpose: to provide my respondents just enough structure to recount their experience of marriage, starting with their memories of their parents and proceeding through their own marital history. This kind of research thrives on considerable intimacy between interviewer and respondent. It requires an eagerness to leap over the "stranger" barrier and make contact with the whole person, summoning one's full intuitive faculties to lead the respondent in whatever direction will be most meaningful. The strategy here is to hone the very subjectivity that is seen in other research as an obstacle to valid findings.

Once the interview phase was completed, I developed a coding operation to help me find things in my data file, which now consisted of over 2,500 pages of typed transcripts. Again I should have known better. I had to pore over at least forty of the 129 respondents' transcripts to arrive at code categories

that seemed usable, and this took a long time. While five coders then devoted a year to coding the transcribed data, I continued to read transcripts and take notes. By the time the coders finished, my own emerging interests in my data had shifted far away from the categories of information they had been coding. I now had a computerized data file that had become partly obsolete even before I had had a chance to use it. This was the period when I could be seen going around muttering, "Qualitative research is not for wimps."

In retrospect, I now realize that these middle two years were not for naught. Reading transcripts over and over again, eventually I became so familiar with them that all I needed was to scan my list of 129 respondents, and I could easily pick out the names of those who had provided information about virtually any topic I wanted to explore. The most important sorting, coding, and storing had thus occurred in my own brain, and this was the "computer" on which I most depended during the two-year-plus formal writing phase, whenever I had to come up with some really engaging case material to bring alive a particular theme.

Three Corners is designed for a variety of audiences. Above all, it is designed to provide anyone with a keener sense of the dynamics of intimacy. It is not the last word on the subject, but it should reward the general reader with some surprising insights about the pushes and pulls in long-term partnerships. The book is written with the barest minimum of technical language, and no special training or background are required to master the contents.

In academia, instructors and students of marriage and the family will find in *Three Corners*, first, a serious attempt to link up the experiences that people have in a marriage with their experiences in their family of origin. Second, I hope they will find the most theoretically coherent and comprehensive treatment of marital dynamics that has so far been developed, joining together "resource theory," Murray Bowen's "family systems" approach, and Dorothy Dinnerstein's and Nancy Chodorow's developmental perspectives. Third, they will welcome a treatment of marital vitality in part III that lays to rest the unfortunate notion that "intrinsic marriages" are all the same.

Instructors and students of human development, adult development, the life span, the life course, and adult socialization will find in *Three Corners* an attempt to demonstrate how fundamental human capacities—most notably bonding and individuation—develop over the life course, first in the family of origin and then in one or more marriage or marriage-like relationships.

Instructors and students of the self, whether from out of a sociological, psychological, or some other tradition, should also find some good use for this book. The unique approach to the self as a dynamic, three-cornered arrangement sees it both as an objective process, reaching out to various "outside" interests that in part define it, and a subjective center, brimming with impulses, urgings, strivings, and yearnings that spring from within. Different marriages give rise to different organizations of the self, and these are graphically explored.

Instructors and students of gender or sex roles should find in *Three Corners* a consistent attempt to show how cultural concepts of masculinity and femininity find their way into married life. Again following the leads of Dinnerstein and Chodorow, I show how gender identities are amongst the most important components of the self's inner-corner, profoundly affecting our approach to both the other corners.

Finally, I hope that those interested in women's studies will find much use for this book. In fundamental respects it has a feminist thrust in its research methods, its mode of analysis, its manner of presentation, and its conclusions. Especially in part IV but elsewhere as well, case studies show how patriarchy is inimical to female and male growth in marriage, creating an unbalanced structure of the self for both spouses, though in different ways. Some of the cases criticize patriarchy simply by transcending it. Particularly in part III, the reader will encounter couples who teach by their various examples that there is more than one way to skin the patriarchal cat.

Outside of academia, *Three Corners* should appeal to marriage counselors and other mental health practitioners. It will provide them with a broader understanding of "baseline" married life, since the data were drawn from a nonclinical sample of couples who were not undergoing any exceptional crisis. It will also offer them some conceptual tools that should prove useful in sorting out their clients' general marital constructs. In my view, these constructs (here called "marital paradigms" and "marriage agendas") are no less important than the actual marital struggles that clients like to recount. Finally, *Three Corners* should help dissuade mental health professionals from the curious idea that increased marital harmony is always played out through virtuoso performances in the art of communication. Frank disclosure of real feelings may of course help, but so can other interventions in the three corners of a married person, and practitioners will welcome a better knowledge of the different areas to which they can direct their efforts. I hope they will then repay the favor by directing their clients to this book.

Acknowledgments

It would be impossible to acknowledge all the people who have helped me with this project, but I can easily skim the cream off the top. First, I am grateful to the University of Maine's Faculty Research Funds Committee, who believed enough in my project to fund me on two occasions. Second, the 129 people who agreed to be interviewed taught me more than they will ever know. They gave generously of their time, and they willingly shared some of their most tender experiences for a few hours. I hope they will find some value in what I have written. To protect their identities I have created fictitious names, and, except in the case of couples who explicitly did not care, I have often falsified other identifying characteristics such as occupation.

xii • *Three Corners*

The transcribing of 129 taped interviews was all done by Perien Gray. Her skill and speed at this task were truly unbelievable. Her work was far more than mechanical, as she had the editorial license to free the transcript pages of "uh"s, "mm"s, utter repetitions, nonsequiturs, and other nonessentials. Her deep interest and involvement throughout this early phase of the research were very important to me. The coding of most of these transcripts was entrusted to five crafty Work Study students, Joan Murdock, Mathew Day, Cathy Begin, Bob Cicogna, and Lynn Eaton. I thank them all for their enthusiasm and encouragement.

Everyone should have a secretary like Sue McLaughlin. She can read the unreadable, turn what is wrong into right, and type it almost as fast as a speeding bullet. She has been most supportive in every way. I am grateful to Carol Nichols for her professional enthusiasm about my figure designs and for expertly turning them into the camera-ready art that appears in the book. I shall be forever indebted to my dear friend and fellow traveler Jim Spates for alerting me to the work of Dorothy Dinnerstein, and also to Ken Edelston, who first brought the work of Murray Bowen to my attention. And I thank Eva Meyn, Julie Watkins, and Ralph LaRossa for support and kindness at various phases of the project.

Prepublication drafts of the manuscript were read by Lila Balch, Cleo Berkun, Jim Gallagher, Bob Milardo, Bethany Spangelo, Martha Spruce, and Ira Weissman, and portions of drafts by Annette Cole, Carol Godfrey, and Kyriacos Markides. These people not only gave generously of their time but often provided warm friendship, useful criticisms, thoughtful commentary, and above all else, enthusiasm. I am also grateful to my editor at Lexington Books, Margaret Zusky, who told me she knows a good thing when she sees one. I hope she is right.

I would like especially to thank Doug Cowan, George Flink, and Ira Weissman for their loving support. Over these years they have never failed to be there for me, listening to my tales of woe all those times I got stuck, and reveling with me in my triumphs when things were rolling merrily along.

My parents, Golda and Meyer Marks, my sister, Linda Marks, and my parents-in-law, Ellen and Fred Kallos, have all been a most wonderful cheering section, always eager to applaud me for any little step of forward progress. My children, Peter and Andy, surely got a raw deal when their father took on this project. They know too well how a book can become a consuming third-corner, but they have typically put up with it in good humor and with loving interest. And my wife Joan Marks—partner, lover, astute critic, good witch, and dearest friend, to whom this book is dedicated, has walked the entire length of this path with me, remaining strong enough to keep it from pulling her off her own course, and devoted enough to stay nearby even at those times when I was too busy running in every direction to see her.

1
Introduction

> We are designed to grow and be strengthened by every event, no matter how mundane or awesome. The flow of nature and seasons, people, extreme contrasts, apparent catastrophes, pleasantries—all are experiences of interaction to be enjoyed and opportunities for learning. . . . With what is human intelligence designed to interact? With anything and everything possible. If there is anything intelligence cannot interact with, that intelligence is to that extent crippled. A fully developed intelligence is one designed to exchange energies with anything existing, without ever being overwhelmed.[1]

I begin with this quote from a favorite modern thinker, Joseph Pearce, whose vision informs much of this book. Any marriage partner provides us with numberless events, most of them mundane, a few of them awesome, to repeat Pearce's words. How do we approach these marital events? Do we do so in a manner "designed to exchange energies" with our partners? If we did so, we would indeed "grow and be strengtehened by" every such interaction. The problem is that Pearce's vision would presuppose that we come to each marital episode already knowing fully how to interact, when in fact many of us became retarded in that life-giving capacity long before we ever met our current partner.

When I began this study, I hoped to find many marriages that could illustrate a vigorous exchange of energies, energies of the kind that coax each partner to periodically dismantle narrow self-boundaries for the sake of creatively integrating the other partner's world. I did hear some impressive growth stories, and these will be noted in the pages that follow. I did not, however, hear them very often, and when I did so, the growth most often occurred in one or two upheavals and then quickly subsided. If marital growth spurts are like the flooding of a river basin, annually bringing life-giving nutrients to the depleted terrain, then even those couples who enjoy them must typically endure subsequent dry spells often lasting far longer than a year. For some couples I could not identify any marital growth or change at all that was significant to them, if not to me. In some cases they grew or were strengthened only by interaction with events outside the marriage; in other cases all of life seemed to be business-as-usual, a set of investments in things-as-they-are without any new interaction with anything.

2 • *Three Corners*

I quickly discovered that I would need to scale down my quest for spectacular growth to plain old ordinary growth. If many people come to marriage already partially crippled in their ability to interact, perhaps some important gains in that capacity can nevertheless be made, and I wanted to be able to recognize growth at whatever level it is occurring. Pearce says that growth can occur "only by interacting with new phenomena, that is, by moving from that which is known into that which is not known."[2] I take this perspective as my point of departure. In any marriage, we have the possibility of moving from what is known of our partner to that which is not known. We frequently come face-to-face with tendencies and actions that are new, unexpected, surprising, unwanted or, in a word, alien. In marital growth we engage this unknown, alien stuff through vigorous interaction with it, and this process is as often painful as it is joyful because it entails a kind of death and rebirth. We bury our old boundaries of being with another person when we open enough to let more of that person be born in ourselves.

Covering fifty-seven couples and fifteen recently divorced persons, this book gives their accounts of their experiences as married people. It concerns both their struggles for growth and their resistance to it, their dealings with new or alien material in their partners and their retreats into the safety of the old. Most often I shall let them speak for themselves. Not having observed their actual marriages, I can only report their own accounts of their marital experiences. Fundamentally, this study is exploratory. Using Pearce's model as a general guide, it simply asks, when do people in a long-term marriage grow and when do they not? And whether or not growth occurs, how does a marriage develop over a long period of time?

The Theory of Triangles

Aside from Pearce's guiding vision, several other intellectual tools have shaped this study. My previous theoretical work on human energy, and on how people manage their multiple and often competing interests, taught me to think in terms of systems.[9] Specifically, I learned that the amount and quality of energy that people have for an interest such as a spouse has much to do with how they evaluate that interest in relation to their other interests, such as a job. Already I was dealing with triangular structures: the striving self on one corner of the triangle, the spouse on the second corner, and the job or some other pressing commitment on the third corner. But it took the work of family therapist Murray Bowen to fully alert me to the significance of triangles in the organization of emotional energy.

Bowen discovered that a close twosome in a family is never an island in itself but is continually affected by other family members who are linked to it as the third corner of a triangle. Not the twosome alone but the triangle is

Introduction • 3

thus "the smallest stable relationship system." Bowen adds that "the emotional forces within the triangle are constantly in motion from moment to moment, even in periods of calm.'⁹ A family is thus seen as a series of interlocking triangles within which spouses are embedded, and the emotional dynamics between spouses are continually fed by, and feed back on, the emotional play of each spouse with every other member of the family.

For Bowen it is inevitable that spouses and other close twosomes will betray each other's emotional needs from time to time. Attempts at confrontation may escalate the ensuing tension rather than relieve it. As tensions and anxieties begin to mount, one or both partners will seek to ease the discomfort by intensifying their connection with various other family members, near or distant. If no family members are available for such triangling moves, a friend or lover or other outsider will do just as well.

While Bowen's work provides the foundation for the theory of marital dynamics to be developed here, my conception of the marital triangle differs significantly from his. Bowen sees spouses as forming two of the three corners of a single triangle, the third corner being the various persons triangled in by the less comfortable of the twosome. In my framework, *each* partner is a triangle, so that a couple is always a pair of interacting triangles—two sets of three corners mingling together—even when they live alone as a twosome. As we shall see, this framework will capture more of the psychosocial complexity of partnerships, as it focuses both on the self in developmental process and on the structures that two selves produce as an ongoing relationship. Put simply, I am offering both a theory of the self and a theory of marriage.

Each partner's triangle is an organization of three points of reference. As a married person, my first corner is my *inner self.* It is "inner" in that it consists of my own private drama, my internal dialogue, and my chatter of thoughts, impulses, and images as well as the flux of feelings that rise and fall to punctuate my mental chatter. My inner-corner is also a focus. That is, my internal dialogue does not dramatize all of my ongoing experience but settles only on that which is of signal importance to me, letting everything else slide by. Finally, my inner-corner is an energy center, creating intensity around the objects of my focus. The very act of focussing is a concentrating and coalescing of energy.

If the first-corner represents my innermost angle, then the other two corners represent two different outward expansions of my personal space. The second-corner is my *primary partnership*—in this analysis, a spouse, though the model can apply to other intimate relationships too, such as close friends who are primary partners to each other. My partnership is that corner in which I coordinate with another person's movements, space, and general existence. The more I dwell in this corner, the more I take account of my partner's presumed needs, demands, moods, whereabouts, and emotional states. This accounting may be positive and loving, but it may also become defensive

and downright hostile. In either case, having a primary partner requires my continual coordination if only through constant acts of attention.

The *third-corner* consists of any other important focal point of my personal world. In Bowen's analysis, the third-corner always seems to be another person, such as a child, parent, sibling, or other relative, or a friend or lover, or even a mental health professional, if no one else is available. Here I shall further extend the analysis to include important third *interests,* such as a job or career, volunteer activity, hobby or recreational pursuit, God, or some spiritual quest. Insofar as people have an ongoing emotional investment in any such interest, it will enter into their emotional dynamics with their primary partners, who must then compete with it if they wish more time and attention given to the twosome, or at the very least they must in some way coordinate with it. Again following Bowen, when tensions mount in a twosome, one or both partners will seek to relieve the discomfort by intensifying their interaction with their third-corners. Even in the absence of any escalation of tensions, however, each partner always has a variety of third-corner involvements, with the ebb and flow of emotional energy among these involvements ever shifting along with the emotional dynamics of the twosome.

I use the term *triangulation* or *triangling* to refer to primary partners' involvement in their third-corners. As we shall see, triangulation is the mover and shaker of all marital dynamics. Like it or not, both spouses are interacting not simply with their partner but with their partner's third-corners. The various third-corners are an ongoing part of the relationship and are not outside it. Depending on the circumstances, the spouses' convergence of triangling moves may calm down a relationship to a level of cool complacency, or bring new energy into it, or heat it to the boiling point, or drive the couple far apart and then determine whether they feel sorry or glad about the situation.

Gender Differences in the Shaping of the Inner-Corner

Along with this theory of triangles, my analysis is profoundly influenced by the works of Dorothy Dinnerstein and Nancy Chodorow.[5] Both writers focus on the forming of some crucial tendencies of human character, tendencies of the sort that eventually guide males and females in their different approaches to intimate partnership and to adult life in general.

In Chodorow's analysis, becoming a female is relatively nonproblematic, straightforward, and uncomplicated, compared to becoming a male. The girl–child discovers that her earliest model—her mother, the person with whom she has had abundant, intimate contact—is someone like herself, a female. She need not renounce her mother's qualities as her own qualities, at least during her childhood. Indeed, her status as a female will be secure if she

Introduction • 5

stays identified with her mother, who in turn makes this connection easier by seeing her daughter as a miniature version of herself. No insecurities of gender identity thus push the girl into individuating or separating from her mother.

The boy–child, in contrast, discovers that his earliest model—with whom he has had the same abundant contact—is, as a female, someone unlike himself. Originally identifying with her qualities, the only qualities regularly available to him, he must soon renounce them for himself in order to become male, once he sees that "female" is regarded by those around him as quite different than "male." Thus he comes to renounce his identification with his mother, who innocently makes it easier for him to do so by treating him more as a "male opposite" than as a miniature version of herself. Strong uncertainties and insecurities of gender therefore push the boy into making some bold steps toward differentiating, individuating, and separating from his mother.[6]

In both Chodorow's and Dinnerstein's analyses, female-governed primary child-care produces male and female sensibilities that are rather alien to each other. (The same consequence would, of course, follow from male-governed primary care, only the gender issues would be reversed.) Females emerge from their youth with a strong, emotionally nurturant capacity and a need to merge with a partner in a way that recaptures and continues their primary bond with their mother. Males emerge with a repressed affective capacity and a strong need to prove themselves as separate and independent, particularly from that female fusion that antedated and appeared to forestall their self-identification as males.

Under these conditions marriage can well threaten both spouses with their respective versions of ultimate self-annihilation. For a husband, the warm, nurturing stuff that marriage conjures up can easily feel like the earlier connective dependency that he has worked hard to outdistance in order to find himself as a male; for a wife, her husband's elusive emotional presence and his apparent determination to carve out a private existence that often excludes her can easily feel like a destruction of the very relational setting she requires to confirm her own being in the world. His craving to separate spells her self-invisibility; her craving to bond spells his annihilation as a male.

Chodorow's and Dinnerstein's works are essential to my own project because the gender differences to which they call attention keep on surfacing as marital issues for the majority of my respondents. It soon became obvious that these different gender emphases—males on individuating and females on bonding—bear much on how husbands and wives project their entire three-cornered arrangement of personal space into a marriage. Even before any marriage, however, specific inclinations toward individuating and bonding become two of the most important components of anyone's inner self, male or female, despite their different emphases. All people need skills both in being

6 • *Three Corners*

separate and in functioning intimately with others. People with good facility in both capacities tend to create "connected" marriages, which I shall define and document later. We shall see that such people are well equipped to handle both a partnership-corner and a variety of third-corner interests without destructive conflicts.

On the other hand, many people, perhaps most of my respondents, do not seem to bring an even blend of bonding and individuating to their marriages. Males are often retarded in their bonding function, and then their individuating becomes compulsive, cold, and emotionally distant. Females are often retarded in their individuating function, and then their bonding becomes obsessive, dependent, and emotionally overdemanding. In either case an inner self that is unbalanced and lacking in equanimity will generate predictable issues in a marriage, and these can be specified as distinct triangular arrangements.

The Plan of the Book

Those readers who are uncomfortable proceeding further with this study without knowing more about its methodological makeup should now go directly to the appendix. There, I discuss the logic and procedure of my selecting two different subsamples of long-term married people, and I summarize some of their characteristics: length of marriage, religious affiliation, regional origins and moves before and during marriage, educational background, and occupational involvements, with brief contrasts with their parents. I also present the history of this research project—its twists, turns, and changes of direction. Finally, I address the issue of generalizability and conclude that while it is not scientifically defensible to generalize my findings to any known population, the exploratory purpose of this study makes that whole issue irrelevant to the task at hand. There is enough diversity among these respondents to generate a new and more theoretically comprehensive understanding of marital statics and dynamics than any the literature now offers. If I am successful, social scientists will emerge with a new basis for conceiving and testing hypotheses, and interested general readers will gain much greater insight into their own and others' developing relationships.

The text of the book is divided into four parts. In part I, I present the statics of marriage—the varied strategies and imagined scenarios that people superimpose on marriages to whittle down the unseemly contingencies and to ward off the unknown. In triangle terms, we shall see that these strategies and scenarios form much of the content and imagery of a person's inner-corner. Chapter 2 shows how people originally create these strategies long before they marry. Chapter 3 then documents how these creations may get hardened into various "marriage agendas" by the time a marriage occurs.

Part II focusses on marital dynamics and development. Chapter 4 introduces the subject and shows how dynamics are always at work regardless of how fixed and frozen a relationship may look. Chapters 5 through 7 focus successively on three different patterns of marital dynamics: romantic fusion, dependency-distancing, and separateness.

Part III explores a fourth pattern of dynamics—marital connection. Drawing intensively on case studies, I devote chapters to each of four different subtypes of connection—balanced, couple-centered, family-centered, and loose. Chapter 12 ends part III with a case illustrating that even solid lines of connection between partners are delicate enough to come undone.

Part IV explores processes of marital exchange. Chapter 13 considers three such processes—appropriation, foreclosure, and challenge—in some detail. Chapter 14 closes the book with some thoughts on the feminist impact on the three corners.

Notes

1. Joseph Pearce, *The Magical Child: Rediscovering Nature's Plan for Our Children* (New York: E.P. Dutton, 1977), p. 25.

2. Ibid., p. 12.

3. See Stephen R. Marks, "Multiple Roles and Role Strain: Some Notes on Human Energy, Time and Commitment," *American Sociological Review* 42 (1977):921–936. See also Marks's "Culture, Human Energy, and Self-Actualization: A Sociological Offering to Humanistic Psychology," *Journal of Humanistic Psychology* 19 (1979):27–42.

4. Murray Bowen, "Theory in the Practice of Psychotherapy," in *Family Therapy,* ed. Philip J. Guerin (New York: Gardner, 1976), p. 76. See also Bowen's "Toward the Differentiation of Self in One's Family of Origin," in *Family Interaction: A Dialogue between Family Researchers and Family Therapists,* ed. James Framo (New York: Springer, 1972), pp. 111–173.

5. Dorothy Dinnerstein, *The Mermaid and the Minotaur* (New York: Harper and Row, 1976); Nancy Chodorow, *The Reproduction of Mothering* (Berkeley: University of California Press, 1978).

6. Chodorow, op. cit., pp. 173–190; 213.

Part I
Marital Statics

Dear Alice,
I just sent
you my example data
with several floral
scents.

2
The Forming of the Inner-Corner

Any marriage is a chain of experience that is embedded in a still longer development of an entire life span. Too often the literature on marriage starts with the experience of courtship or marriage itself, as if the time before then is insignificant in structuring the ensuing marriage. "The marital status involves a separation from what went before," writes Joan Aldous.[1] Can this be true? Have we not learned anything prior to our courtship about how to be married? Do we not extend the past into the future at least as much as we separate from it? In fact my data suggest that for most people the important learning (and for some people the only learning) about being married has been gained long before any serious courtship. It is true that people sometimes manage to unlearn their premarital training; nevertheless, any marriage is necessarily built on the past. It is the coming together of two unfolding life-patterns that already have their own biographically shaped tendencies—tendencies that lead each partner to seek whatever materials will continue that unfolding in the most desired direction. And of all the legacies that bear upon the chosen direction of this unfolding, none is more important than a person's family of origin.

Marital Socialization

Our foremost marriage teachers are our parents, not so much through what they say as through what they do. Our earliest images and concepts about marriage are formed in reaction to them, as we watch them enjoy or struggle through their own marriages, or move in and out of them, or perhaps strive to do without marriage altogether. Their marriage is almost always the first marriage we ever witness, and most often it is the only one prior to our own that we witness pretty much as insiders. All children know more, see more, hear more, and feel more than their parents would ever dream they do. A woman speaks of her parents:

12 • *Three Corners*

My father had a good job and led a highly social life, and my mother stayed at home, because she wasn't at all that way. It led to a lot of friction. My father was involved at times with different ladies.

This was known to you and your mother?

It was known to me because of the fights I used to lay in bed and listen to them having. No other way would I have known. Maybe I was just nosy, or maybe I listened too much. At times they had terrific fights.

Another woman, Carla Dean, speaks of a growing gap between her parents, and she relates her unspoken knowledge about how her mother dealt with it:

She spent a great deal of time lying on the couch, or talking on the telephone. I can't help but feel very strongly that my mother had fantasies about some of the men she met. I'm sure neither she nor my father ever went outside of their marriage, but I even know who a couple of the men are. Mother never discussed any of her frustrations with us. Once in a while she'd cry, and she'd try to explain it, but she tried to keep the real problem from hurting us. She just found outlets in her fantasy world.

Has she ever admitted these fantasies? How do you know she had them— intuitively?

Yes, and the way that mother acted. Because I've had a couple of this type of fantasy thing during my own marriage, and I recognize it. And things she'd say, also. When you talk about somebody that you're having a fantasy about you sort of describe them in very glowing terms.

"Mother never *discussed* any of her frustrations with us," nor, presumably, her fantasies; yet her daughter Carla clearly sensed them, knew about them, and has thought about them. She may even have unwittingly copied her mother's model for dealing with frustration when, years later, she found herself likewise struggling on occasion with persistent fantasies about other men. In one such period, Carla had been married for four years. She had two small children; her husband Jerry was engrossed in his work, and she was feeling lonely and overwhelmed with the responsibilities of caring for the house and children. Carla began to go alone to a couple's group at her church:

The minister convinced me that he could help me with all my problems. He paid a lot of attention to me, and I was flattered by it, I'm sure. I asked for a pastoral call, and he made a pass at me which I repelled. But after about three days I called him up and told him I was sorry I had been rude. . . . It was about 95 percent on the telephone, and it lasted about a year. I looked

The Forming of the Inner-Corner • 13

forward to the telephone call that came usually around ten every morning, and it seemed like the bright spot of my whole day. And then I would take the kids out into the front yard in the afternoon and he would drive by and I'd chat with him.

Notice how in this account, Carla's awareness of her mother's fantasies must span a long period of time. She "recognizes" something her mother did many years ago on the basis of much later going through the same experience herself. Over and over again I heard stories demonstrating that as we make our way through a marriage, we continue to interact with our parents' model, the most important one we know. Even years into our own marriage, we still evaluate our parents and how they lived, as if we can only locate where *we* stand in relation to *them*. Here is a woman married fourteen years, describing her mother and then her parents' relationship:

> Her personality is such that she tends to play the role of the martyr and Goody Two-Shoes. Any infraction of the rules and she was ready for a lecture. . . . I never could find out what their relationship was. I still haven't figured it out. The only thing I can think of is they thrive on discord. I guess some people do! I've begun to realize that. Being away for eleven years, it was kind of nice to ignore the whole situation, and now I'm coming back and I'm getting a different perspective. She hides the candy so that he can go find it, and he's diabetic so he's not supposed to eat it, so she will lecture at him that he's not supposed to eat it, but why does she bring it in the house in the first place? That's why I think they thrive on discord.

Clearly, this woman has figured out more than she gives herself credit for, and while the parental model that she sees is not one she wishes to repeat, it is nevertheless her point of departure. Our parents neither cause nor determine our marriages, to be sure. But our experience in and around their households is already part of our unfolding life-pattern, and any later development we go through as a married person must necessarily build on that experience.

Marital Paradigms

It is useful to think of our premarital notions about married life as forming a paradigm. Thomas Kuhn writes that a scientific paradigm is a set of rules and standards for "normal" scientific practice. It specifies model types of scientific problems and their model solutions.[2] Similarly, I define a *marital paradigm* as a set of procedures for "normal" marriage practice, complete with a vision of model problems and their typical solutions. Our marital paradigm is the picture, the set of images we have formed about how marriage practice might be or seems to be done, for better or worse.

14 • *Three Corners*

Such paradigms are formed as a consequence of two kinds of experience. First, even before we learn to speak we have already become well-practiced at partnership through our own relationship with one or both parents. Childhood and adolescence are like arranged marriages insofar as we are thrust into partnerships that we have no recollection of choosing. Once embedded in these minor "marriages" to our parents, we gain some initial practice at structuring the triangular arrangement of personal space referred to earlier. That is, we attempt to preserve the integrity of our own inner-corner and its internal drama, to maintain a viable partnership-corner with one or two parents, and to carve out a variety of third-corner interests, all at the same time. Whether this first attempt goes roughly or smoothly, these early "marriages" leave us with powerful imagery, upon which we abundantly draw later when we structure our "real" marriages.

The other source of our marital paradigms, mediated to us through our parents' example with each other, was described in the previous section. Neither paradigm source—our own relationship with our parents or their marital partnership with each other—results in any final set of images. From birth on, our marital paradigms are refined, revised, or transformed in the light of whatever subsequent experience we gather. By the time we approach the age when we marry, our paradigmatic images are vigorously stamping their imprint on the kind of reality with an intimate partner that we are open to experiencing.

In order to uncover my respondents' familiar paradigms, early in the interviews I asked them a set of open-ended questions about their childhood and about their parents' marriages. I began by querying, "How do you remember your childhood," followed by, "How do you remember your parents' marriage?", questions that allowed them to express some of their images of partnership with minimal interference and predefinition from me. Whatever they said that seemed to be of significance to them, I followed up with further probing questions, inviting them to clarify it further, tell me more about the surrounding context, talk about the way they felt about it at the time, and so forth. Even when this line of questioning had produced an abundance of material, I still asked at least two more companion questions about their parents, probing their answers for still more detail: "Was there anything in your parents' marriage you were determined *not* to repeat in your own," and "Was there anything in their marriage you were *eager* to repeat in your own?"

The responses I got ran the gamut of feeling and reaction. Marital paradigms are a composite of a wide variety of images, some positive, some negative, and some neutral. Premarital life experience is rarely uniform or totally consistent, particularly in and around the home, so each person's paradigm will usually reflect this variety of elements. Nevertheless, most people either have a conscious, overall feeling about what they already know about partnership, or at least they have a tendency to attend to one or a few

The Forming of the Inner-Corner • 15

dominating elements of their familiar paradigm. Specifically, some people are inclined to embrace the paradigm, some reject the paradigm, others are not consciously aware of it and hence invariably fall into the paradigm, still others approach/avoid certain paradigm elements, and finally, some transform the paradigm. These standpoints may change in the course of a person's marital career. For example, many people who begin by rejecting key paradigmatic images find themselves falling into that pattern later on. And many who begin without conscious knowledge of any pattern wind up eventually becoming aware of it and then transforming it.

Whatever respondents could tell me about their childhood and their parents must surely be like the tip of an iceberg: the known and visible tip of course affects them, but the unseen mountain underneath may have an even more momentous impact. Of course, some respondents managed to become excellent "divers," determined to fathom more and more of the hidden territory. Others seemed to steer their awareness clear of both the tip and the drama below, and accordingly they found little to tell me. Fortunately for this study, these latter people were a tiny minority of those I interviewed.

I am soundly convinced that regardless of what people think they are doing in their marriages, the path of least resistance is to fall back into many elements of their familiar paradigms, repeating what they have already seen or done, and usually doing so without much awareness of it. As an analogy, consider embarking on winter driving trips from driveways with well-worn grooves, left in the ice and snow by those who have gone before you. You can "embrace" the grooves and try to ease your way through them. If they still work, all well and good. But your wheels may not be able to maintain their grip on the hardened ice in the groove; you may begin to skid or get stuck. You must then try to "reject" the grooves, but it often happens that the harder you try to get out of them, the more deeply you seem to fall into them; the gravity of the groove keeps on pulling you back in. It may then require some special finesse to get yourself out.

Parents cannot help but leave their imprint, and all children must to some extent negotiate the pathways forged by their parents. Indeed, it is quite striking how people often seem to select the very partners who will swiftly jerk them right back into the grooves of the familiar paradigm, despite the fact that this return may be very painful. It is as if people *want* to re-experience any pain from their earlier development that they were unable to surmount, as if, in embracing that pain still another time, they have the chance of finally transcending it.

Lyle and Kathy Remick, married for eighteen years when I interviewed them, both seemed to fall back into painful yet familiar elements of their respective paradigms, and they will provide us with an initial opportunity to see how the process works. Lyle's parents split up when he was thirteen, and he recalls his family life before then as a "stormy time. Barricaded doors, I can

16 • *Three Corners*

remember, and pounding on doors and screaming and yelling. Really quite a traumatic time." Kathy's parents remained together, but their marriage was no more enviable than Lyle's parents'. Kathy recalls "terrible scenes. At four in the morning we'd all be up crying, that kind of thing." She remembers her father as:

moody and disagreeable, a perfectionist. . . . I can remember when we were little and he'd take us for walks, and if we didn't all behave, which we never did, we were in for trouble. You could never relax around him or just be yourself. Everything was really regimented. Christmas morning we all had to get up and get dressed, line up at the head of the stairs, and come down in a certain order. Literally! Maybe he had this image of what a perfect family should be and was trying to whip us all into it, but it never worked. . . . I think he would blame me and say things were my fault. He would say negative things to me anyway. He thought I was a lot like he was, and that if he would just criticize me enough, I'd shape up and be something better.

Not surprisingly, Kathy emerged from her youth feeling that "everybody else was better than I was. I wanted somebody to love me, but I didn't think it was possible."

Whereas Kathy's father had an image of a perfect daughter, an image that Kathy always failed, Lyle came to marriage with an image of a perfect wife. "I think I fantasized about having some ideal woman who was going to be a companion," Lyle recalls:

Someone who was poetic, outdoorsy but at the same time pink, light, and feminine, like Jack London's wife. I remember a picture of her with him, and they were in this sloop, and she was in an oil slicker and he was in an oil slicker, and they were bending over, looking over a chart, and the look of equalness, of companionship, and the capability and femininity at the same time, and the complete mating of male and female but also a real genuine friend type relationship in the world of the outdoors. That struck me very much, and I thought Kathy was like that. . . . I have always been capable of using my imagination to create the world as I want it to be. I think I did bring in preconceptions to the marriage. I look at a person and I see something, and that doesn't mean that it's there. I probably did that with my wife; I probably envisioned her as being what I wanted her to be.

The stage is thus set. Lyle retreats from his uncomfortable everyday life and his mistrust of marriage into the fantasy of the perfect female companion; Kathy yearns for someone to love her as she is, but she feels destined to fail at marriage because who she is has always seemed defective. Together, they hook each other right into the most painful grooves of their familiar paradigms. Kathy tells the story of their meeting:

The Forming of the Inner-Corner • 17

I can remember the first time I saw Lyle, and it's very interesting. We worked at American Airlines. I was sitting in the lunchroom one day. Lyle came in and I noticed him, and he had a very unhappy look on his face, and he was very intriguing to me. Physically, he fit my image of what I liked in a man, but it was mainly this expression in his face that appealed to me, and I feel now it was at a preconscious level. My father was never happy, and I could never do anything to make him happy; there's a chance for me to try again. Maybe if he'd come in with a sunny smile on his face, I wouldn't have found him so appealing.

In the ensuing eighteen years, Kathy once more fails at making the man in her life happy, and Lyle finds that the reality of married life repeatedly fails to measure up to his fantasy of it. They quickly fall back into the "terrible scenes" that both recall in their parents' marriages. Lyle speaks of a loss of self-respect in the midst of these battles:

The arguments remind me of my youth, and I'm thinking, "I don't need this all over again." And at those times I'm thinking about splitting or being an independent person, where you come home at night and you've got a quiet place with the clock ticking, and you can read a book, and you can have a glass of sherry if you want. You have at least the decency of being a member of the human race. Whereas when you're having these arguments, you reduce yourself to nothing.

Again, a marital paradigm is a collection of images that describe pathways through partnership and also a set of procedural rules that specify how those pathways might be travelled. While the content of all these images is tremendously varied from one person's paradigm to another's, I find that there are a limited array of issues that lend structure to these diverse contents. Generally speaking, marital paradigms portray attempted solutions to issues of bonding and individuating. In triangle terms, marital paradigms depict strategies for managing all three corners—the inner self, the partnership-corner, and the various third-corners. In the remainder of this chapter, I shall document ways in which each of the three corners is formed, and indicate some of the typical issues upon which they center.

First-Corner Issues

Like all people, parents have inner selves that are laden with feelings of comfort or fear, stability or insecurity, potency or powerlessness, adequacy or worthlessness, with all shadings of gray in between these and other inner polarities. Because parents so often see their own marriages as opportunities to actualize their inner strivings, they cannot help but transmit these urgencies

18 • *Three Corners*

to their children, and some do it quite deliberately. Carla Dean is fifty-five years old and has been married for twenty-nine years. She is the woman of chapter 1 who in earlier periods of her marriage repeated her mother's pattern of extramarital fantasies, acted out largely via the telephone. Throughout her life, securing a sense of personal adequacy and social respectability has been a major theme, overlaid by fantasies of glory and adoration. It is easy to see the origins of these inner-corner issues and their influence on Carla's choice of her mate, Jerry:

My mother had a queen complex. She had always dreamed of living in a really nice home. We did have a nice home, but it wasn't elegant, and my mother had always wanted that kind of life. She never discussed things with us, never really helped us to grow up and face life, and face limitations and reality. . . . Mother never allowed us to have our school friends in the house, and she always talked so reverently, almost, about the wealthy "400" of Portland. So you can see how we all felt inadequate. [Carla had three sisters.]

We didn't go to Mountcrest School—at this time it was very elite, and Mother kind of worshipped that kind of thing. We got from her the desire for elegance. . . . When I worked for my father, I had to answer the telephone a lot, and many of the people who ordered things were people that Mother thought so highly of, monied people, and I just dreamed that I would be one of them. I used to envy those people; they sounded so cozy. . . .

My mother was not a good housekeeper at all, and we did almost all of the work that was done around that house, and Mother would be on the couch, and she'd look at *Good Housekeeping* magazines and dream. When my grandmother was there it was as if somebody had waved a magic wand; within half an hour of the time she came, the house was neat, and you felt as though things were in good hands. I never felt that way with my mother.

If Carla's mother focussed only on the silver-lined side of life and presented everyday reality as tarnished, Carla's father carried on about the dark clouds:

My father twice a year would talk to us in the evening. It took the whole evening. He would never say "boo" to us between these tirades. He would spend the whole evening warning us about the perils of the big old bad world out there, and also the dangers of spending ten dollars when you only have five, and we'd always invariably wind the evening up with all of us in tears, including Mother, and Dad would be in the middle of the floor on his knees pounding on the floor to make his point.

Growing up with these prominent images, it is not surprising that Carla fell into her mother's style of fantasy to bolster up her inadequate self and her gloomy, unacceptable everyday world. After high school and a failed romance, she yearned to become a singer:

The Forming of the Inner-Corner • 19

I lived in a dream world all the time, of being adored by all these fans. I just couldn't face normal humdrum living. I tried desperately to adjust, and I joined the YWCA and played badminton and volleyball and softball. I did some sewing. I was just so intent on "adjusting." Jerry was the first one who made life seem exciting to me at all. And we both had dreams of having a big home like this. He used to work for my father as a delivery boy just so he could be near me. Making deliveries to these mansions, he just made up his mind he was going to have a mansion like that.

Jerry not only fed Carla's fantasies but fueled them with some of his own. Carla relates:

I inherited some of my mother's queen complex, and Jerry has always made me feel like a queen. To this day he tells me I have no faults. He is so accepting of me, and I feel so unaccepted outside of the home, usually. Jerry makes me feel so good about myself all the time, no matter what I do, what kind of mood I'm in. No matter how sick I am, Jerry's always made me feel very beloved.

Carla's account reminds us that the inner-corner is in part a dialogue between our own impulses and the messages about ourselves and the world received from significant others. It is not completely clear how Carla's mother transmitted her own sense of inadequacy and her yearnings for social recognition to her daughters; what we know is that somehow, these urgencies become Carla's urgencies, in large part constituting her private drama and shaping her need for a particular kind of partner.

For some respondents, inner-corner issues arose not from adopting their parents' urgencies, as Carla did, but from striving to escape the difficulties of their own partnership with one or both parents. Brenda Davis is one such respondent. Her mother divorced her father when Brenda was ten, and remarried a man who was violent. Brenda recalls her ensuing home life as "turbulent":

While my mother was with my stepfather, I just had a very strange childhood. He didn't drink, but he'd get violent every once in a while, and he'd cause an uproar, and we had to live through that. He didn't hit me too often, just a couple of times. He'd throw things, he'd be destructive. I can remember his chasing me with a gun once. He'd threaten a lot of the times and he wouldn't do anything, but he'd do it to scare her, to get at her. He used us or anything else that he thought she cared about. Like if there was any furniture that he thought she liked, he'd destroy it.

For Brenda, there were two dominating inner-corner issues. The first was a lack of basic safety. Filled with paradigmatic images of how a violent partner can ruin a family, she focussed her marital sights on "someone who would be quiet. I didn't want it to be anything like my mother's marriage to Gene. At the

20 • *Three Corners*

time I didn't realize what 'quiet' would mean in a marriage. What it meant to me was no arguing, no fighting. And I always said I'd never get a divorce. It was so hard growing up with Gene, and so I said I would never get a divorce and put my kids through all that."

The other inner-corner issue plaguing Brenda was a lack of any real sense of adequacy and efficacy, an issue that arose more from her relationship with her mother than from her stepfather's destructive influence. She recalls her mother as "the dominant one in the family" while she was married to Brenda's natural father. Early on, Brenda must have learned to deal with her mother's criticism by conducting herself outwardly in a manner beyond reproach and by inwardly hiding her real feelings about things. These tendencies have become clearer to Brenda because she sometimes re-enacts this drama with her own daughter Allison:

> When I get angry it's almost like Allison tunes me out, and she won't argue with me. She'll go upstairs. *I used to do things like that.* . . . I remember so much about my mother that I didn't like. Like this look that she has, this disgusted look, when people aren't doing what she thinks they should be doing. . . . My mother didn't want me to marry Glen, and I married him anyway. She said, "He's not right for you; you're not going to be happy," and I was going to prove her wrong. So even though I was unhappy in my marriage, I wouldn't have left for the world [emphasis added].

Not only did Brenda stay in an unhappy marriage for seventeen years before getting a divorce, but even throughout her four-year courtship with Glen, she knew that her basic emotional needs were not being met.

> I often wondered why we ever got married. He never treated me special. He was never on time; he never paid me a compliment. He never acted like he really cared whether I was around. So I often wondered what kind of need I had to allow that to go on and marry a person that I got so little from emotionally. He never built me up or encouraged me. It was like he found every opportunity to put me down. I think he was insecure and he didn't want me to feel good about myself because then he couldn't feel superior in any way, and I might realize that I didn't need him. If I expressed any particular like, he'd find a way to put that down.

What kind of need did Brenda have to enter a marriage based on such an unsatisfying courtship? When we look closely at her account, what appears to be an irrational mate-choice had a certain rationality to it, geared to filling the two gaps in her inner-corner. On one hand she could finally feel safe, away from the torments of her stepfather: "It was bad at home, and I just needed someplace to belong. I knew Glen well enough to know that he wasn't violent, and it seemed like a safe type of relationship. He was quiet." On the

The Forming of the Inner-Corner • 21

other hand, she could feel more adequate and competent away from the critical scrutiny of her mother: "He didn't ask anything of me. I didn't feel put on the spot, or I didn't think he'd make any demands that I couldn't fulfill. Even though emotionally he wasn't good for me and he put me down, I could do what I wanted around the home; he'd allow me to take charge of the home. I think the attraction was more the home than him—to belong somewhere."

Of course, the initial vision proved much better than the reality, and Brenda could not seem to avoid falling back into paradigm elements relating to her inner sense of inadequacy that was reminiscent of her failure to meet her mother's expectations: "Glen put me down all the time. If there was dust on the floor, or the way I said something—I always felt like I never quite measured up. And it's like I always had to do everything better all the time, to get to some ideal place where people couldn't find any wrong at all."

In summary, the inner-corner may come to focus on such needs as basic safety and minimal comfort, but above all else it is a set of strivings based on our vision of personal adequacy. That vision may differ for males and females. In a patriarchal setting female adequacy will often center around attractiveness and desirability, on caring for others and being attuned to their needs, or on being tidy, responsible, and accommodating. Male adequacy will more often focus on independence, on ability to command others' allegiance, on task competence, and on being decisive, cool, and in full control. While these respective emphases pervade and largely constitute patriarchal culture, they can only start constituting the *person* insofar as they are mediated to us through watching and interacting with our most significant early partners, especially parents. And once these inner-corner strivings (or perhaps our rejection of them) are firmly fixed within our own personhood, our later intimate partnerships cannot help but reflect them, as we saw with both Carla Dean and Brenda Davis.

Second-Corner Issues

Often, there is no hard and fast line between inner-corner and partnership-corner imagery. Does our sense of adequacy and competence belong to our inner-self, or to the kind of affirmation we are used to receiving from intimate partners? Our images can focus on the issue from either direction or from both. Is a sense of safety and security an inner-corner issue, or does it relate more to a strong history of comfort in the company of others? Because intimate partnerships stand so close to our inner core, it is not always easy to separate the one from the other. Nevertheless, I shall treat them as separable for the sake of analytical clarity.

As with the inner-corner, partnership-corner images may be summarized as a set of implicit polarities. Here, the issues seem to be attachment and belonging

22 • *Three Corners*

to someone versus aloneness or abandonment; love and affection versus cold-ness or aloofness; peace and quiet versus conflict and confrontation; dominance/subordination versus equity in decision making; availability and active companionship versus inaccessibility. Marital paradigms are filled with such images about partnership interaction, and again, these images are primarily remnants of what our parents modeled with each other and of our own partnerships with one or both parents or parental surrogates.

Attachment

Perhaps the most basic second-corner image has to do with attachment versus abandonment. Many respondents recounted a strong sense of secure connec-tion in their family of origin, a feeling that their parents would always un-questionably be there for them and for each other. These respondents did not specifically refer to "belonging" per se, having always taken that for granted. Typically, they singled out a feeling of closeness. "My parents always ap-peared to derive a lot of satisfaction and comfort from that close relationship," a thirty-three-year-old man told me. He added, "I saw the shar-ing that they had together as very important in marriage. They were both even-tempered and got along extremely well together. I enjoy my parents' company. We have a close, strong relationship."

Other respondents felt little of this security in belonging. Rejecting some painful paradigm images, they told stories that focussed on aloneness or abandonment. A woman expressed this theme of abandonment in terms of parenting:

> It was super-important to me to marry someone I could depend on in terms of parenting with me, because I knew I wanted children. I didn't want a man who would leave when I was pregnant. My natural father deserted my mother when she was pregnant with me. I had all kinds of irrational anxieties with each of my own pregnancies, because I've never really worked all that through.

Another woman, Angela, spoke of her father's navy career and eventual divorce from her mother:

> Even before their separation and divorce he was gone most of the time; he was usually aboard ship. We always stayed home. I've never had a relation-ship with my father, and that is something that I have really missed. I got married with the idea that I would never get a divorce. Never! But as I have gotten older I understand it more than I did then, because when you're a kid you don't ever expect your mother and father to split up. And I think it's an awful blow when they do. . . . My childhood is something that I want to forget. My mother had to work, for one thing. I used to come home from school and there was nobody there, which I swore would never happen to

The Forming of the Inner-Corner • 23

my kids. Whenever I seemed to need somebody or wanted somebody, they were never there. I had nobody to really turn to.

Angela married Joe after a four-year courtship, and following a one-week honeymoon, Joe went overseas with the army. Familiar paradigm images of abandonment then came back to haunt Angela, who spoke of the ordeal of the ensuing two years:

> I felt very, very lonely while he was gone. I don't know if I'd do that all over again. It was a very lonely time. And there again, I had the feeling that when I really needed somebody he wasn't there. I didn't blame him, I just felt like, all my life it's been that way. I was frightened of being alone, because I felt like I was the only person in the world.

In general, when respondents came to marriage with a strong history of security-in-belonging, their partnership-corner imagery reflects an eagerness to share their life with another adult with whom they can recreate that comfortable closeness. When they came, like Angela, with considerable fears of being abandoned, their approach to partnership is more protective. They somehow manage to recreate the very circumstances that perpetuate their fears, often choosing a partner whose third-corner management is most likely to provoke anxieties that are all too familiar.

Affection

When parents give their children abundant affection and show it for each other, their children form some of their most vivid and powerful images of partnership. Many of my respondents fondly embraced these familiar images, carrying them into their own partnership-corner:

> My parents are still very loving, and I always saw them that way as a child. He'd come in from the hayfield and put his arms around her, and I remember saying to myself, "That's just the kind of husband I want." I guess you'd have to know my dad. He just gets a thrill and a kick out of life, and he was always like that—a great joker and a teaser, and that's the way I remember him with my mother. . . . Every idea I had of marriage I learned from my parents. I think I figured all marriages were happy like that, and that would just come automatically. I couldn't imagine not being happy. [Forty-three-year-old woman, married twenty-two years]

Even when respondents chronicle some deep-rooted disturbances in their parents' marriage, they still recall whatever episodes of affection and levity were there. Carla Dean, who told me that her mother was quite unhappy in her marriage and that her parents grew farther and farther apart, nevertheless remembers some affectionate moments that seemed to make a strong impact on her:

24 • *Three Corners*

When my mother was working over the sink, my father used to go over and play with her breasts, and that always made me feel good. She'd giggle and say, "Oh George, stop, in front of the kids!" and this and that. . . . There was kissing. He never went to work without kissing her goodbye. Up to a certain age he used to kiss us goodbye every day, and mother never went anywhere without doing the rounds. . . . They would invite their friends to come over Sunday with their families for a big dinner, and they'd stay the afternoon and then we'd all go to bed, and we could hear the parents downstairs laughing and giggling. But when these families, friends, would leave, almost always my father would put his arm around my mother's shoulder and they'd stand together like that until the people went. It was jovial.

A number of respondents did not have even these ephemeral episodes of affection in their paradigmatic imagery. Some of them, like Bonnie Macklin, became aware of having missed out on something, and early on they decided that their own marriage and child rearing would be different. Bonnie told me:

My parents lived very separate lives. They didn't have any communication at all that I can ever remember. My father never really listened—to her, the kids, anybody. I wanted someone who would be gentle to me, and not be afraid to show his love, and if we had children, who wouldn't be afraid to pick the kids up and take them someplace, or just hug them, or play with them. My father *never* played with us. And I never saw him hug and kiss my mother, never. . . . He was extremely, extremely strict. We always asked my mother, "Could we go to a dance?"; we *never* went to my father. And God forbid we should talk to him before he ate supper! We would get our heads chopped off.

Conflict

Perhaps the most frightening images that people carry into their partnership-corners are imprinted from scenes of confrontation in their families of origin. Many of the respondents who spoke most positively about their parents and their childhood mentioned the absence of overt conflicts in their homes. Here are two examples:

I grew up in a very calm home situation. There was never an angry word, never a raised voice between my parents. So my assumption was that marriage was a calm, tranquil situation. [Forty-four-year-old woman, married twenty-four years]

Everything just seemed to be so perfect. I can only remember my parents quarrelling once, and I don't remember what it was about. I didn't realize that other people quarrelled, and I didn't realize that other people had problems. I guess I just lived a very sheltered life. So I carried that on into my own marriage. [Thirty-five-year-old woman, married fourteen years]

The Forming of the Inner-Corner • 25

Not everyone who embraces their familiar paradigm does so by reference to an absence of quarrelling in the parents' marriage. Here is a man whose model of marriage includes both closeness and some conflicts:

> My parents were very happily married. I inherited a very intense feeling of family. We were very close; there was a great deal of affection. There's always been a lot of support over the years, and all three of us always felt very special in the eyes of our parents. We go down to visit them every year, and they used to come to Maine in the summer. . . . My mother is a very strong-willed person; she's domineering but very loving and supportive. Arguments were always a staple in our family; there was anger expressed, but it was never destructive anger.

In his own twenty-five-year marriage, this man has not needed to shy away from conflict, because his paradigm instructs him that one can quarrel vigorously and still have a good marriage.

> My wife and I both have strong ideas, and when they clash, the fireworks go. We're volatile. The fireworks fly, but then they die very quickly. Sometimes we feel badly about having had a shouting match, but it ends quickly.

Other respondents, who grew up with an abundance of conflicts in their homes but without any positive, counterbalancing influences, became convinced that conflict in a marriage can only be destructive, and they intended their own marriages to be totally free of it. Frank O'Brien is one such respondent. As is often the case, the conflicts he remembers were aggravated by alcohol:

> It was a stormy household. My mother was an alcoholic of many years standing. There were a large number of tensions, alleviated by the fact that my father wasn't home much. He was a periodic heavy drinker too. Being Roman Catholics, they'd never consider divorce; one got used to living with situations that were incurable. . . . I inherited the basic cultural set that marriage is final; you work things out, period. Until I left my home community I'd never met a divorced person. Divorce was something that happened in books and movies; it didn't happen in our neighborhood. [Fifty-two-year-old college professor, married twenty-seven years]

Filled with images about the damaging impact of conflicts, while expecting that no matter how his marriage turned out it would have to be final, Frank was determined to avoid any semblance of confrontation. Courtship became a testing ground to verify that it would not happen. He told me, "The things that would be irritating would show up in courtship. That's what courtship is for: finding out whether you can handle each other's sharp edges." Once

married (to a woman who grew up in a home that was totally devoid of expressed conflicts), Frank maintained a stance toward conflict that was consistent with his paradigm-inspired philosophy:

> Storminess occurs when one forces issues. I don't force issues in my marriage. I don't force a decision on a conflict. My wife does the same thing. Conflict can resolve itself if you leave it nebulous. It becomes irrelevant, or you gradually resolve it, but not through confrontation. Confrontation resulted in storms in my parents' marriage, and there were a lot of confrontations. They never solved anything.

Frank's rejection of any conflict scenario seemed likewise to guard him against too much emotional disclosure; revealing deep or unsettled feelings could hurl him back into that quarantined territory of marital struggle. Asked if he thought he and his wife Laura knew each other's deepest strivings, he replied, "No, that's what one loses when one doesn't have confrontation. In confrontation one finds out the other's deepest strivings." Thus, when the death of a close friend threw Frank into an emotional crisis some fifteen years into his marriage, it never was talked about with Laura:

> I went through a couple of years of withdrawal. I went on Valium for a couple of years. Sexual withdrawal was part of it. There were relatively strong emotional changes. I don't even know if Laura noticed them, but I think she did. She knew something was going on but she never pressed me about it. I guess we both figured it would work itself out, and it did. It was a two-year episode, at the end of which we began to get back to a relationship that was more normal for the marriage.

Apparently, Laura never asked and Frank never told, both honoring the implicit contract not to pry into each other's inner-corner, making certain to preserve the peace and keep the demon conflict at bay.

Power and Decision Making

Even if parents do not model overt conflicts, marriage always raises issues of who decides what. Children form clear images of which parent led and which parent followed, of who was dominant and who was submissive, or of decision making as a shared enterprise, if that was the case. They themselves also participate in a power structure with one or both parents, an arrangement that usually generates strong feelings, sometimes positive, sometimes negative, but rarely neutral or indifferent. All of this gives rise to paradigms of marital power, which are among the most central of the second-corner images to which people address themselves in structuring their own courtships and marriages.

The Forming of the Inner-Corner • 27

Many of my male respondents had fathers whose presence was the dominant one in the home. Where such patriarchal dominance remained uncon-
tested and confrontation was therefore absent, these men generally embraced
their familiar paradigm images and expected that they would likewise be the
leading authority in their own marriage. As Paul Carter put it:

> There were very few arguments in my youth. My mother never talked back
> to my father, so I was definitely not expecting to have a female talk back. It
> was pretty much a man-is-head type marriage situation. Whatever was neces-
> sary for the man to get ahead, for the man to basically be happy was what
> was supposed to be the standard by which the family functioned. And the
> woman basically supported that. [Forty-two-year-old electronics teacher,
> married twenty years]

It should not be thought, however, that men who grow up in a male-governed
household embrace everything about this arrangement for their own marriages. The rule here as elsewhere is a simple one: only those paradigm elements
that appear to work comfortably are adopted without much forethought.
Those elements that seem to work but also to produce some unseemly consequences are treated according to the perceived severity of the discomforts. People make diagnoses about what they think was unhealthy in their families, and
they arrive at some prescriptive remedies which they intend to apply to their
own marriages and families to eliminate the discomforts. For example, a
respondent told me that his parents' relationship was "very good. He was a
leader and she was a follower; she was happy doing whatever he thought right."
This man added, however, that while he "wanted the obvious relationship [his
parents] had," he wanted a wife who was not quite as dependent as his mother
had been: "I know if he had made her more self-sufficient, it would have been a
great deal easier for her after he died. He would do the shopping because she
didn't want to do it, and simple things like that she should have been doing, she
just didn't have any inkling about at all" [forty-eight-year-old store manager,
married thirteen years to second wife].

Scott King is another respondent who describes these elements of patriarchy:

> It was not an equal marriage. He made most of the decisions. When he died,
> she still did not know how to keep a checkbook even though they'd been
> married twenty-six or twenty-seven years. When she worked, her money
> came home and went to him and he spent it. He was the one who made deci-
> sions. He bought most of the groceries and brought them home. He didn't
> stint her with money, and I'm sure she was very, very happy. But he did
> make most of the decisions.

Since there was little conflict in Scott's home, and Scott felt well connected to
both parents, it might be expected that he would structure his own marriage

28 • *Three Corners*

along the lines of his familiar paradigm, adopting his father's model of authority for himself and making only minor changes. The situation was far more complex, however, because while Scott's working-class father was the unquestioned decision-making authority, his mother came from a different background and was the unspoken intellectual and cultural authority of the family—an active reader, "a fairly accomplished musician," a person with "a good deal more catholic taste." Scott's father developed a drinking problem, in large part, Scott thinks, because he could not overcome his insecurities about his wife's intellectual superiority: "That was a realm that he just didn't understand or know at all. It was difficult for him to know that she had a world that he couldn't enter. He must have feared that being so cultured, she could easily take over all the decision making, and then he'd be left with nothing. In drinking, he could escape from all this."

While Scott was enough identified with his father to appreciate the privileges inherent in domestic power, he soon became even more identified with his mother's intellectual world, so much so that he ultimately chose an academic career. In his own marriage he became more than willing to trade away domestic authority for active leadership in intellectual enterprises. Intellectual pursuits spelled danger, however, since in Scott's familiar paradigm, friction in a marriage arises when only one partner has an intellectual life. His preventative medicine, therefore, was to choose a wife who would not only agree that intellectual authority might be assigned a higher value than domestic authority, not only be an eager and supportive "ground crew" for all the intellectual missions he might launch, but also be strong enough to stand on her own two feet intellectually and thus protect their marriage from the extreme intellectual inequality that plagued his parents. In his words, a satisfying marriage would be one:

> in which the female partner buoyed me up as I needed it [much as his mother always had], a marriage that would have a high intellectual quality, a continuous intellectual quality. That was one thing I wanted that was different from my parents' marriage. I didn't want that superior/inferior [intellectual] relationship that they had, because I thought that was the basis of some of their other problems [Scott is a fifty-year-old-college professor, married for twenty-seven years].

Those men who grew up in an uncomfortable patriarchy and had a negative or nonexistent relationship with their father became highly conscious and critical of their family's power arrangements, rejecting specific paradigm elements for their own marriages and/or parenting. Depending on the circumstances, such a rejection can focus either on a husband/father being too tyrannical or a wife/mother being too weak or submissive. It can also focus on both, as it did in the case of Hal Stern, who describes his home life growing up near New York City:

I remember my home as not a very friendly place. It was the kind of place where people came to do battle with one another, particularly at mealtimes. It was a constant kind of thing. Something was always in the air. My father was the protagonist always. He favored one of my older brothers and continually put down the other one. There was a lot of conflict between my father and my older sister too, and my mother always kind of played the role of trying to smooth things over. For me there was always a problem there in trying to fit in. I think I spent most of my time growing up avoiding conflict. I became very independent as a youngster and moved in my own circles, as kind of a protective situation. . . . It was an authoritarian family, and decisions always rested with my father. And I was determined not to provide that kind of a model in raising my own kids. I felt that a sense of fairness should be instilled in the family: for decisions that affect the family, people would have something to say about them on an equal level.

So far, Hal's account faults only his father and his autocratic tendencies. Elsewhere, however, Hal focusses on his mother. He was close to her emotionally, and she was "more interesting intellectually than [his] father was"; he can remember having discussions with her. But she was likewise unable to protect her own space from her husband's tumult and tension, and she wound up in a mental institution for many years. Hal was then left without an ally or companion. Marriage came to mean "an image of security. It meant that I wouldn't be alone anymore, that there would be somebody who I could trust and could really care for me as a person and that I could share that trust and caring." As much as Hal rejected his father's model, he also faulted his mother for her contribution to their dominant–subordinate pattern of marriage. Had she not been so weak, she would have stood her ground with her husband, and then Hal would have retained the emotional support that she alone had to offer him. Asked what qualities he wanted in a mate, Hal replies: "I didn't want anybody who would fall over. I wanted somebody I could press against emotionally as well as intellectually, somebody who would stand up and have some guts and say what they wanted to say and not be afraid of me. I didn't want to duplicate my mother in the woman that I married."

Hal's story brings out many complexities of how familiar paradigms lend structure to a person's inner-corner, with all its hidden drama and kaleidoscope of emotions. In one package Hal has organized not just his second-corner images of power dynamics but also of conflict and caring, aloneness and abandonment, trust and security. Having made a considered diagnosis of the ills of his parents and of his own childhood situation, he carries his intended remedy into his marriage. But it took many years for Hal to move significantly in the direction he wished. It proved a lot easier to fall into the familiar paradigm than to transform it. Alone and powerless to get his needs met within his family of origin, it became all too tempting to pick a spouse who would not offer too much resistance, who would at least back down if

30 • *Three Corners*

not "fall over," who would let him dominate enough to secure his needs but would not become so dysfunctional (like his mother) that he would be left without a companion. In other words, it was easier to adopt his father's stance of dominance than to trust that a wife's strength, power, and love could be relied upon to make him feel secure. "Hal's quite domineering," his wife Paula says. "He figures what he thinks is right. I was always afraid to say whether I thought I was right or not." Hal himself concedes, "I always pressed my concerns and needs and what I wanted."

Still, Hal's initial vision of a more equal marriage was never totally lost. Paula was eventually able to convince both herself and Hal that she did indeed have some valuable strengths. "I used to be more dependent on Hal. I think I was looking for somebody to take care of me. I'm more independent now. I'm more aggressive than I was." For Hal, Paula's strength became more credible during a period when he and Paula lost three people who were close to them, including Hal's mother. Perhaps her death was also the symbolic death of Hal's fear of ultimate abandonment at the hands of a female, for it coincided with the emergence of his wife being unmistakably there for him to lean on:

> I was really feeling kind of lost. It was very hard for me to handle. Being able to talk to Paula about that, *and having her continue to function* made me feel good. I didn't have to carry the two of us, and we could share and somehow get through it. And so now when something happens that's emotionally rending in the family, I feel a kind of confidence that we'll be able to handle it together [emphasis added].

This new sense of emotional equality and trust apparently spilled over into the whole area of power dynamics, for Hal no longer has to push so hard to secure his own needs. "I'm more able to listen to her concerns and feel that they're as important as mine. Now, what she's saying is equally important, and I listen and respond and show some caring. That was probably a major change for me as a person." Paula seems to agree: "I don't think he's so bossy any more. I think he respects my feelings a little more."

Women are no less variable than men in their ways of forming images of domestic power. Again, their "diagnoses" will reflect their level of comfort in their families of origin—the goings-on between their parents as well as any leftover issues between themselves and their parents. Chodorow's and Dinnerstein's analyses suggest that males and females develop different approaches to power, notwithstanding the great variety of family issues that either gender may have experienced by the time of marriage. Because men as infants are originally bonded to and identified with a female, securing a masculine status eventually requires a vigorous assertion of independence from that relationship. To be sure, men still want the nurturance and support that they got from their mother; nevertheless, with one eye fixed on their father's third-corner independence, they cling fast to their hard-won freedom

The Forming of the Inner-Corner • 31

from a woman's power, a power that once bent their will to female-defined purposes. If being nurtured comes only at the cost of a man's freedom from female domination, men are willing to do without the nurturance. Hal Stern could focus so much attention on a wife being strong enough to properly nurture him only because he never doubted his own power to initiate and rule in matters of greatest importance to him. And Scott King could marry a strong woman who would take full charge of the domestic front because his sense of power and authority was exclusively tied to his intellectual prowess, and he knew that if push ever came to shove, his wife would subordinate her own domain of power to his. Patriarchy is the safest path for men, and female attachment to a man's apparent strength is the time-honored arrangement in which male independence from females is combined with nurturant female service.

As Dinnerstein notes, patriarchy is also the safest path for women, who often stand ready and eager to take their place in this arrangement. Regardless of what they saw played out at home, female gender security does not require any wrenching apart from their earliest bond with their mother. Rather than following the path of sharp differentiation that boys take, girls continue to invest in that primary connection that was their original source of security. Blending and harmonizing with a stronger partner, pleasing someone else rather than seeking separate distinction, a girl learns to make her partner's needs her own.

When mothers assume this stance of devoted service toward their husbands, daughters form especially clear images of wifely attendance to a man's needs. Norma Parker recalls that she and her siblings "were always secondary" to her mother's relationship with her father and later her stepfather: "When my mother and father were communicating the children were shut out; we weren't allowed in the house when he came home from work so they could sit and have a drink." Rather than fault her mother for neglecting her, Norma idealized her, hoping to finally get her needs met in her adult life by likewise pleasing a man.

> I held my mother in high esteem all through my childhood, and looked to her as a model of the perfect wife. She was always willing to give in and do what her husband wanted—which I certainly changed my mind about. I think that was the downfall of her first marriage. For instance, he'd say, "I really like blond women," and she'd dye her hair blond. It never was good enough. She tried to be what he wanted, sexually or whatever. I saw that as a good and noble characteristic and modeled myself after her. She continues to do that sort of thing with her second husband. She has very good qualities.

Though Norma always tried to please her own husband Bud, in the first five years of their marriage his professional insecurities often left him depressed and ill-humored. Norma felt resentful; a man is supposed to be strong and decisive, and if something goes wrong in his life, a wife is supposed to make

32 • *Three Corners*

it right for him. By paradigmatic rule, a man who is not pleased must not be pleased with *her:*

> In those days it put a heavy blanket over everything. He would grump and slam doors, and sometimes cry. Most of the time it was directed inward; he hurt himself a lot and thereby hurt me. The reason I couldn't cope with it was that I felt the wife should help the husband and I could never get through to him to help him. So I said, "If I'm having no effect on the marriage, why should I stay in it?" I didn't know what to do. I just felt inadequate, like it must be my fault.

Surely patriarchy is in full gear when females are ready to assume responsibility for the difficulties of their male partners.

Unlike Norma, some girls struggle with a long-standing history of conflict with a critical mother. Not idealization but opposition or fear is then their pattern of response to her, and fathers sometimes get pulled in (or rush in) to fill the vacuum. To be sure, if fathers are accessible and congenial, both boys and girls will tend to shift their allegiance to them, given aggravated conflict with their mothers, but there are important differences. A boy's conflict with Mom becomes fuel for an organized campaign of masculine differentiation from her female world, and his link to Dad does not so much focus on nurturant connection as it does on Dad's model of third-corner distinction and independence. A girl's shift to Dad is typically devoid of these vigorous strivings for separation and independence. She is far less likely to take Dad as a model of freedom than she is to seek his nurturant care. He can harbor her from the gusty winds of Mom's criticism, but he does not typically inspire her to become a more autonomous, individuated female person.

As Chodorow points out, "He is not her primary caretaker but comes on the scene after his daughter's relationship to this caretaker (her mother) is well established."[3] Since, therefore, he "has never presented himself to [her] with the same force as her mother,"[4] he "does not serve as a sufficiently important object to break her maternal attachment."[5] Of course, he can start her on a career of pleasing men. Fathers often see their daughters as darling little girls and encourage them to cultivate a seductive female selfhood. Getting rewards and approval for seductive femininity may feel better than a mother's harsh criticism, but when female security rests on the shallow roots of seductiveness, it is too fragile to stand on its own solid ground. In any case, a mother's vision of her daughter will usually count more in the long run because a mother's involvement with her has usually been much greater. Even if her expectations are too harsh and difficult to meet, she is the one who most knows her; she is her daughter's first and most intense love. Comfort with Dad may soothe a daughter, but it does not solve her problem of autonomous female identity. In her heart she would still like to authenticate herself by convincing Mom that she is really okay.

The Forming of the Inner-Corner • 33

In short, girls find it extremely difficult to differentiate themselves from a critical mother's expectations. While a boy has the luxury of escaping an overly critical mother by hastening into his masculine oppositeness from her, a girl who would distance too far from her mother's scrutinizing eye is in danger of losing the only concrete vision of adequate female personhood she knows.

Small wonder that young women with a history of struggle with their mothers often pin their hopes on a strong man who will love them, lead them, guide them and care for them. Failure to satisfy Mom has left them feeling shaky, unlovable, insecure, and inadequate as a female self, and poorly equipped to garner the personal power to initiate projects without someone else's direction. Now enter the White Knight to take charge.

Ruth Hawkins was one respondent whose story closely follows this scenario. Recently divorced after a fifteen-year marriage, Ruth had hoped her ex-husband Ken would be her liberation from demon Mom. Marriage spelled the chance "to get out of that restrictive, hostile, arid, barren place that I grew up in." As the oldest of five children, Ruth must have caught the full force of her mother's harsh expectations: "My mother is a very strong-willed, dominating, domineering person who needs to exercise a tremendous amount of control over the people who live in her house. When I was growing up, I felt 99 percent of the time that I was a problem, that I wasn't good enough in terms of behavior." To make matters worse, Mom's bite was just as bad as her bark. Here Ruth invidiously compares her mother's style of discipline to her father's:

> I was terrifically afraid of my mother. I never felt threatened when my father was hitting us, because I knew my father was a very controlled person; he knew when to stop. Whereas my mother, you didn't know. She might beat you right into the ground. . . . My mother is not a sensitive person. I think she'd like to be, but it's not there inside of her. My father has it inside of him. My father had a gift for making you feel loved, even when he was giving you a licking, whereas when my mother gave you a licking, you knew it was done with a vengeance and she meant to do it because she wanted to release all of that hostility and resentment that you were the cause of.

Here as elsewhere, Ruth's account signals a sense of defensive alliance with her father, whom she sees as the saving grace of her childhood. Yet, it is clear that she saw her father neither as a model to emulate in her own adult life nor as a desirable model of what her husband should be. If anything, her father was a negative example of the husband she would need, because, as Ruth puts it, "He gets overpowered. I don't think he's particularly good at defending his position. I probably was looking for someone *not* like my father so that I wouldn't be like my mother." Ruth's thoughts about marriage were thus a dialogue with her mother's version of female adequacy. Mortified

34 • Three Corners

by that unlovable and faulty female she was in her mother's eyes, yet also horrified by the prospect of being that unloving and fault-finding kind of female that her mother represented, Ruth had no apprehension of her female personhood that could differentiate her from her mother.

In the end, it was her mother's critical judgment that Ruth bought the most. Her premarital courtships were marred by the conviction that her basic female self was defective. Speaking of one suitor, she recalls:

> I was very, very drawn to him and he to me. But I couldn't trust this person enough to open up, to talk to him, to tell him who I really was. And the closer we became, the more time we spent together, the more closed up I became. I was so afraid of this person getting to know me and seeing how little I had to offer. This is how I felt at the time. He couldn't possibly want to know me, to be with me.

After several such courtship experiences, Ruth met Ken, and their relationship developed on the basis of Ken's appearing to understand the difficulties Ruth had been having with her self-esteem.

> We would talk about my feelings of inferiority, and he seemed to be sensitive to things that I was going through. He used an inherently good and caring kind of trait in a very destructive way, but I didn't know that then. The more he knew about what was going on in my mind, the easier it was for him to manipulate me. What I thought then was that he was taking care of me. I didn't have to make, really, any decisions. At the time I looked upon that as a caring kind of thing.

Not only did this white knight Ken seem to be nurturing but he also appeared (in the fashion of all white knights) to be powerful. "I think that's one of the things that attracted me to him—he had power, and I didn't." With his power, he could define her, direct her, make her whole, tell her what she needed, since she herself felt too powerless to know her own needs, and too weak, in any case, to take the strides required to get them met.

It was not long before Ruth became a prisoner of her own powerlessness, for Ken was neither nurturing nor inclined to lead Ruth in ways that would bring her to greater wholeness. Far from liberating her from her critical mother, this white knight turned out to be the demon mother in disguise. His expectations were likewise insatiable, he was abusive, and he found nothing but fault in whatever Ruth did, probably because he depended on her inferiority to nail down his own elusive sense of male importance:

> It was horrible from the very beginning. He did such a good job at always putting me down and belittling me and reminding me that I was inept and incompetent and stupid that I never focussed on what my strengths really were.

The Forming of the Inner-Corner • 35

I was constantly trying to become better and better and better. He could come home and reel off the things I hadn't done right, and rant and scream, and the next day I'd do it the way he told me to, and then *that* was wrong! I could have put the salt on the wrong side of the dish—and I'm being literal. I mean, it started there and worked it's way up, and infiltrated everywhere in the relationship. I just was not living up to his expectations, and I thought there was something radically wrong with me. I had failed as a daughter; I never did anything right when I was growing up; I never pleased anybody when I was growing up. And now I was in this situation again. I just beat myself silly for many, many years.

The circle is thus complete. Ruth fell back into the paradigm she knew all too well: When your partner expects the moon, you shoot for it, since the glimmer of a chance for success is the one chink of light in an otherwise black abyss of inadequacy. There really was no choice. Only an autonomous person could carve out her own direction; one who remains undifferentiated from a stronger partner's directives does not know how to be a self without that guidance. The alternative is the nightmare of being alone with oneself, a self who knows itself only as incompleteness, and who therefore lacks the wholeness of vision that would have rendered a white knight unnecessary in the first place.

In summary, second-corner paradigms focus on the things that are supposed to happen (or, just as importantly, *not* happen) when intimate partners deal with one another. We have explored the themes of attachment/abandonment, affection/coldness, conflict/harmony, and power/deference. Others might have been considered as well. It has not always been easy or possible to clearly distinguish these second-corner themes from inner-corner themes. Perhaps the difficulty arises because the self is just one self, so when we talk of its three "corners", we are not dealing with separate "things" but with three different angles of vision the self can adopt as it makes its way in the world. Now we shall consider the third-corner.

Third-Corner Issues

Before proceeding, perhaps a conceptual reminder will prove useful: A "third-corner" refers to any recurring interest that "triangulates" one partner's attention away from the other partner. Jobs and children are surely the most frequently held third-corners. Most partners have, in addition, various leisure interests, one or more friends, parents and/or relatives, religious or spiritual interests, and so forth. Any third-corner of one partner may clash with the other partner's second-corner (partnership) needs and expectations. Leo Farnum recalls one such conflict from early in his twenty-year marriage to Maureen: "I established a habit that bugged Maureen: reading the paper at

the breakfast table. She complained about this, so I gave her part of the paper." As seen here, any third-corner can be done jointly or independently of one's partner. Leo retained his third-corner morning interest by simply converting it from independent to joint activity: both partners were now reading the paper instead of just one. Of course, joint third-corners still shift the partners' energy away from each other, but they may also provide the common focus for expanded partnership interaction. Leo and Maureen might, for example, begin to chat about some newspaper story. In the same way, children create the potential for joint triangulation, although they often seem to become the wife's independent third-corners rather than truly joint ones.

A partner's independent third-corners always heighten the potential for conflicts because of the chance that the other partner will feel excluded, jealous, deprived of attention, or abandoned. Such feelings may indeed have a basis in reality since there is always the possibility that a partner will become so enamoured of some independent third-corner that she or he will lose all interest in the partnership-corner, perhaps even permanently. A lover is of course the classic example here.

As mentioned earlier, triangulation is the mover and shaker of marital dynamics. How partners handle their third-corners always creates repercussions for their partnership-corners. But the reverse is also true. Many of the second-corner arrangements described in the previous section bear greatly on the way that partners structure their third-corners. Of these arrangements, power relationships probably generate the most far-reaching third-corner consequences. Power in a partnership is not just power over the twosome when the spouses are together, or over the inner workings of their household. It is also the power to determine one's own movements in third-corners away from the partner, and to give or withhold permission to the partner for such movements. In other words, the taking of independent third-corner space is not just a mark of freedom but a badge of power. With power, one can say successfully, "I'll do what I want. You can't tell me what to do." With power, likewise, one can say, "You may do only what I want you to do."

If second-corner power creates more space for third-corner independence, that independence creates the basis for further expansion of the power that gave rise to it. Willard Waller pointed out this relationship years ago with his "principle of less interest": the partner who is less involved and invested in the partnership always has more power.[6] What Waller might have added is that less interest in the partnership typically rests on some greater relative interest in one or more independent third-corners and in the resources they put at one's disposal. Herein lies the staggering advantage of economic independence over economic dependence on a partner. Such independence is usually secured on the basis of an income-earning job, which may itself offer abundant third-corner stimulation, esteem, and belonging, thus opening up the flow of rewards from beyond the control of the partner alone. But even

short of these less tangible resources, jobs offer money, and in a consumer society money is power. Ultimately, money is the power to say, "I can pay my own way if I must, so if you value my partnership, you must pay heed to my wants and my needs and not just to your own."[7]

The strings of patriarchy have always been pulled through the purse. Women find it easier to resist male arbitrariness when they are economically independent of any would-be puppeteers. I asked fifty-six-year-old Thelma Jensen if she "backs down" more than her husband Ben does. "In the beginning, I did," she replied, "but not any more. I think going to work did that for me." Thelma went on to recount some often humorous episodes in which she and Ben have been at odds with each other. Notice how she herself appears fully aware that her third-corner independence in the economic sphere is directly linked to her emerging power:

I used to think of Ben as a fuddy-duddy. He was so much more conservative than I about a lot of things. Our friends kid him about it. But it's him. For instance, he's so cheap. Like, we play poker about every Saturday night with the same people—we've done it for years. At the end we play showdown, and Ben will never bet a side bet. We used to go out with people and have a drink, and he'd never have a second drink. If I have a second drink, I pay for it myself.

He looks for all the cheapest brands. We always shop together, always have. (We do everything together, really.) He likes smelly cheese and I don't, and I like strawberries and he doesn't. So he'll pick up a cheese, and if I pick up some strawberries he'll say, "What are you buying those for?" *Before I worked, I'd put them back. I don't now. Every so often I have to remind him that I earn as much as he does. It bugs him, and I don't do it often.* [emphasis added]

He'll only go fifty-five miles an hour. When I'm driving I go faster, and as long as he's sleeping he doesn't notice it. He likes to sleep in the back of the truck. I told him when we got it that I refuse to sleep in the back of the truck. So we stop at a motel. Before, he used to get the cheapest motels. I couldn't say anything, because we didn't have much money. Now I say, "You can't take it with you. And I won't sleep in the back of the truck."

The kids gave us tickets to a concert and $20 for dinner once, and my son said, "Now Mother, don't let him take you to Bonanza!" This sort of thing. And yet he's so great in other ways. But it's ingrained in him. It's the way he was brought up. His mother would roll her own noodles to save money.

When people marry, they do not work out their third-corner management strategies from scratch. Once again, they are informed by paradigms— the familiar images that linger on as traces of what they experienced prior to marriage, particularly at home. Essentially, there is only one third-corner drama, notwithstanding its enormous variety of scenes and stagings: accessibility versus independence. The most aggravated struggles of partnership

revolve around this issue, with children having ample opportunity to see the associated tensions heat up and to form notions about what, if anything, they wish to do about it in their own married lives.

If husbands and wives are either equally accessible or equally inaccessible to each other, the resulting symmetry and balance will keep their relationship on an even keel. Such is rarely the case, however, and Waller's principle of less interest reminds us that one partner is usually less accessible than the other. Under conditions of partriarchy, wives have typically been the more accessible ones. Their exclusive responsibility for child-care anchors them to the home and leaves them economically dependent, while husbands' occupational third-corners keep them inaccessible to the home and give them the economic leverage to maintain domestic power. This arrangement is ultimately more satisfying to men than to women. Males leap into third-corner independence and limited accessibility to females; boys who were reared by a female crave activity away from female control in order to confirm their masculinity. Females often leap into total accessibility to males, having been geared principally for partnership, but if they cannot tame their husbands' inaccessibility, their yearning to be nurtured and not just be nurturing may remain frustrated. Numerous studies show that wives score lower than husbands on almost every measure of mental health and life-satisfaction.[8]

Many of my respondents retain vivid images of the conflicts between their mothers' wishes for more nurturance and their fathers' craving for third-corner independence. Daughters typically remain identified with their mothers in this conflict, unless their connection with the latter has been weakened by excessive frictions. This identification is not simply some abstract loyalty to their gender but is a product of their close relationship with their mothers as well as their own experience with their fathers. Like their mothers, daughters may feel deprived of attention and consideration from the man of the house and be alert to the dangers of a man's third-corner independence. Nellie Green is one respondent whose familiar paradigm provided her with abundant material in this regard:

My father was married to his job and spent a lot of time away. I didn't want that [in my own marriage]. I don't think my mother got much emotional support. My father wasn't cold, but his warmth was given in ways other than what I like to get. He was not affectionate or emotional with us. . . . When tension occurred it was always about his spending more time at his job than at home. It didn't happen often, because my mother was used to it. He's been dead for seven years now, and when she talks about their marriage it's all in Utopian terms. She said to me recently, when my sister met a man and married him in two weeks, "I met your father and felt the same about him, and look at the wonderful life we had." I felt tempted to say, "Cut the shit, Mother!" . . . There was a lot of love between them. The conflict came when she couldn't put up with not getting her needs met anymore. It would

The Forming of the Inner-Corner • 39

happen at 10 P.M. when Mother was in the kitchen banging pots and pans and he was drinking coffee. They'd argue about it.

Nellie is rather pointed here in debunking what to her are some fanciful mystifications on her mother's part. In the same vein she says, "I've always had the seed for being independent and self-sufficient, and not being like my mother, depending on a man to make me happy. That's one thing I was determined to avoid."

But Nellie's analysis is perched on the hindsight of her own ten-year marriage, and it took her at least half of those ten years to begin to break out of her mother's pattern of dependency. It is true that her first year of marriage to Ron was marked by excitement and a sense of independence, as she worked on a master's degree. Still, this is a woman who had thought marriage "was going to be absolute Utopia, the answer to all my hopes and dreams," who yearned to be "well cared for and adored," whose mother was "a Wonder Woman homemaker" devoted only to her husband and six children and who "cried for days" after Nellie, her oldest daughter, left home. When Nellie got pregnant just as she was finishing her degree, all the fun seemed to be instantly gone. "Reality set in. I went through a conflict of wanting to be taken care of by men. That was part of what hit: not only was I not going to be taken care of (Ron is very independent of me, both in getting and giving), I was going to have someone else to take care of. I wasn't ready for that." Once the baby came, Nellie stayed home and Ron continued to work. Nellie grew more and more frustrated:

> I was insecure and uncertain. I felt I had no meaning or purpose in my life. I expected Ron to make me happy, and it wasn't happening. I bitched a lot. The worse I got, the less he gave, and the more I wanted. I wanted him to tell me I was beautiful, bring me a present—I had this whole list of things. I'd decide what he had to do when he walked in the door in the evening, and if he didn't do it, I'd be angry. Of course, I didn't clue him in! I didn't tell him what to do, but I told him afterwards what he hadn't done. And no matter what he did, he couldn't meet my expectations.

Plainly, Nellie's "seed for being independent" was simply washed away by those countertendencies that were more in keeping with her familiar paradigm. Rather than rejecting her mother's model of dependency, she ended by amplifying it, as if to say, "Mother was right in what she wanted but she wasn't demanding enough. I'm going to insist that my husband adore me properly."

It is unusual in my data for men to renounce their third-corner independence. The men who reported some confrontations initiated by mothers about what their fathers were doing outside the home rarely had sympathy for their mother's point of view. Instead, they tended to criticize their mothers for being too demanding or domineering, and they did their best to find

40 • *Three Corners*

more compliant wives. In American culture, men have always assumed that outside third-corners are their right, especially activities that can be broadly construed as work-related, but even some independent recreational interests are held to be perfectly defensible. Here is a man who sides squarely with his father:

> My mother was an extremely jealous woman, and that made for some fights, but with seven children, my father had to work a lot in the paper mill. His job in the mill was always a day job, and he would start at five or six in the morning and get done about noon, and then he would either cut wood or he did gardens, or he had a Caterpillar tractor and he dug foundations and did grading. He was ambitious.

So there was no basis for your mother's jealousy?

> No, she was jealous of other women, but he was always busy on jobs and she just fantasized. That's the way I look at it.

Notice how, in siding with his father, this man chooses to believe that his father "was always busy on jobs," without, presumably, having any more evidence than he thinks his mother had. Another respondent saw his mother as being out of line for keeping his father too confined to the home:

> I think my mother was more the ruler than my father. Sometimes I didn't particularly care for that. Like if I wanted to take him to a ball game, she would put up a stink, and of course my father would say, "All right, I just won't go." I feel that this won't happen with me. If I'm going to make a decision, I want her to go along with it.

To be sure, men do not always ally themselves with their fathers. Many of my male respondents had considerable issues with their fathers, and some felt the same lack of an adult male presence in the home that was mentioned by female respondents. Hal Stern was one of the more articulate men in discussing his father's inaccessibility:

> I remember reading my father's obituary, and it was an interesting obituary. He had been a member of this faculty and that faculty, and done this and that, and nowhere in there did it mention his family. Well, it did; I think it said that he was "survived by"—and that's just about it. We were able to survive his career! And that really struck me, that the model I would like to create for our family is that my obituary would read, "He was involved in doing this with his son, with his daughter, with his family," and that there would be very little mention of any national associations or anything like that.

Hal's remarks are indeed pointed, but the fact remains that American culture holds out tremendous rewards to men who will singlemindedly devote

The Forming of the Inner-Corner • 41

themselves to their career or at least to earning a living. Just as a woman who renounces her mother's dependency finds it difficult to avoid falling into it, so a man who renounces his father's inaccessibility often winds up repeating that pattern. Hal himself did not realize the extent to which he modeled himself after his father: "I think I was looking for a woman, at that time, who would support *my* interests and give *me* support during the time that I was getting my education and pursuing my career." Later in the interview he talked about "the pressure and stress" that he carries into his family from his job:

> I find that a lot of times my mind might be working on problems left over from the day, and I think that interferes with our communication. I know it does. This weekend I took Friday off and we went down to the cottage for the weekend. When we got there I realized I was having trouble leaving the problems of my job behind. I managed to do it but it was hard. When I get up in the morning my mind is on what I'm going to do at work.

Bud Parker was another respondent who often felt neglected by his father throughout his childhood:

> My father was so busy that he didn't have a lot of time for the family and for me. I was an only child, and I would have liked to do things with him, but he didn't get home until eight or nine at night. It also bothered me that he wasn't spending more time with my mother. She's a very intelligent woman, and I can now see that she learned over the years to accept his dedication to his work. He's a very responsible man, and when he's committed to something he does it, even if his time with family has to suffer. I was determined not to get into that.

Despite his best intentions, when Bud began his career of college teaching, he found it all too easy to throw himself totally into his work:

> That first year was extremely difficult. I had never taught before, and I had to spend six hours preparing for each hour of class. We fought more that year than we ever have, because of the stress I was under. I remember Norma being angry at me for the amount of time I had to spend, but I had to spend it to meet my responsibility.

Sounds like your father!

> It does. I couldn't imagine not teaching well. I'd always wanted to be a teacher. Yes, it does sound like my father. I'd say the biggest strain we have is my overcommitment to my job; and yet I like it.

Norma's account indicates that the pattern has not changed a great deal over the years.

42 • *Three Corners*

He makes an effort to say no more to committees and such. Each year he feels he'll have more time with the family, but it doesn't turn out that way; something at school always fills the time. We're learning to accept that he just won't have the kind of time we'd like. He does make the effort to be around more. And I'm more accepting of how things are. But it can still be a sore point.

Notice the parallel between Norma's response—"I'm more accepting of how things are"—and Bud's own account of his mother's response to his father—"I can now see that she learned over the years to accept his dedication to his work."

Thus far we have looked only at those third-corner issues in which "female" needs for nurturance come into conflict with "male" needs for third-corner independence. Of course, wives too may have independent third-corners, and husbands sometimes struggle with their partner's inaccessibility. In a culture of patriarchy, however, female third-corners are rarely carried to the extremes of independence that male ones are. One reason is because female-reared women tend to crave partnership more than independent activity. Often, wives' independent third-corners are other partners, such as a mother, a sister, or female friends. These alternate partners may sometimes occasion some grievances from husbands, but since under patriarchy wives still give top priority to making themselves accessible to their husbands whenever the latter might want them, issues between spouses in this area are usually avoided.

As the literature often notes, the tie between married women and their mothers frequently remains a close one. A girl's mother is her first love, and unlike sons, daughters have no gender-inspired motive to emotionally separate from that bond. Married daughters whose mothers remain close at hand ideally have a reliable and proven source of support, a third-corner partnership that antedates and is independent of their husbands. This bond may be even stronger than usual when it is fed by circumstances that throw a mother toward her daughter as her only significant support.

Such circumstances are well illustrated by Ruby Nelson, an only child whose mother had her at the tender age of fifteen. For the first five years of her life, Ruby and her mother lived alone with Ruby's grandmother. Then her mother married an abusive man, whom she divorced when Ruby was a senior in high school. It was a turbulent, difficult marriage. Ruby's stepfather was "a drinker and a gambler" who would pick fights with her mother, while Ruby would "stand in the corner and scream." Ruby recalls that her mother dealt with her own unhappiness by turning to her. My mother and I were very close. She was like a sister to me. She was quite possessive, and that did cause tension in our marriage.

When Ruby's mother remarried a year after her divorce, she moved to Florida for a short time. Ruby then married Greg, in part because she had no home, and she did not want to be alone.

The Forming of the Inner-Corner • 43

I did love Greg at that time, but another reason was that my mother had just remarried. I could have gone to Florida for the winter with them, but I didn't think it was fair to do that. I didn't have any money, I was young, my mother was leaving, and I didn't know what I was going to do. . . . I kind of resented my new stepfather. I wanted my mother to be happy and secure, but I missed having her close and being able to talk with her.

The fact is that Ruby and her mother had developed a long-standing, dependent alliance with each other. Ruby emerged with two working elements or rules in her marital paradigm. The first rule was drawn from her own experience and told her, depend on your mother for getting your emotional support. The second rule was drawn from what her mother modeled, and told her, when your husband becomes hostile, unavailable, or inaccessible, depend on your daughter for getting your support. Ruby's marriage conformed to her paradigm.

Greg did become fairly inaccessible, pursuing a job on the road that typically kept him away from home except on weekends, and when he went through a psychotic breakdown in the second decade of their twenty-five-year marriage, he became extremely hostile to her, just as Ruby's stepfather had been toward her mother. Ruby's predictable response was to draw on both of the familiar elements in her paradigm. On one hand, she continued to get the emotional support she had always gotten from her mother, who had long since returned from Florida; on the other, she also began to lean on her relationship with her own oldest daughter, just as her mother had done with her. And there are recent signs that this mother–daughter alliance pattern is being carried into a third generation. Ruby's second oldest daughter, Sheila, who had been extremely rebellious and rejecting of her parents throughout her teens, has recently married and provided Ruby and Greg with their first grandchild, as fate would have it, another girl:

I told you how Sheila had rejected us and the home when she was younger. Now she keeps saying how much she loves us, and every time she has a problem she calls home. Before she didn't want us for anything, and now she can't seem to see us or call us enough.

In a patriarchal setting, women like Ruby whose strongest third-corners are their mothers or children do not usually threaten men, because as wives they continue to reserve their highest priority for their husbands. Economically and emotionally dependent on their marriages, they lack the autonomy to make vigorous claims on behalf of any needs that are independent of their husbands or children. In contrast, some women come to marriage already equipped with a spirit of third-corner initiative and a determination to develop some talent or capacity that may have little to do with any partnership per se. As we shall see, these women may easily offend their husbands' sensibilities, particularly if the husbands are governed by familiar paradigms

44 • *Three Corners*

that instruct them that a wife is not supposed to have individual needs other than marital and family service.

The circumstances that may lead a girl into third-corner autonomy are several. Perhaps the most important contributing paradigm element is a mother who consistently modeled female involvement in some strong, independent third-corner of her own. For example, when Gail Jordan's father died the year after she was born, her mother never remarried. Gail's paternal grandmother, who lived with them, was the one who did the daytime childcare and housework, while Gail's mother held a full-time job. Seeing is believing, and Gail grew up watching her breadwinning mother maintain a regular third-corner outside the home. With this familiar paradigm, Gail simply assumed that it is perfectly appropriate for females to have an active outside life. Even in her childhood she found it natural to cultivate third-corners away from the home that were not simply extensions of some partnership.

> I didn't give much thought to marriage. When I was growing up I was very active and interested in things at school, belonged to clubs, was in athletics, and went camping, so when I thought of the future, I thought about what I wanted to do. I wanted to be a nurse and then a vet. In sixth or seventh grade I got very interested in sports and got into leadership positions in athletics. For quite a while I was more competitive with boys than interested in them.

Gail's husband Brian was anything but prepared for a wife with such an independent stance toward her own third-corner activity. His familiar paradigm was far more in keeping with the traditional patriarchal arrangement. He says:

> The role of the wife that I observed in my mother was what I assumed a wife would be: picking up, having meals prepared on time, spending a lot of time taking care of the home, etcetera. Those notions have been the cause of problems between me and Gail throughout our relationship. What I wanted in a wife didn't jibe with her assertive personality. My mother had been submissive with my father. Gail was not that way with me, and it was confusing to our interaction.

The basic conflict between Brian's and Gail's familiar paradigms led to some predictably stormy episodes, first during courtship and then continuing into the marriage. Brian recalls:

> We were two very strong-willed individuals, fighting it out. We had a lot of screaming arguments about small things, like whether or not to stop along the road when we were going somewhere. She'd want to stop, and I like to get where I'm going. A lot of clashes of will. It was like we were both saying, "Why don't you do it the way I want to?"

The Forming of the Inner-Corner • 45

Gail remembers similar episodes:

> We had minor hassles, and one really bad fight that first year of marriage. It was about something I was determined I was going to do, and he was determined I wasn't, and he physically blocked the door so I couldn't get out. I decked him, and he decked me back. . . . My concerns about being married had to do with how free I'd be, whether I'd have someone who'd tell me what I could and couldn't do. That was probably the real issue behind the fight. . . . The most difficult thing for me was having to check in with someone as to where I was and how long I'd be. Brian would always call to let me know where he was, and I didn't like having to do the same.

Recall that unlike Brian's, Gail's life-experience had never exposed her to significant female figures subordinating themselves to a man or even needing to coordinate their own movements with those of a man. It then becomes clear how truly paradigmatic her conflicts were with Brian. Both were simply drawing on the images that were most deeply imprinted from their earlier experience, and seeking to translate the seemingly workable images into their own married lifestyle.

Notice, once more, the intimate connection between third-corner independence and power in a partnership-corner. If patriarchy means lopsided male power, and if power in a marriage rests on the chance to secure important life resources in independent third-corners, then women with their own third-corner resources have, like Gail, the basis not only for making counterbalancing power claims in their marriage but also for more actively meeting their own needs. A wife with such resources may not necessarily love her husband less, but she may need him less. Her inner-corner has expanded and grown more complex, so that marital and family service may not alone express the fullness that she holds within her. She may require some outside corners to externalize her inner urges, capacities, skills, talents, and impulses.

If a mother's modeling is the most typical influence on a girl's third-corner habits, the second most prominent influence comes from her father. When a father responds to a daughter only as a cute little thing, the girl gets the message that rewards will flow to her through pleasing a man with her seductiveness. But some fathers stand ready to see their daughters as active agents in the world, as independent centers of power and initiative, not simply as repositories of charm, sweetness, and service. If such fathers are also ready to translate this vision into ongoing activities with their daughters, activities that lead to the cultivation of particular skills or talents or capacities, then the daughters may form strong habits of third-corner independence by the time they marry, even if their mothers never themselves modeled such third-corner interests.

Kelly Sampson nicely illustrates this pattern:

> My father was the dominant figure, and my mother was the subservient housewife dedicated to his endeavors. I didn't want to marry a dominating figure,

46 • *Three Corners*

because I had ideas of my own and I didn't want to have to fight to get them out. I knew I had more on my mind than just wanting to sit home and be a housewife. My mother could never really express her own endeavors or be her own person.

Though Kelly does not sound very sympathetic to either her mother or her father, she told me she felt more closely identified with her father. "I think my relationship with my father was always closer. I was never close to my mother and never would discuss my problems with her." The father–daughter closeness did not appear to stem from any greater ease in discussing her problems with her father. Rather, it arose from what they did together. Kelly's father was a high school physical education instructor, and his devotion to sports apparently spilled over into his family activity:

We were very involved as a family unit when I was growing up, especially through his sports years. [He later became a principal and superintendent.] My two brothers and I were always involved in sports. I never thought about marriage at all. I was always too involved in what I was doing—sports, and majorette in band in high school, taking lessons myself. I had a steady boyfriend in high school, but that became a convenient type of thing, having a social partner. He was also involved in sports. That's always been an equalling factor for me. In college I was involved in gymnastics. I met my husband on a trampoline our third day of college.

By the time Kelly married near the end of her college career, her third-corner habits of independence had long been established. Later, we shall see in another context that once her first child came, she could not seem to avoid falling into her mother's "subservient" pattern of housewifely dependency for a time. The important point here is that her familiar paradigm always included these other countertendencies of independence, aided by her father's encouragement, and they remained valuable resources to draw on whenever she chose, as she eventually did.

Aside from a mother modeling third-corner independence, or a father helping his daughther to develop it, a girl can form strong third-corners through other pathways as well. Older brothers sometimes help sisters develop athletic or other physical skills. Some girls who have difficult relationships with their parents escape into independence through some consuming pursuit such as tending and riding horses. "As a teenager," Janet Murray told me, "the biggest thing in my life was being able to have a horse and mastering horsemanship and finding rewards there, and that took me through an awful lot of rocky roads that other kids were having difficulties with." For Janet, as we shall see, horsemanship was not simply a childhood pursuit but has remained a lifelong passion.

The Forming of the Inner-Corner • 47

Other female respondents found an independent niche through their accomplishments in the school system. "My mother's values were alien to me," Alice Berger told me. "I'm more like my father. It irritated her that I read all the time. My father used to escape from her nagging by working in the garden and reading." Alice's penchant for reading carried her through some difficult years in secondary school:

> I was Franco-American, and when I went to Lewiston, from a French parochial school, they automatically put me in the lowest division. I was ten years old, in the sixth grade, and I was with kids who were about sixteen, waiting to get out of school. Fortunately I had a good teacher who understood. She pushed the work to me, and I thrived on it. When I was in junior high they didn't want me to take the college course because they thought I'd just get married and have kids, but a teacher intervened and let me take it. I graduated eleventh in my class. I wasn't accepted by the crowd I'd have liked to be in, so I read and sewed.

By the time she graduated from high school, Alice had already formed strong habits of self-reliance, well-defined personal traits and proclivities, and an enormous array of skills and talents. She went on to become a registered nurse, but after she married Tim, she only worked for a brief period until their first child was born. Then, with a move to another state, no job, no neighbors, two small children, and a husband who was gone from dawn to dusk, Alice still flourished in a situation in which many women would have languished. Her third-corner independence and resourcefulness were more than enough to sustain her:

> I channelled my energy into working on the property. I dug trees from the wilds and landscaped and I grew a garden. We worked on the house as we had the money. I sewed and refinished furniture. I never remember a time when I got bored.

Twenty-two years of marriage to Tim have not changed Alice's third-corner autonomy. She appreciates whatever attention he gives her, but she does not seem to crave very much because she is essentially self-stimulating:

> I think of myself as myself, not as Tim's wife or the kids' mother, and Tim sees me as myself too. In all these years I haven't distracted him from ball games and he hasn't changed my taste in reading. I still like classical music, but I listen to it when he's not around. He's very interested in ball games and needs that outlet, and I don't resent it as other wives might. I wanted to go to Spain a couple of years ago and he didn't, so I went with his mother. . . . I wish Tim liked to read and go to art shows. I do those things alone, but I'd like his company if he enjoyed them. But he'll never change.

48 • *Three Corners*

Alice shows us, once more, how the three corners of one's personal space play off of each other. With many independent third-corners and a partnership-corner that is comfortable despite its limitations, Alice can feel good with or without her husband's presence. In turn, the balance between her two outer-corners (second- and third-) keeps her inner-corner free from fusion with either of them.

To summarize the thrust of this chapter: We have seen that a person comes to marriage with a knowledge of how it might work, does work, should work, and should not work. This practical knowledge, which I have called a marital paradigm, is profoundly shaped by whatever life-experience precedes the marriage, and particularly by the living example of marriage modeled by one or both parents. The familiar paradigm includes imagery about all three corners of a married self, and we have explored some of the themes of each of the corners. The list of themes is not exhaustive, and the case materials are only illustrative. The purpose is to suggest a few ways of linking marital issues with premarital history, not to provide a comprehensive treatment of all the territory to be found on the map.

Notes

1. Joan Aldous, *Family Careers: Developmental Change in Families* (New York: Wiley, 1978), p. 133.
2. Thomas Kuhn, *The Structure of Scientific Revolutions* (Chicago: University of Chicago Press, 1962), pp. viii, 10–11.
3. Nancy Chodorow, *The Reproduction of Mothering* (Berkeley: University of California Press, 1978), p. 128.
4. Ibid., p. 140.
5. Ibid., p. 128.
6. Willard Waller and Reuben Hill, *The Family: A Dynamic Interpretation* (New York: Holt, Rinehart and Winston, 1951), pp. 190–192.
7. The idea that marital power is determined by the partners' relative access to resources outside the marriage was first developed by Robert Blood and Donald Wolfe in *Husbands and Wives* (New York: Free Press, 1960). Now outdated because of the authors' premature declaration of the death of patriarchy, this work has been superseded by the research of such sociologists as John Scanzoni. See his *Sexual Bargaining,* 2d ed. (Chicago: University of Chicago Press, 1982), and his "Social Processes and Power in Families," in *Contemporary Theories about the Family,* vol. 1, ed. Wesley Burr, Reuben Hill, F. Ivan Nye, and Ira Reiss (New York: Free Press, 1979), pp. 295–316. The link between work, income, and marital power has been explored more recently by Philip Blumstein and Pepper Schwartz, *American Couples* (New York: William Morrow, 1983), especially pp. 51–111, and 139–145.
8. One of the more notable studies is Walter Gove and Jeanette Tudor, "Adult Sex Roles and Mental Illness," *American Journal of Sociology* 78 (1973):812–835.

3
Marriage Agendas

To this point, my focus has centered on two aspects of the images that people bring to their marriages: first, the paradigms themselves (the actual pictures that people have of how their three corners might be arranged), and second, their feelings about these arrangements—the standpoints that people adopt toward the scenarios they know, as seen in their tendencies to embrace, reject, or fall into them. I now introduce a third aspect through which people organize and flesh out their images of marriage. A *marriage agenda* is a mental outline of the type of work or "business" that people seek to transact in their marriages. It is a set of intentions through which they translate their stance toward their familiar paradigm into an actual program. Marriage agendas thus reflect what people want to do in light of their knowledge and feelings about what might happen to them in a marriage.

Like the marital paradigms that underlie them, marriage agendas may be simple or elaborate, strongly or weakly held, implicit or remarkably explicit, as when couples actually draw up a marriage contract. Some people are fully cognizant of what their marriage agendas are, while others are unconscious of them, believing that they would never have constructed such a thing. These latter people may, in fact, be fairly free of agendas for marriage. Often, however, agendas are carried unconsciously, and they are hidden from awareness only because their implementation is smooth, easy, and unchallenged.

Before looking at some actual marriage agendas, we might consider why such agendas commonly arise. Immediately, we are struck by a paradox. On one hand, most people who contemplate marriage see it as a fresh start, a chance to do something new and different. On the other hand, everything said here so far should indicate that in marriage we continue to interact with the old and familiar. Both sides of the paradox are in fact true. Marriage is indeed a new chance to deal with old issues, and though many people fancy marriage to be a great escape from these issues, they often revert back into old strategies after all.

The crux of the matter is that people often have some pressing needs before they marry, and getting married does not make these needs magically go away.

The late psychologist Abraham Maslow often wrote about deficiency needs and growth needs, and his claims are useful in coming to terms with the marriage agendas I found in my data. Deficiency needs are basic needs like safety and security, love and affection, and self-esteem. If these needs have never been properly gratified, the person is left in a relatively deprived frame of mind. In contrast, growth needs focus on realizing one's potential through the free exercise of one's creative capacities, and these come to predominate only after the basic deficiency needs have been at least minimally gratified.[1]

People who, as children, never felt safe or adequately nurtured or respected seem to act so as to secure these needs for themselves as adults, and creative self-expression may get temporarily if not permanently postponed. They may then bring this deficiency motivation into their marriages, beginning with their actual search for a partner. The greater their deficiency, the more sharply focussed their marriage agendas will be, restricting their vision only to those potential partners who seem willing to attend to their deficits. With good reason Marvin Goodman found that people who score low on measures of self-acceptance tend to select partners who narrowly complement their own needs, while high self-accepters seem to be open to a much wider and more random range of possible partners.[2] One woman in my sample mused:

> My personality has always been "will of the wind." When I'm with various types of people I can do what they're doing and enjoy it. I could have married several kinds of men and fit into their life-style. Eric isn't that adaptable. He wouldn't have been able to get along with as many kinds of women.

These are clearly the words of a basic need-gratified person whose agendas for marriage are open and flexible. Her vision of partnership did not have to be narrowed down for the sake of filling a particular deficit. The difference between open and closed agendas—between growth-motivated and deficiency-motivated agendas—will become clearer as we look at the full range of agenda types I found in my data.

Avoiding the Demon

The marriage agenda that can perhaps become most rigid and inflexible is *Avoiding the Demon.* Typically, this agenda is held by people who soundly reject some elements of their familiar paradigm. They have powerful images of one or more disaster scenarios which they saw played out at home. There were traumatic childhood or adolescent scenes either for themselves or for one or both of their parents. In some instances, these scenes left them with some unmet basic needs, and marriage is then seen as a chance to fill the deficit—to be finally safe instead of unprotected, or loved instead of unloved, or attached

Marriage Agendas • 51

instead of abandoned, or respected instead of scorned. Typical demons to be avoided are alcohol, confrontation and conflict, divorce, undesirable power relationships, unseemly dispositions in a partner, extramarital intimacies, and abandonment. Several of these themes are often found together, as in the case of Morris Gorman, a thirty-eight-year-old businessman, married fourteen years:

> My parents were divorced when I was quite young, and we kids were put into state homes. Then my mother, my real mother, had some illegitimate children, so I have half-sisters and half-brothers. My mother used to come see me once in a while. She had a lot of problems. Even at five or six years old I knew things wasn't right. My mother had a lot of men calling and that didn't set with me.

Here we see themes of divorce, abandonment, and extramarital intimacy, all coming together to form Morris's disaster scenario. His strategy for dealing with this scenario became obvious when I asked him if he knew what qualities he wanted in a partner. He replied, "I wanted a pure girl: I didn't want someone that flaunted herself around. I didn't want to be married to a barmaid. And I certainly didn't want to be divorced." For Morris, whose childhood was fraught with so much uncertainty and instability of parental figures, marriage is largely seen as a chance to be permanently attached instead of abandoned, and to be attached to someone whose moral values would make it unthinkable for her to repeat what he sees as his mother's pattern of betrayal.

People with strong agendas to avoid some demon are often recognizable through their courtship processes. For them, there are certain behaviors that they will simply not tolerate in a partner, and any potential mate who displays these behaviors during courtship will be eliminated from consideration. On some matters they may expect to compromise, but there are bottom-line requirements that are nonnegotiable. "Almost everything that I didn't want in my marriage had to do with alcohol," said a woman whose childhood was split between her aunt and uncle's home and her father and stepmother's:

> My uncle was a drunk. He abused my aunt at times, but they ignored each other more than anything else. My uncle went on binges. My father drank from Friday night at five until he wasn't aware of anything Saturday night. Then he slept until it was time to go to work Monday morning. I didn't want to marry anyone who was interested in liquor at all. It was the source of all the disruption of my childhood.

Another woman said, "I knew I definitely didn't want to marry a playboy." Her father had died when she was an infant, and she had heard "a few negative things" from her mother concerning his infidelity. "And I made some inferences

52 • *Three Corners*

in my own mind that—well, I don't think I would really like that kind of life-style."

Clark Mason's demon to be avoided centered on conflict and confrontation. The sixth of seven children, Clark was only six years old when his mother divorced his alcoholic father after twenty-five tumultuous years. As he sees it now, Clark got caught in the fallout of his mother's anger and frustration:

> My younger brother and I never could figure out why my mother always appeared mad at us. Much later I realized that her living that long with alcohol had to make her angry, and I think that just carried right over. Even after they were divorced, I think she was still angry, and I think we took a lot of that for a lot of years, and really didn't understand it. . . . The way that I dealt with her anger was by running away from it as much as I could. I'd be out of the house a lot. I worked all the time. When I was going to high school I'd start work at four in the morning, I'd go to school, and I'd work at night. That's all I did until I went into the service.

By the time Clark married, he had formed a marriage agenda that was a direct response to his experience with anger and conflict:

> In my mother's second marriage she was still angry, and there was always a lot of hollering and fighting back and forth. I was determined that that would not be the case in any marriage that I went into. Whoever this would be would be someone that's pretty mild-mannered and wouldn't be taking to fireworks.

Clark's courtship with Henrietta was appropriately calm, cool, and low key, with the added benefit that Henrietta helped convince Clark that his potential for success in life was far greater than his low self-esteem would allow him to consider. Their marriage lasted for eleven years before Clark filed for divorce. For the first ten years, Clark studiously avoided coming to grips with the enormous differences between them. Henrietta hated Maine and wanted to live in the South; Clark had no interest in leaving. She did not want any children; he came to want them, though he had earlier agreed not to have any. He wanted to live in the country; she wanted to live in town. He wanted to own a house; she wanted to rent. He wanted an active social life; her style was more reclusive. He wanted some outside athletic activities in his leisure time; she was more of a homebody and had no interest in athletic pursuits. She wanted to travel during vacation times; he often would have preferred to stay home. With the exception of continuing to live in Maine, Henrietta got her way on all these differences. Clark now faults himself for not being aggressive enough:

> If there was a problem, I think that it was with me, because she communicated what she wanted. She made it clear what she wanted, and I didn't communicate with her the way I should have on the things that I wanted. I let myself get

pushed around. I'm sure I felt some resentment, but I don't think it was strong, because I accepted getting pushed around.

Clark cannot recall a single argument in their eleven years of marriage. Henrietta may have been more vocal in expressing her tangible wants, but she likewise steered clear of any confrontation, and both partners made hardly any emotional demands on one another. Clark summarizes:

> Our whole marriage was smooth, except for the last year. When I said I wanted someone that didn't fight with me, that's exactly what I got. That was a big problem. There should have been some fighting, and there wasn't. We'd just walk away from each other. There was absolutely no exchange. If there was something difficult to talk about, we just wouldn't, rather than risk getting into a fight. . . . I was very successful in my business and everything in my life was running smoothly—I'm sure that's what I wanted to happen. There was no conflict, everything was going fine, and I accomplished the things I wanted to do. From what my mother and father went through and what all my brothers and sisters were going through [four of the six of them have been divorced at least once], why, this felt, well, this must be right.

I shall not detail the process through which Clark became dissatisfied with his conflict-free and emotionally vacuous marriage, nor his efforts to extricate himself from it. My purpose here is to show that demon conflict may become so dominating in a person's familiar paradigm that successfully avoiding it can emerge as the only blueprint for constructing and maintaining a marriage. The fact that Henrietta and Clark both had strong, independent, professional third-corners spared them many of the one-sided partnership investments that plague other couples, and their marriage thus lumbered along for ten years.

Nevertheless, third-corner symmetry alone is not a sticky enough glue to hold a couple together. When both partners adhere only to their own interests, with neither a vital partnership-corner nor any ongoing joint third-corners such as children or mutual leisure interests, the centrifugal force of separate concerns can stretch a marriage precariously thin. For Clark, the success of his marriage agenda ironically spelled the demise of his marriage. Avoiding the demon conflict worked so well that his vision of partnership was eventually freed up to focus on other needs and potentials for a marriage. Now in his second marriage, he cherishes the many ways that he and his new wife can connect together, and he has put aside his fear of conflict: "I always assumed that if you had confrontation, you were going to come out loser. I don't find that to be the case now. If anything else, I think if you get on out through it, it strengthens things."

For some respondents, courtship screening out of unwanted demons was not successful, and that demon later managed to rear its ugly head. Some

54 • *Three Corners*

respondents who wanted no part of alcohol in their lives wound up struggling with a partner's drinking problem or their own. The same was often true of conflict. A male respondent who had hoped in his own marriage to avoid his father's withdrawal from discussion of marital issues picked a wife whose passion was to question and challenge everything. This man soon found himself feeling that he was the target of criticism even where none was intended. He reacted by withdrawing and becoming noncommunicative, much as his father had, and it took him many years before he could stop repeating that pattern. As we have already seen, the path of least resistance is to fall back into the most central elements of our familiar paradigms, and this is no less true of negative paradigm elements than positive ones. A persons's marriage agenda is binding only on the level of intent, and people do not always get what they intend. It all depends on the paradigms and agendas that one's partner brings to the marriage, on how skillful one is in discovering what these are, and on the dynamics unleashed by the convergence of these two unfolding life-patterns.

Finally, while Avoiding the Demon may sometimes create some tunnel vision because it focusses mainly on negative scenarios, people who successfully carry it out are not necessarily cast with partners whose only asset is that they will not do the demonic deed, whatever it is. Sometimes, ruling out that deed through good courtship screening may be enough to fill some deficit left over from childhood, and the person may then be able to shift from deficiency motivation to growth motivation in the field of intimate relationships. Such a shift will be difficult if neither parent modeled a partnership role that could be comfortably emulated. But if just one parent did so, or if other significant marital models were available with truly formative intensity, then the person may be able in his or her own marriage to resoundingly transcend everything that was played out between the parents. A forty-five-year-old business manager speaks of his parents:

> They had an unhappy marriage. They were not compatible, but they stuck it out. My mother was a very cantankerous person—I couldn't live with her either. My father was very easygoing, and he and I did a lot together. My mother and I didn't have that type of relationship any more than she and my father did. I'm sure my father was a very unhappy man because of not having a relationship with my mother, either physically or socially.

Strongly identified with his easygoing father, this man avoided the demon of a cantankerous wife by choosing a mate who turned out to be unabashedly thrilled to be married and dedicated to doing everything she could to make it work. Moreover, his wife had also been his childhood sweetheart, and from an early age he was able to lavishly secure from her all the warmth and nurturance that he missed from his mother. He worked several summers for her father, and he spent a lot of time around her house, finding in her parents'

marriage a really positive, comfortable model, just the opposite of his own parents'. His wife remembers the first year they were married:

> Alan grew up where home didn't mean that much; he didn't have the love I did growing up in the home. Listen! That first year we were married, you just can't imagine! He'd come home at night and he'd say, "I can't believe it." He was just so overwhelmed by the happiness, to have a nice home. And it pleased me so much that I wanted to work even harder to make this happy for him, to make it a good marriage. To come home and have a hot meal at night, and a loving wife—he'd just never seen anything like this. And he still loves it [after twenty-two years of marriage], I think. And I love having him come home. I'm so thankful for our marriage.

Safe Return Home

Some people have an idyllic image of their parents' marriage and hope to recapture it in their own. Their marriage agenda is diametrically opposite to Avoiding the Demon. Far from rejecting their familiar paradigm and steering clear of some disaster scenario of marriage, they embrace what their parents did and seek a partner with whom they can recreate it. Their image of marriage is not demonic but cozy and comfortable; they want to make a *Safe Return Home*.

For people with this agenda, marriage does not stand alone but must be linked up to the larger extended family circle. Marriage creates a new home and family, and thus a larger basis for solidifying one's place in the entire kinship network. The pattern described by Elizabeth Bott applies here: People who have been residentially stable and who have always found ample social support in their kinship network will not tend to disrupt that network for the sake of a marriage. Rather, the marriage will be "superimposed" (Bott's term) upon the pre-existing tightly-knit kin network.[3] Thus it is not the parents' marital relationship alone that gets focussed on in this agenda, not the special qualities (if there are any) of their emotional partnership, but the embeddedness of a family in the safe confines of the larger kin network: "My mother's mother and father lived downstairs," recalls Mike McCarthy, a thirty-seven-year-old store manager, married twelve years. I asked him if they ate meals with his grandparents:

> Always. We did everything with my grandparents. Everytime one of them had to go somewhere, I'd be tagging along with them when I was younger. . . . On the weekends we used to go on picnics, go down to Belfast and have lobster feeds, and dig our own clams. A good twenty relatives would get together. A lot of my grandmother's brothers and sisters would come. We'd go out in a field and have cookouts. I had lots of uncles who did things with me too.

Mike's marriage to Jill had a rocky beginning, due in part to his reluctance to give up his previous life-style revolving around sports and his male peers. Jill got pregnant right away, and there was a brief tug of war between the interests of his new domestic life and those of his male peer group. Safe Return Home then came to the rescue, with the birth of their first child:

> I think you can go right back to me wanting to start right then and there bringing my kids up the way I was, as far as being loving and affectionate. Ellen [the baby] was a big change for us. With the baby I had to stay home more. I think Ellen was the reason for us doing things together. And then when Suzy came along we did a lot more. . . . We moved back up over my grandparents where I was brought up, in the same apartment, and my wife thinks a lot of my grandmother, so I think that might have changed us a little bit for the better.

Recall that in Mike's familiar paradigm, children are often given over to their grandparents and other extended family members. New parenthood, with its creation of a new generation, thus anchors a person more firmly into the extended family circle, and one's place in that home-centered world becomes still more solidly grounded.

Safe Return Home is most often a working-class phenomenon, although we may find it held by anyone who has reason to downgrade the value of career success or who believes that existing kinship bonds are the only safe "haven in a heartless world," to use Christopher Lasch's lyrical phrase. Then too, any person who has been greatly sheltered as a child or adolescent or whose life has remained comfortably confined to a limited milieu may have little reason to envision forsaking that milieu for the great unknown. Among my respondents, Safe Return Home is commonly found in working-class rural or in small-town settings, although I would expect it to be common in the urban working class as well. Working-class worlds are *sometimes* "worlds of pain," as in Lillian Rubin's reckoning—worlds replete with economic insecurity, alcohol abuse, and violence.[4] But Rubin ignores just how often they are worlds with their own brand of comfort, with zones of safety defined in large part by continuing ties with one's family of origin. Gil Hopkins, a thirty-five-year-old truck mechanic, describes how he discovered his profound link with his parents:

> I was pretty strongheaded and my father wasn't too much for tolerating too much bull. That's the way he was brought up, so it passes on. I thought for a long time, where he was so tight, that he didn't care too much about us at all. As I got older things started changing. I didn't realize that I was close to my folks until after I was married, and I got drafted. When I got away from home, I felt an awful empty spot. There was a lot more feeling there than I ever knew there was. Growing up, you know there's something there, but you can't put your finger on it.

Safe Return Home does not necessarily imply an overly idealized conception of the parents' marriage. Gil remembers some tensions:

> I knew that spats were flying and words were going. They both worked real hard [he as a truck driver, she in a factory] and they were tired, and it didn't take very much to set off a fuse. They were working long hours and the wages weren't that great.

Despite some quarrels over money, their marriage has nevertheless been a positive model:

> I did look forward to getting married. I looked forward to having a nice home, and a nice person to be good to my kids, keep things straight, and if necessary work along with me to help get us through—more or less the same lifestyle that I had been used to, my mother and father out working.

Gil's first attempt was short-lived. He married a casual girlfriend after she became pregnant, and when the draft called him away she wrote him that "she didn't want to be tied down." Following their divorce she gave up custody of the child, not to Gil but to his parents. Before long Gil remarried, this time to his childhood sweetheart. I asked him if there were any surprises at the outset of his second marriage: "The only thing that was surprising was being so content." His contentment was surely aided by how easily this marriage could be intertwined with their respective families of origin. "Even when we were dating we more or less stayed at her place or we'd come down to my folks and visit," a pattern that has continued throughout their ten years of marriage. His parents' custody of his first child seemed to solidify his Safe Return Home:

> My mother has custody of my daughter from the first marriage. I can see her whenever I want to. She stays here a lot of weekends, and we're always down to Mom's and Dad's, so I know she's being brought up right. . . . My parents were more than willing to have custody, since my daughter had lived with them ever since she was born. To my mother and father she seems just like one of theirs.

Notice how once again, the creation of a new generation is what stabilizes the agenda to make a Safe Return Home, even under these unconventional circumstances.

Some respondents seemed to hold this marriage agenda precisely because their own home was not safe, and they yearned to create for themselves a secure family haven through their partner's family. Hal Stern, the man who remembers his home as "the kind of place where people came to do battle with one another," speaks of how he dealt with the situation: "I became very

58 • *Three Corners*

independent as a youngster and moved in my own circles, as kind of a protective situation." One of his agendas for marriage was thus colored by deficiency motivation, by the need to fill the deficit of emotional security and safety:

> I just had an image of security, that I wouldn't be alone anymore, that there would be somebody who I could trust and who could really care for me as a person. It was something that I really desperately needed, too, and I saw a marriage relationship as providing that. And I was looking for someone who came from a strong family; that was important to me. I remember relating as well to her family as I did to her. I felt very comfortable with her family and they with me, and so the whole thing kind of came together as a replacement for something I didn't have, growing up. And her family had acceptance in the society that they existed in. I never felt my family had acceptance from the community they lived in, from neighbors; there was hardly ever anybody in my house. There were very few friends that I can remember. I was looking for greater depth in a family relationship and found that in my wife's family.

Clearly, Hal saw in his wife's family a safe *arrival* home, given that his own family did not lend itself to the notion of a safe return home. Right after marriage, he found his first home in an upstairs room of his wife's parents' household, and while he remembers wanting more privacy and a place of their own, his living with them must have spoken to a long-standing fantasy wish to be comfortably enmeshed in a tight family circle.

As with most marriage agendas, Safe Return Home does not focus on needs within the partnership-corner per se but looks to a third-corner to shore up the foundations of individual security. For many people, partnership alone is too empty a concept in which to invest one's adult sustenance, either because they witnessed too many failed relationships or simply because they lacked any model that could lend concreteness to the notion of partnership as a self-contained frontier, which is the modern "therapeutic" conception of marriage. In many respects, "marriage" is always a code word for adult security, and because dependence on only one person increases feelings of vulnerability, people tend to translate "marriage" into something more than partnership alone. Safe Return Home, with its focus on kin-based third-corners, is only one of several such translations. As we shall now see, the other marriage agendas are also translations of partnership into larger commitments and obligations, though the particular third-corner focus may differ from one agenda to another.

Religious Calling

Some people see their marriage as a *Religious Calling*. They want to align their marriage with the convictions and principles drawn from their church or creed.

Marriage Agendas • 59

There are several pathways that can lead to this marriage agenda. For some of my respondents whose home life was comfortable, a marriage with religion at its center was modeled in their family of origin. An engineer, married twenty years, immediately translated a question I asked him about his parents' marriage into a statement about their family life and religion:

I don't ever remember any problems with their marriage. We did everything together. My father, when he was a boy, had to walk five miles or so to get to Sunday school, and he never missed a Sunday. . . . So as we were growing up our parents always took us to church and Sunday school. They never left it to us to decide if we wanted to go or not. They went with us, so we always had that relationship together. And Sunday afternoon after church, they used to take us on picnics and so forth.

For this man, embracing a religious-centered marriage meant referring to religious standards as the only rightful guides to conduct both for marriage and for courtship. I asked whether his courtship was a high-intensity sort of experience or more low key. He spoke of a time when the physical attraction between them began to grow more intense and how religious principles overruled their sexual desires:

As we were growing up we were both going to church. We were both involved at this time in a youth group, and our parents and the people in the church were all brought up not to compromise but to believe the Bible and believe that what it says is absolute. That was what you set your standard by, not by what other people were doing or because if-it-feels-good,-do-it. So we always had a good guide to decide for ourselves whether what we were doing was beyond the limits of what God wanted for us.

Some respondents arrive at a religious agenda for marriage through rejecting their familiar paradigm, not through embracing it. Religious Calling may then be combined with Avoiding the Demon as a plan for marriage. Morris Gorman, who was mentioned as wanting to avoid divorce and extramarital intimacies after having spent most of his childhood in a succession of foster homes, spoke of having had "some false notions" prior to his religious conversion:

I had Satanic notions. And then I decided, here I am, I'm seventeen, and if I want to end up the way my father did I can continue. It wasn't so much my behavior but my attitude. I seemed to have a guardian angel. I couldn't seem to find the type of behavior I was looking for, the activities I wanted to get into. So the missionaries of the church came along, and I wanted to emulate them. I said, well, if I want to be like them then I have to follow their way of life, and if I want to end up the way my parents have, then I can continue their way. So I made that decision when I was seventeen years old to change

60 • *Three Corners*

my attitude and my thinking and my outlook on life, and so that's when I joined the Church. . . . About a month before that I was out one night and I drove into the restaurant and saw the guys. They said, "Come on, we've got a hot broad over here in cabin 8. You want to go out?" I goes out, and I was very abrupt. I opened the door, and I took my clothes off, and I says, "Let's go." They'd been banging her all day—it was about two in the morning—she wasn't in any mood to have any more callers. And I thought, "What the hell is this anyway? Is this what I want out of life?" From that day on I decided maybe I'd do something different in life.

Armed with new-found religious principles, Morris indeed did "something different." He found a woman who shared his religious faith, one whose religious scruples would have made it inconceivable for her to repeat the sexually promiscuous pattern of his mother, the pattern that (at least in his own mind) had led to his earlier abandonment to foster homes:

> In the church we have a lot of qualities that we look for: a person with a strong conviction in their religious beliefs, and a person that has a strong conviction of the Savior and the teachings of the church, and is willing to live them and not question them. The Lord indicated to me that Becky was the one; it was nothing flashy, the Lord just pointed her out to me. I just had a warm feeling.

A third pathway to marriage as a Religious Calling also entails a conversion experience or at least an intensification of religious commitments, only it occurs after the marriage has been formed. Here, Religious Calling is paired neither with avoiding some demon nor with Safe Return Home, although in some instances the person may have had considerable religious exposure as a child. The essential fact is that religious principles now provide a new framework for interpreting past, present, and future marital events and for coming to terms with the meaning of one's life.

Faith Dickson, a respondent married fifty-three years, told me that she sees two basic phases that her marriage has gone through—a ten-year period of frequent though unexpressed resentments followed by a forty-three-year period in which her principal focus has been, in her words, "to know and do the will of God."

> I think that I really was a selfish person when I was first married. I was always thinking of what he should do for me instead of what I should do for him. When things didn't go my way I became resentful. And my husband is a very bright engineer, and I think he made me feel inferior. I think it was his attitude. He's very quick, and some of us do not learn as quickly as he does. His tone of voice—if you didn't understand something right away—would show you that he was impatient and thought you really were a little slow. [Chuckles.] I know it gave me that feeling. Then when I read these devotional

books it made me absolutely realize that Jesus loves me, even if I'm not as brilliant as Stuart is. Stuart is an impatient man, and I have had to learn to live with that. . . . I think you have to learn to accept the person as he is and to appreciate him. . . . It was not until I read these books that I began to see my faults. See, I was blaming him for everything that happened. . . . Later, I don't know as he even knew that I felt better. We never did quarrel much. I would just close up and not say anything. I never told him my real feelings, which was bad.

Notice how, in Faith's account, there is no indication that Stuart's impatience or any other of his previously objectional behaviors ever changed. When marriage becomes a Religious Calling, one has a new frame of reference, a new translation for understanding marital events and for gauging the rightness of one's own behavior, and this development need not entail a single change in any of the externals. In some instances, however, when this agenda is adopted by both partners together, there may be profoundly dynamic changes in both of their partnership-corners. Such is the case whenever the new religious principles actually direct the couple to perfect their marriage so it can serve as an instrument of God's will. This situation is especially fostered by the Marriage Encounter movement, and will be discussed later.

Economic Calling

In American culture all adults must in some way be concerned with their economic status. A "living" is something we "make" through "earning," and this earning is held to be each family's private problem. In this sense every marriage is an economic enterprise. For some people, however, earning a living seems to be elevated into the defining essence of what a marriage is. It is as if the very purpose of intimate partnership is to jointly accumulate material possessions, and the progress of the marriage can be marked by the major purchases that stand as tangible milestones. For these people, marriage is an Economic Calling. Such people were sometimes recognizable through their eagerness to show or tell me about their most prized possessions, or to recount the sequence of job advancements that made these purchases possible. In no case did I ask for the elaborate information about consumer spending or job mobility that I sometimes got, although I did seek minimal descriptions of a person's job history. What was so striking was the tendency of some respondents to spontaneously translate questions I asked them about different phases of their marriage into statements about their economic changes of fortune. Men who strongly identify with the breadwinner or provider notion of a husband's role were especially likely to make this kind of translation, and to have begun to do so even at the beginning of courtship. Here is a respondent who immediately makes the economic translation, when I asked about his courtship:

62 • *Three Corners*

It was a lot of fun, although there wasn't much money to throw around. I was getting $20 a week from the service, and there was very little work available. I did a few crazy things. She loved dogs and I bought her a registered cocker spaniel for $35, which was a lot of money for me then. Another time she saw a quilt she wanted that was $15, and I had $17 in my pocket and I bought it for her. And that's pretty much the way things have been. Of course after we got married she knew what the finances were and wouldn't ask for something we couldn't afford, but for the most part whatever she's wanted I've gotten for her.

It sounds like it's been very important to you to provide materially for your wife.

Absolutely. I think that's reflected in this home that we have. I built this house. I drove every damned nail in it. I've taken a great deal of pride in everything I have here, and I think that a great deal of that stems from the fact that I did without so much in my younger years. I'm going to have what I can afford to have.

"I did without so much in my younger years"—the inner feeling of many of the men who see marriage as an Economic Calling. A number of these respondents grew up in an atmosphere of privation, whatever the actual facts were of their parents' economic situation. Accordingly, they bring to their marriage some pressing deficiency needs that focus on material progress as the only way to fill the deficit. Economic Calling is then the remedy for Avoiding the Demon of privation. The man just quoted was born in 1929, and remembers his parents being "preoccupied with trying to eke out a living."

We grew up on a farm and had hired men living with us at times. My father and mother both worked in a shoe factory. We had a few head of cattle, a few horses, about 100 chickens and a couple of pigs, mainly for our own use. Dad had about a five-acre garden. They both worked full-time. It was a hard life. I know what it is to do without, but we never went hungry. I wanted to do more for Margie and my children than obviously my parents were able to do for me.

Another man, born the year after this one, tells a similar story:

If my children had to live their childhood the way my wife and I did, then things would have been a lot different for them: hand-me-down clothes, corn chowder, potato soup, oatmeal for supper, things like that. But I had what I considered a happy childhood. When I was real young there was only one man in the family that was working, and the whole family lived together. When I was in kindergarten I came to school on snowshoes.

Marriage Agendas • 63

Who was in the household?

My grandmother, my great-aunt and -uncle, their son, my mother's brother and his wife and child, my folks, and me and my brother. This was in '34, '35, '36 during the Depression. My dad happened to get a job at the shipyard by being in the right place in the line waiting for work. The rest of us lived off the farm. You counted heads for Sunday dinner and then you went out in the chicken coop and picked out the biggest rooster! We never went hungry. We always had clothes to wear. We didn't wear shoes in the summertime; no one did. I can remember when I was six years old going up into the woods to help gather firewood. We burned wood—we had three big woodburning stoves in the house. The family used to go hunting. We had cows, we had a horse. Things that kids don't have now.

This man remembers a happy childhood, and he thinks his parents had a very good marriage. But he naturally brought to his own marriage a keen sense of the precariousness of economic safety. I asked him about any expectations he may have had for his marriage:

Nothing would be wasted. And even now it disturbs me to see things wasted. I hate to see people blowing their money. The kids now have no idea what they can do with a dollar. . . . I think Tess probably represented everything I expected in a woman. She could cook; she could sew—she was a pretty girl, too. She didn't strike me as anyone who would be wasteful with things.

I asked, "How do you remember your first year of marriage," and almost immediately he translated my question into a series of economic statements:

That's when the daughter was born. We had a three-room apartment. I was bringing home just under $40 a week. We had all brand-new furniture—we had been paying for it for about a year before we were married, so we had it pretty well paid for. We had a car that we owned. We had a new refrigerator. We were paying rent, paying our utilities and heat, and we were putting money in the bank.

For the most part, the men in my sample who see marriage as an Economic Calling have been upwardly mobile from humble origins. They are proud homeowners who are living out the American dream of active membership in the consumer society. But even when they have become quite affluent, they seem to retain a vision of marriage that puts it to the service of relieving their basic sense of economic deficiency and insecurity. Not the objective reality but the subjective sensibility makes the difference here. Regardless of how safe from absolute privation people may be, they are often measuring their progress by comparison with those around them. Preoccupied with economic

64 • *Three Corners*

standards of comparison, people may feel safe if they can simply avoid privation, but if they are to feel esteemed in their own and others' eyes, they may need to accomplish some rather virtuoso economic performances. Here is a man thirty-four years of age, married thirteen years, a manager for an industrial firm, and the son of a tool- and die-maker, talking about his wife's family:

> I felt a strong sense of competition from her dad and her brothers. To this day she does not understand my feelings in that respect. She thinks it's silly of me to feel that way. Janet's dad was very successful; I can't think of anything he's done wrong. He flew airplanes, which is a fond dream of mine which I've never been able to do. He was a pilot during World War II, was shot down twice—a hero. Then he came back after the war and got a job, and very quickly moved up in the business, and had a beautiful house and a swimming pool and a twin-engine airplane. And her older brother was pretty much in the same mold, a very competitive individual. Financially he made the right decisions all the time; he flew an airplane. Her younger brother, he's a pilot in the navy. He's probably of the three of them going to be the best. . . . It's a very athletic family. So I always felt that I had to do at least as well as they did, or I would be letting my wife down, or my girl. I still feel it to a certain point to this day.

This man has already risen far above the level of earning and consumption of his own father, but that level is no longer his benchmark for measuring his own economic progress. When he was eighteen his father died, and at that point Janet's father "took me under his wing, because of my dad not being around." Given his craving for parental guidance, it then became easy to adopt Janet's father's model of financial success.

Clearly, the standard of economic deprivation is a relative one, as sociologists have long pointed out. At every level of the socio-economic hierarchy, marriage may become an Economic Calling, and people at each stratum will be making different kinds of comparisons in order to determine whether they are more or less "worthy" than those around them. Women, too, may see their marriage as an Economic Calling, even when their husband alone is responsible for generating the family finances. I asked fifty-year-old Sandy, a woman who lives in a low-rent public housing development, if she felt her marriage was in some way special compared to the marriages of other couples she and her husband Billy know. Notice how she immediately translated my question into economic realities:

> The people we see out here? I certainly do think our marriage is special. They're very content with nothing. If you could see the people around here you'd know. What they have in the house is nothing. And they have no ambition to try to make it better! They're satisfied to live like that. We're always trying to have something a little bit better. This couple we've known about maybe a month or so—she comes over, and my God, she never knows enough

to go home; she'll sit for hours and hours and hours! This is something that I wouldn't want, and Billy's not like that either. Billy doesn't want to sit around and waste his time when there's so much you could be doing! But they have nothing, and they never expect to have anything.

There's one couple that's living on meager social security, but a few days after his check comes he's always up here wanting to borrow money or wanting cigarette money. Ther's a limit to how much you can endure. But rather than say anything, we give him sixty cents. This is what Billy and I see in other couples: lack of ambition for one thing. I learned my lesson with those two, and I'm not about to branch out and ask any more to be friendly. [She tells another story about a woman who borrows and never pays anything back.] This is how we feel different from a lot of people, in that we can make our money stretch to pay for what we need, and we don't have to beg from others.

For the Children

The vast majority of American people want to have children once they marry. All fifty-seven of the couples I interviewed either bore children themselves or adopted them. Most of them knew even before they met their partner that having children would be a high priority in their marriage. In this sense, it could be said that *For the Children* is a marriage agenda held by all my respondents. For most of these couples, however, For the Children is not the defining essence of marriage but takes its place among an assortment of images that help define what a marriage is. When asked, "What notions did you have about marriage?", one woman replied: "I've always been a romantic. Marriage, family—*babies*! I was one of those kids that always played with dolls." Her three children have no doubt fulfilled this part of her vision of marriage, but it is also clear that her vision included a lot more. When her husband became, in her words, a "shiny new minister who was going out to slay dragons in the world," he became less and less accessible to her and their first child.

> It wasn't exactly the way I thought it was going to be. I was kind of a romantic, and that meant that he was going to be around a lot. . . . Yes, I did confront him. I don't know where I got the courage; I never had any. I guess it meant enough so that I knew we just had to back up and look at things again. . . . I discovered that I had some things that were important to me. I wasn't willing to share so much of him with other people.

Her husband's testimony confirmed her own. He conceded, "I was a pompous ass, like anybody who just comes out of seminary and believes God has peculiarly ordained him to solve the world's problems. And my wife was shut up in a horrible apartment."

66 • *Three Corners*

I shall not dwell on couples like this one, for whom marriage comes to mean something more than raising children, however important that may be. Rather, I shall focus on those respondents who seem to turn child rearing into a sort of mission and marriage into a vehicle whose overriding purpose is to serve that mission. Marriage for the children, in this sense, seems to have several possible origins. For some respondents this agenda is an outgrowth of rejecting the paradigm modeled by their parents. Thinking that one or both of their parents made grievous errors in their own upbringing, they are determined to correct these errors through providing different experiences for their children. It is as if child rearing provides an opportunity to relive their own childhood. By becoming the kind of parents they never had, they might vicariously become the kind of child they never could be. A respondent named Louise Miller said that her father was so engrossed in his work that he spent little time with her, "and this certainly played a part in my looking at people in terms of who I might marry." For her, the focus was not on mothering differently than her own mother but in finding a husband who would be a different kind of parent than her own father.

> When I was thinking about getting married, I was very eager to have a family and to see that my children would have a daddy that they could climb into his lap and snuggle up to him, who was around to do things with them on a continuing basis, who would deal with them like real, live people from the day they were born. My husband is very unusual. Ask a dozen people in Portland who Superdaddy is and they'll say "Jake Miller." . . . My father did not have a lot of that sensitivity toward children; I don't think he really thinks of children as people until they're able to carry on an intellectual conversation, or play a game at his level.

At this point in the interview, Louise provided a recent instance of her father having the kind of interaction with her children that demonstrates his lack of sensitivity to them. Clearly, the unspoken message behind the story—indeed, behind much of her vision of marriage—is that her father failed to be sensitive to *her* in some important ways. Just how much pain and anguish she had to endure in consequence is not clear; she is quick to gloss over any lingering resentments she may feel. What is clear to her is that where her own children are concerned, she and her husband will make any necessary sacrifices as a couple so that their presumed needs will be met.

> The overwhelming reason why I think we're as happy as we are is because, when it came down to the decision to have and to be involved with children, we've both, independently, almost always reached the same conclusion when it comes to "what are we going to do with this block of time?" If I'd like to spend a day playing golf with him, and he'd like that too, we both almost invariably decide that what we really ought to be doing is spending the day

Marriage Agendas • 67

with the children. We don't have those kinds of incompatibilities which I see among some friends we have. We put our children first. We both do it together. We may think there's time for us to play golf alone, but we'd rather teach our children to play golf together, frustrating as it might be. We want to do things with our kids. We opt to vacation with them. My job right now is to see that these kids get the best possible start in life that we can give them; and he feels exactly the same way. And that makes the difference in our marriage.

Louise's husband Jake did not feel "exactly" the same way, for reasons that will be explored in another context, but his account did square essentially with hers. And he provided additional information that showed just how singlemindedly this couple structures their marriage For the Children. For example, their relationships with other couples must eventually come to rest on those couples' values about children. I asked, "When you see marriages that lack what yours has, what's lacking?" Jake replied:

A sufficient commitment to the kids, to helping the kids get through things. What both of us focus on when looking at other people, in terms of whether we will spend time with them, is how they interact with their kids. And we draw a lot of conclusions about people from how they treat their kids and get along with their kids.

Religious commitments also get made on the basis of the presumed needs of the children. "I'm very atheist," Jake told me, "but we go to a Protestant church. I'm not sure how religious Louise really is, but she thought it was a good influence for the kids, and I agree, so we go without my having any strong commitment. I like the routine, and I like to sing." Louise's account was similar: "I feel very strongly that the children should have some sort of religious training. We are pursuing it for that reason. If we didn't have kids, we might not be pursuing it at this particular time."

Louise and Jake represent an almost pure case of For the Children as a marriage agenda, certainly the purest case in my sample. To be sure, all couples with children find themselves periodically structuring their marriage in terms of their children's needs, particularly when the family is large and when at least one child is still a preschooler. A woman whose three children range from age six to eleven put it this way:

I read once where somebody said, "If you have to pick between your husband and your children, you should pick your husband." And I feel that in a sense that's true. But when the children are small, they need you. Maybe if your children are teenagers or adults, then yes, your husband should definitely come first in all instances. We both feel that most of the time the kids come first because they need to come first.

68 • *Three Corners*

It may well be that in the more active child-rearing phase of each family's life cycle, For the Children tends to take center stage as the dominant marriage agenda for most couples, certainly for most wives. Nevertheless, there is still a difference between marrying for the children and marrying for the partnership, even when, in the latter instance, the prerogatives of the partnership itself are willingly suspended for the sake of the children's needs. Here, I shall stick to those former cases in which people are eager to translate marriage into a set of parental obligations to their children.

A common origin of this agenda is the arising of a sense of disillusionment about how the couple relationship is going. It is as if the person says, "My partner cannot or will not be there for me; therefore my domestic life will focus on my children." The marriage may have been formed for the partnership, but when that falters and divorce or separation is not a serious consideration, For the Children comes to be the defining essence of the marriage. This outcome will be more likely of course, if the person's parents also modeled a marriage that revolved around children, in which case it may become easy to fall into that familiar paradigm in response to an inaccessible spouse. Women are especially likely to adopt this agenda wherever traditional cultural patterns still govern the prevailing assumptions about what it means to be a wife or husband. Then, a wife may see it as her duty to rest content with maintaining the home, raising the children, and supporting the husband's total absorption in his independent third-corners, even at the expense of any intimate couple partnership. Ruby Nelson, a forty-eight-year-old woman, married for thirty years to a man whose job often kept him out of town during the week, recalls some disillusionment when she realized that her husband Greg had so little time for her:

> Greg is very ambitious. When he does something for his career, he puts his whole heart and soul into it. After I had my second child [they have four] I kind of felt neglected, and I was a little unhappy. I always seemed to come down at the bottom, and I was stuck right at home. This caused a few little heartaches. I kept arguing with myself, trying to convince myself that it didn't matter. I just felt I always came last.

In time Ruby grew resigned to Greg's minimal daily involvement with her and their children. She then became more dependent on the children to meet her need for some companionship:

> I think I've leaned on my children an awful lot; I've depended on them, especially as they got older. When Greg would be off somewhere and I had something to discuss or some problem, and I had no one to talk to, they were always here just to put my arm around them and give them a kiss, or tell them I love them, or squeeze their hand, or go to a basketball game. . . . I just feel that Greg's missed so much, being away so much because they're only young once, and then they're gone. My children have been a big part of my life.

In one form or another this scenario was recounted over and over again by women in my sample. But it should not be thought that marriage For the Children is something that women do only as a secondary response to an inaccessible husband. There are enormous cultural pressures that coax women to throw themselves headlong into child rearing independently of how accessible their husbands are. A number of men complained that their wives' absorption in the children was above and beyond the call of duty, and they felt that their wives stood less ready than they did for intimate partnership once children came. Clearly, women who have no career or other meaningful third-corners may come to see in children their best chance as a married person to have something important of their own. And for women who come to marriage lacking a solid sense of self-esteem, child rearing may seem the only way to fill the void. "I felt more a member of society," one woman told me. "I took great delight in my baby, and I felt more comfortable in a way, more relaxed, more accepted in the eyes of the world." Her husband spoke frankly about his own feelings:

My wife is an excellent and perfect mother. My daughter Helen was always absolutely clean and perfectly cared for, and I think I probably felt a lot of jealousy, a lot of resentment even though I loved my daughter very much. My wife could almost be offensive about it, to the extent of saying, "Helen is everything to me, and you're nothing." She has actually said that to me. She might come back later and say "I didn't mean it," but I did get that message for a long time. . . . When she became a mother she was something entirely different than that soft, very feminine companion that I wanted in my fantasy of a wife. She was this creature who was walking around with pins stuck in her shirt, totally absorbed in being a mother.

I heard no accounts of men having this same level of singleminded absorption in their children; when one thing alone is their "baby," it is typically work. What I did hear from several men was their crediting the ongoing presence of children as the basis of their marriage's durability, given that the strength of the couple relationship alone would not have been enough to sustain it. A handyman for a small business reflects on his twenty-four-year marriage:

She would want to go around the world this year and go someplace else next year. I think she could travel the rest of her life. I don't want to go down the end of the street. We have different thoughts on a lot of things. She said one kid would have been enough, and when she gets mad, she wishes she didn't have any. And I wouldn't have been able to survive without them—just us two. You have to have something to do in between everything else, and the kids fall in that role with me. I enjoyed every minute of it—two a.m. feeding, it didn't matter. Maybe because I can think on their level I can relate to them.

70 • *Three Corners*

Another man, married twelve years, thought that the arrival of children had driven his wife and him apart but had also kept their marriage together at the same time:

> Every kid was another phase, I guess, another headache to a certain degree. Don't get me wrong; I wouldn't get rid of them for nothing, but you'd get tied down a little bit more. She changed quite a bit. Her patience was gone. And we didn't sit down, we didn't talk. I'd stay up late; she'd go to bed early. We basically just stopped going out as much. If the kids weren't around, I don't think we'd be together, just because I think we would have parted over something small.

Has either of you ever mentioned the possibility of divorce or separation?

Yeah, in an argument. Her, more so than me.

Does it end with the argument, or does it come up again?

> It comes up in another argument. Not for a long time. The kids have kept us together. Plus I won't leave; I've got no place to go. I don't know why we stay together. There's love there, but some of the fights we've had have been enough to split us if the kids weren't around.

In the long run, marriage For the Children is by itself an unstable agenda. Children grow up and move out, so eventually the couple is left alone again. The man just quoted has three children, none of whom are yet ten years of age. As they get older and then leave, his marriage relationship will surely change. Either the "love there" that he spoke of will be renewed, or the accumulated gaps and resentments between him and his wife will drive them further apart. Whatever the outcome, it will be fed in large part by both of their stances toward their familiar marital paradigms.[5]

Safe Haven

Some people see marriage as a comfortable old shoe that can provide a homey and tension-free refuge from the outside world. Marriage is not the main platform from which these people launch their struggle for growth and achievement. Rather, it is a *Safe Haven* to which they can retreat and get recharged, enabling them to return to the all-important outside struggle with replenished vigor.

This agenda differs from Safe Return Home as it lacks the latter agenda's continuous influence of one or both spouses' extended family network. Indeed, the Safe-Haven agenda, with its typical emphasis on career achievement,

often removes both spouses from any intense kin activity, just because career advancement so often requires that people relocate far away from their families of origin. While Safe Return Home tends to be a working-class phenomenon, with generation after generation often laboring for the same local employer, Safe Haven is more often a middle-class agenda, held by those whose occupational chances are considerable enough that they can willingly forsake the security of their extended family ties.

Safe Haven bears a resemblance to marriage as an Economic Calling. In both agendas the issue of what should be happening in the partnership itself gets subordinated or at least referred to some central third-corner away from the partnership. With Economic Calling, that third-corner interest is success at earning an income and accumulating the material possessions that mark one's progress. With Safe Haven the occupational activity itself—the course of one's career development—is the primary concern. The income and material possessions earned in the process may become important, but they tend to be more taken for granted. Social class backgrounds make some (but not all) the difference.

As mentioned earlier, people who see marriage as an Economic Calling are usually upwardly mobile from working-class backgrounds, quite happy to be participating more actively in the consumer society than their parents could. Their Safe Haven counterparts usually come from middle- and upper-middle-class backgrounds, where parents teach children that an occupation should be deeply meaningful, and that one can only measure one's worth by the scope of the contribution one can make to one's occupation. Regardless of the amount of income earned, if a career is not deeply meaningful or challenging, it should be abandoned for the sake of one that is.

Still, some of the respondents who had this sense of devotion to the inner meaning of their work came from family backgrounds that were more solidly working class than middle class. As youngsters, several of these respondents sought refuge from tensions at home by immersing themselves in books and intellect—interests which easily fed into success in school, then entrance into the world of college, and finally, involvement in a career that offered the same measure of absorption as did intellectual pursuits as a child.

Frank O'Brien, the professor who grew up in an Italian and Irish working-class neighborhood, escaped his parents' alcoholic and conflict-ridden world through reading.

> I've been an intense reader all my life. The reading child was probably committed to the priesthood by half the families in my neighborhood; that was part of the reason I ran off to the navy. My models weren't from inside my family culture; they came from literature as much as anything.

From the navy he went to college and then graduate school, where his intellectual interests crystallized into a career. Science and politics have always

72 • *Three Corners*

dominated his interests as a married person, while marriage is a tension-free space in which to rest and relax. Emotional intensity is to be avoided, as in his mind it probably leads to the explosive confrontations his parents always had. He is grateful to his wife Laura for her calming influence:

> I get rather stormy, and Laura is calming. Emotionally I found a lot of support in marriage. It was nice to have someone you could be stormy with and who would not take offense. I found marriage a secure haven from the very beginning. . . . What we do together is not exotic; it's beach-walking, collecting specimens, reading in the same room. We both enjoy eating and cooking. We are sports fans. We go to football, basketball, and hockey games together. We don't feel a need for anything else. We don't need any wild emotional climaxes. We're mutually supportive, and that's enough for us.

Another man learned to seek in books a much needed refuge from his overbearing father, a railroad brakeman:

> My father was quite dominant and I found it difficult to do things right for him. In fact, that ultimately drove me into situations in which he had no knowledge; there was no way he could argue with me then. He had difficulty getting through high school, spent five years to get his diploma. . . . I learned that book knowledge and working in areas that he knew nothing about brought me more joy, because they didn't bring with them the problem of him being able to tell me that there's a better way of doing this.

This man became deeply involved in a demanding navy career, and his agenda for marriage was that it should comfortably fit into a life-style that took him away from home for even months at a time.

A second pathway to career-absorption and marriage as a Safe Haven, among those from working-class backgrounds, does not begin with the need of some refuge from tensions at home, as does the first one. Rather, it entails one or both parents helping to steer the individual into directions that later lead to upward mobility and career-mindedness. Scott King, an English professor whose father had had a whole array of working-class jobs, from farmer to butcher to painter and paper-hanger, described his early home life with great fondness. He remembers being "very, very close" not only to both his parents but also to many aunts, uncles, and all of his grandparents. These are conditions which, for many working-class boys, would culminate in a marriage as a Safe Return Home—as described earlier. Indeed, in speaking about the different direction that he chose to move in, Scott seems to sense very clearly the type of life he had to give up in the process:

> By the time I was thinking about marriage, I was already beginning to think about no longer living in that area [an area he describes as "extreme rural

isolation"]. I was thinking about pursuing intellectual life in some form. I was already looking for a marriage that would have a high intellectual quality, a continuous intellectual quality. That was one thing that I wanted that was different from my parents' marriage. On the other hand, I really did like the concept of the closeness they had with their brothers, their sisters, mothers, fathers—that extended family closeness. I liked that. I haven't repeated it much, but I still look at it with a great deal of fondness. It's something that, if I had an opportunity, might have been useful.

It was Scott's mother who apparently influenced him to forsake that life for a more intellectual one:

My mother was intellectually stronger than my father was. She read more than he did. She had a good deal more catholic taste. She was a fairly accomplished musician, belonged to a fairly good musical society, and played. . . . My mother's father, although he didn't go to college, was a good musician in his own right. He was a strong believer in intellectual values. He introduced me to Dickens, for instance, when I was twelve. He had read most of the great world's classics.

Whatever the social class origins of people who hold this marriage agenda, they can often be recognized through their tendency to translate questions about the phases of their marriage into statements about their career history. Because these people measure their life satisfaction first and foremost in terms of career accomplishments, they find it difficult to recall how their marriage was going at a given period of time without first anchoring themselves in the memory of where they were in their career development. I asked a history professor if his twenty-five-year marriage has gone through any phases. He began by speaking of the "graduate school experience, where you almost have to be selfish in order to get through." When I asked him when this first phase of his marriage ended and the next one began, it became clear that the graduate school pattern of intensive career preparation extended full steam into his actual career activity. "Sheila was always involved with the children and I was busy this, busy that. I was a good family man in the sense of being a provider, but I didn't really have as much time for Sheila and the family as I do now."

Most of my respondents who see their marriage as a Safe Haven and their career interests at the center of their lives learned this marriage agenda by watching their parents. Men with fathers who had both successful careers and comfortable, low-key marriages were especially likely to embrace this paradigm for themselves. The model that they have internalized, often without any direct teaching from their parents, is that a man gains esteem from others and can feel good about himself through career achievements. To be sure, many men were aware of having missed out, as children or adolescents, on

74 • *Three Corners*

the attention they craved from their career-absorbed fathers. "He spent very little time with us," one man told me, echoing the account of many others:

> We ended up with Mother a lot more. When he was available to do things, the things he did did not include the family. I'm not sure I had any judgments at that time, but I do now. Maybe I might have felt irritated, a little left out. . . . Several memories jump to mind from my early childhood, and one of them was my mother going, "Shh! Your father's sleeping!"

Whatever irritation he felt about his father leaving him out, it was apparently not enough to prevent him from falling into his familiar paradigm, once he married and was trying to finish up his college degree:

> I very quickly learned that wife and children can get in the way of doing the things that you want to do. I moved to the periphery of the situation. When our first child Ellie arrived, her bedroom and my study were the same room. That term I almost flunked out. During the break I realized I was being interrupted every time Ellie cried a little bit. I'd say, "Jane, Ellie's mumbling," and it would break my line of thought. My solution to the problem was to rent a cheap room elsewhere in the building, and I proceeded to go there to study.

Even when men had had strained relations with their fathers, and wound up rejecting a lot of the tendencies their fathers had modeled, devotion to a career seems to be the last element of the model to get rejected. Brian Jordan, a psychology professor married nineteen years, spoke of his father's impact:

> We had a stormy interaction, a conflict of values. I was people-oriented and he was thing-oriented and very strong-willed. He was a contractor and builder who never completed high school. But he was a person of quality; he looked for excellence in craftsmanship, and he was known for being a craftsman in the renovation of older homes. I didn't have a very positive relationship with my father. He wasn't interested in much that I was doing as a kid. I played football until my junior year, and his attitude was that I could be working with him if I wasn't engaged in sports. He felt that one should be working rather than recreating. A lot of that is still in me. Anything I gained from my father is in terms of work and the quest for excellence.

Did you have notions of what marriage would be like, before you met Gail?

> Yes. The role of the wife that I observed in my mother: picking up, having meals prepared on time, spending a lot of time taking care of the home, etcetera. . . . My mother had to be home when my father came for lunch, and if ever she had to be away, she left everything all prepared for him. That's quite an extreme from where Gail and I are. But early on, that was my image of a wife.

Marriage Agendas • 75

Later, I asked Brian, "What in your current life gives you the most satisfaction?" He replied without hesitation:

My job. At times I catch myself, remembering my father who worked so hard that at the end of the day he didn't have time for me, and I play golf with the kids or something like that. I'd like to think of myself as getting more satisfaction from the family, but I really haven't put as much time in on the family as I have on the job. Learning to temper my life and take more time off for recreation is something I'd like to do better. But I get such a charge out of my work. I never find it boring.

It was not only men who reported such high levels of devotion to their careers. Many women also had career-focussed lives, as did Gail Jordan, the wife of the man just quoted, the same man whose mother always had to be home to serve his father lunch. Gail got a Ph.D. of her own. Here she describes the family strategy that she thinks makes it all work:

We're in the process of applying for license plates, and we want them to say "WIN–WIN," because we've tried to make that a motto for our family. It's been increasingly more difficult when you get more players, now that we have five children. There might be a period of time when it would be WIN–LOSE. When Brian went into his doctoral degree, I really played support all the way. I had some problems with that at the time, but then we reversed it, and he played support while I went for my doctoral degree. That was the beginning of it, I think. Now, whenever we have a decision and a problem facing us, we call a family meeting, and we try and make it WIN–WIN. And if it is WIN–LOSE, it will only be that way for a certain period of time, and then we'll reverse it.

Having gotten her Ph.D., Gail became top administrator for a lucrative grant. Brian describes the impact on their lives:

How that affected the marriage is that Gail has taken on all the things I don't like in myself, in terms of working. She goes off at 8:30 a.m., before I do. Our youngest goes to the children's center here and that's worked out well. Gail brings home a lot of work now. She's very much involved in her job. She always was the balance for me, saying, "Don't work that hard," and now I don't have that check. We used to belong to the country club, and Gail got me a set of golf clubs in an effort to get me to relax. The most frustrating thing for me now is that I wish Gail weren't so wrapped up in her job. But I can understand it, in that it's the first major challenge she's had since earning her doctorate, and it's exciting for her. I'm proud of her for her achievements, but it's been exasperating.

To some, it may seem foolish to see this marriage as a Safe Haven or as a marriage at all, given the fact that both partners seem so single-mindedly

devoted to their work. To be sure, I spoke with several career-devoted people for whom marriage could not have been described as a haven, career being the only meaningful sanctuary in their lives. But not so for Gail and Brian. Safe Haven may indeed mean a lot of career-absorption, but it does not spell a lack of caring and concern for the marriage as we shall see when we look at the Jordans in some more detail. Similarly, Betty Hill, a successful writer with a fifty-year marriage, spoke candidly about her own intense ambition and then about the haven-like elements of her marriage without seeing any serious conflicts between career and marriage:

> It made a big difference when I started doing so much travelling and writing, because I have a different life for myself. We've adjusted to that pretty well. I've been gone for long periods of time, all over the world. . . . He hasn't enjoyed my being away, but it's been fortunate that I could do all this, because I'm ambitious—much more than Roger is—and self-centered, and selfish. I like to write and make a name for myself; both are very important to me. If I hadn't been able to do this, I wouldn't have been happy. It may have meant some sacrifice to him, having me away so much. . . . Sometimes I wonder what I'll be like in the future, when I don't have all this hoopla, going around showing slides and so forth. But I know I'd be completely lost if anything happened to Roger. For one thing, there wouldn't be anybody to share anything with. We have the comradeship, the understanding. I wouldn't have anybody left; I'm the last of my line. You need somebody who loves you and cares about you. Caring is so important in a marriage, particularly if you don't have brothers and sisters, like me.

Finally, to see marriage and family as a Safe Haven is not to see it as the only possible haven in a heartless world. The world outside may often seem difficult and intractable, but one's career efforts can suffuse it with ample "heart"; one can depend upon one's own talent and competence to negotiate one's way through the outside world with a sense of confidence and even comfort. Safe Haven, then, does not necessarily imply that the outside world is unsafe. The safety in this view of marriage inheres in the opportunity simply to relax from the pressures of performance, unwind, and ease off a little from the gravity of all the meaningful work that awaits one's return.

Hedged Bet

Some people come reluctantly to marriage. They are willing to enter it even while they retain grave doubts about its workability. Their doubts are nagging enough that they need to keep some emotional distance from marriage, as if their investment will backfire the moment they step closer than arm's length to the naked reality of partnership. To protect themselves, they adopt

a life-style or at least a point of view that enables them to feel less vulnerable as a married person, should the whole thing come tumbling down. For them, marriage is a *Hedged Bet*—hedged by whatever interest or philosophy they evolve to lessen the risk. If the marriage should then falter, at least they will have the hedge instead of nothing at all.

Virtually all the respondents who held this agenda had negative feelings about the marriage paradigms modeled by their parents. Most of them could not comfortably identify with either their mother or their father, and so their vision of marriage is colored more by an apprehension of its inevitable pitfalls than by anything else. In this respect Hedged Bet resembles Avoiding the Demon, only there is a sense in which those who hold the latter agenda are more hopeful. For them, marital salvation is at hand if they can only avoid the specific folly that got their parents (and themselves, by implication) into trouble. In contrast, those who require a hedge to bring themselves to bet on marriage at all have a more generalized sense of difficulty surrounding the institution. They do not want to go through their adult life alone, as almost all of the rest of the world seems to marry, but they have deep-rooted suspicions about their capacity to get through the experience of marriage unscathed. A hedge then lends a certain feeling of safety by fixing their focus on a strategy of protecting themselves from marriage, once they enter into it.

Perhaps the most common hedge centers on an ideal of independence that remains untarnished by marriage. The notion here is that one should tough it out alone and endeavor to safeguard one's freedom from being coopted by excessive responsibilities to one's spouse. Lyle Remick, whose parents divorced when he was thirteen, formed a negative image of marriage. He recalls an unhappy early childhood with "a lot of tension and strife" that was accented by his father's alcoholism. For him, marriage becomes hedged by an almost obsessive attachment to his own independence, about which he speaks through some strikingly vivid images:

> I had a strong feeling of wanting to be an independent person, a strong desire to be a bachelor. I don't know how much of this I got from the negative marriage of my mother and father, and how much was my own character. I felt very dubious about my own ability to make my way in the world, and I certainly didn't want to be responsible for someone else along with it. I had strong feelings almost against marriage. I can remember the family going to the beach, with all the paraphernalia, when I was twelve or fourteen or so. I can remember seeing some guy come down with just a comb stuck in his bathing suit and a towel and I thought, "Boy, that's the way to go; you're not hampered by all this crap." I didn't want the paraphernalia of marriage or the responsibility of it. It was something that I thought would be a nice way to be: to have it all together, to travel light and have mobility, and that's something that I have always sought and somehow it always seems to evade me. Even at that age it occurred to me, "Why do you need all this paraphernalia?"

78 • *Three Corners*

I mean, we probably wouldn't have this house if it weren't for my wife. I'm glad we've got it now. But I never wanted to crowd my life, if I could avoid it.

Another man held to the same hedge of independence. He too witnessed his parents divorce and the fact that "they grated on each other" long before they finally parted: "I probably was concerned that getting married would tie you down. I was the type of person that wanted to try all kinds of different stuff. My parents seemed to be tied down by each other all the time." When he married, he remembers "a hard time adjusting to each other."

> I'd been a bachelor for a long time [he didn't marry until age twenty-nine] and I was used to coming and going when I felt like it and doing things when I felt like it, and doing what I felt like. I guess I carried that over. I just wasn't used to having another person to coordinate with. . . . I guess I expected that it would be like it was before we got married, when you're not with a person all day; you're with them a few hours at night. Then you get married and they're there all the time.

His wife of eleven years came to marriage with the same hedge of independence. Her parents have remained married, but she remembers her childhood as unhappy, and her parents' marriage was laden with unexpressed grievances and bad feelings. I asked her if there was anything in their marriage that she wanted to avoid in her own.

> Yes. I always felt that if there were problems, I wanted them out in the open. . . . I didn't want to be financially dependent on anybody; I wanted to be able to earn my own way. . . . My mother was financially dependent on my father. She didn't have any training, any education. Even if she had wanted to go on her own way, she didn't have a choice. . . . When I was a teenager, I used to feel sorry for the girls who didn't have anything else on their minds except when they were going to get married and have children, because it tied you down and I knew it even then. I wanted to be independent.

What did independence mean to you at the time?

> To be able to come and go whenever I wanted to, and not answer to anybody.

Most of the respondents for whom marriage was a Hedged Bet had, at some point or other, serious doubts about whether they would ever marry at all. Most of them married much later than average. Given that their marriage paradigm is negative, they were in no hurry. I asked Janet Murray if she had any notions of what marriage would be like, before she met her husband Alec.

> Yes. I hoped that I would never have to get married! I wasn't in any rush, I really wasn't. I found that I was very happy doing what I was doing. It seemed

to be a status symbol to have relationships with the opposite sex, but that didn't concern me, because I wasn't interested. I wasn't thinking in terms of marriage. I always had thought that I'd like to have a family, but as far as settling down and actually doing it, it wasn't an obsession on my part.

Her father, a periodic drinker, would become extremely combative at times when he drank. "If I had something to say, I'd better say it and run like heck, or just hide. I didn't care to be around when he was like that, and made myself pretty scarce." Apparently, Janet's mother did not offer her much comfort either: "Her personality is such that she tends to play the role of the martyr and Goody Two-Shoes. Any infraction of the rules and she was ready for a lecture." Feeling that her home was not a terribly safe place, Janet did her best to construct a life for herself in outside third-corners revolving around horses. "As a teenager, the biggest thing in my life was being able to have a horse and mastering horsemanship and finding rewards there, and that took me through an awful lot of rocky roads."

Janet thus was able to hedge herself from the seemingly inevitable pitfalls of intimate partnership by fixing her attention exclusively on the world of horsemanship, a world that must have felt eminently safer. When Alec appeared on the scene and was clearly interested in her, she accepted this perilous development only because he was willing to have a courtship that would not interfere with her consuming third-corner interest in horses. "Courtship wasn't necessarily 'going out.' If I needed hay for the horse, we hauled hay. If we were going to a horse show, he'd haul the saddles in his truck and the horses would go in the other truck."

In this way the relationship grew for six years before Janet and Alec married. Sex came very late in the courtship, she having "to subdue my thoughts and fears" and he being "very patient." Again, the paradigm modeled by her parents offered no positive guidance at all. "Sex was never talked about. It was a dirty word. And I didn't see any affection in the family. I didn't know how to accept it, I didn't know how to give it." I asked Janet if she ever struggled with the question of whether she was really "in love" enough to marry:

> I think I struggled with the question of "what is love?" It was something I had to answer in my own mind. And I think what I came up with was related to what I had experienced: I had a dog, I loved the dog; I had a horse, I loved the horse. It was a feeling of caring and wanting to do the best I could for that particular animal, and I just applied it to the human, and I said, "It's got to be the same thing. How could it be any different?" That's the only answer I could come up with: loving is caring.

Here we have a wonderful instance of creative hedging: Horses start out in Janet's experience as a third-corner hedge against an unhappy home. The feelings that she then generates about horses become so positive that she is

moved to generalize them into the very setting—marriage, family, home—that stood in need of some hedge to begin with! As we shall see later in another context, Janet has continued throughout her fourteen-year marriage to make use of her interest in horses as a kind of hedge against investing too much in marriage, but as the marriage has turned out to be more and more satisfying, the hedge-like character of this third-corner seems to recede.

Most people who see marriage as a Hedged Bet not only begin with grave doubts about the workability of marriage, but they are also plagued with doubts about their own worth. Indeed, if marriage is a dubious investment, it is largely because they fear that their own deficiencies and quirks may bring the marriage to ruin. Janet was true to form in this respect. I asked her why she decided to marry:

> I don't know. I did not have a very high opinion of myself. I think that Alec thought more of me than I thought of myself. And I knew that I couldn't love him until I liked myself. . . . I said, "Geez, if he likes me well enough to take me, by God he's going to get me! He's going to have to suffer it out!" He made me feel good about myself when oftentimes, if I was around my parents, they just tended to criticize. It was just a good thing.

Kathy Remick told a story with similar ingredients. She too had parents with an unsatisfying marriage, one ending in divorce. They were also very critical of her, particularly her father:

> I think he would blame me and say things were my fault. I really wanted to get married because I wanted somebody to love me but I didn't really think that anybody would. I had no self-esteem. I expected marriage to be rocky. . . . . My mother's kind of a cold person—not really very sympathetic or understanding, and I think I had the feeling that it was weak to want to be loved and to love somebody. Both of my parents gave me that feeling. And I think it had something to do with the picture my mother presented as a woman. She was not really an emotional person at all. I remember one time Lyle and I were sitting at a party, and I said to him, "Gee, your eyes are so blue," or something like that. And for some reason I repeated this remark to my mother, and she thought that was a weak, stupid thing to say! I guess there was this feeling that marriage was a necessary evil.

Having inherited her parents' notion that marriage for anyone is a necessary evil, Kathy not only had a negative marriage paradigm, but she also feared that she was so replete with defects that no one would ever want her for a spouse: "I think that the thought that anybody would love me and marry me was such a high expectation for me that it didn't come down to reality at all. I wanted it, but I didn't think I was marriage material." When Lyle came along, there was a brief period of fun and romance, succeeded all too quickly

by letdown, periodic break-ups, conflict, and extreme moodiness on Lyle's part. When he would become morose, she would feel responsible for his moods, try to lift him out of them, and then feel guilty for failing to do so. Then Kathy became pregnant. Again she felt her own basic defectiveness was at work. "I felt ashamed of being pregnant, with people that I worked with. I felt everybody would say, 'Oh, that's the only way she could get a husband.' I did not want to get married. I didn't want anything to do with it. But I couldn't see any other way out of this dilemma." Her ensuing marriage began on the same note of conflict and despair that marked her courtship, a seeming vindication of her parents' sense that love is an affliction and marriage a necessary evil:

> I didn't think it would be good, but I didn't think it would be as bad as it was. I was much more unhappy than I expected. We had a yard, and I would sit out in the yard and I just wouldn't know what to do or how to cope with my situation. I was completely bewildered, and I felt that I had weights on my mouth, pulling my mouth down. I guess no matter how unpleasant our courtship had been, I still wasn't prepared for the reality of the unpleasantness of the marriage.

Notice Kathy's sense of passivity and powerlessness in this account, for here is a clue to the Hedged Bet nature of her agenda for marriage. Unlike some other respondents, she did not have an external hedge like a horse, or a notion of needing to preserve her individual freedom and third-corner independence to do this or that after marriage. But she did retain her own sense of unworthiness and defectiveness, and she married under circumstances that left perfectly intact her earlier doubts about being able to sustain a marriage. Kathy's hedge, then, was a totally internal one. She stood more ready to bet on her inadequacy than on her marriage-ability. Even as she entered marriage, she had already gone a long way toward emotionally distancing herself from any real possibility of success. Thus when matters became still worse than she feared, she could only cast herself as a spectator to her own misfortune, fall into bewilderment, and feel powerless to effect any significant changes.

It might be said that everyone hedges their bet on marriage to some extent, that most of the marriage agendas portrayed earlier have at least some flavor of diverting a share of the burden of emotional security from the lap of just one person in order to redistribute it somewhere safer. But there is a difference. Hedged Bet carries with it a fundamental sense of the problematic and troublesome nature of marriage. There may indeed be an element of evasive maneuvers vis-à-vis one's spouse in the other agendas too. Those who invest heavily in children, or career, or extended family, or religion, or the consumer society may do so with something of a defensive posture, and when this posture comes to dominate, their investment then too becomes a hedged

82 • *Three Corners*

bet against marriage. But the fact remains that these investments in career or children or whatever are often found side by side with an underlying vision of marriage that is positive, optimistic, and sanguine. In contrast, Hedged Betters are pessimistic about marriage and resigned to its frailty. Hence their need for protection from it is basic, and they require some central, arm's-length strategy to lessen their vulnerability.

Open Agendas

Are there people who carry no images of what marriage should be? Is it possible to bring an agenda-free standpoint to marriage? Surely this prospect is most difficult. Not only does everyone dwell in a culture, thus absorbing the popular knowledge about marriage, but everyone also has a personal history that is laden with vivid imagery about marriage, derived from direct, face-to-face illustrations of married life, particularly as provided by our parents. Given all this imagery it would be strange indeed to find people who have remained unmoved by it all, who can truly put aside everything they know about marriage and venture into it with a totally open mind.

Nevertheless, some people are relatively agenda-free. They too have some agendas; they look for certain outcomes and they want their marriages to speak to certain needs. But their agendas do not grip their vision of marriage with the same tenacious hold that we find among other people. The crux of the matter is that marriage agendas may become hardened or softened in our awareness. Their texture may be rigid and unyielding, or flexible, bending, and malleable. In the latter instance, we can speak of *Open Agendas*— agendas that are flexible enough to be transformed, or even yielding enough to be abandoned.

Those people who already have Open Agendas by the time they marry almost always come from homes that were emotionally comfortable. They recall secure and happy childhoods, and they see their parents as having had excellent marriages together. As adults, they now think of their parents, if they are still living, as friends. The reservoir of good feeling between them leads to enthusiastic visiting and a continuing congenial relationship. These people do not have many lingering "deficiency needs"; they have a strong history of feeling safe and secure, loved and lovable, and highly esteemed. From this platform of strength, they come to marriage with an extremely positive, optimistic outlook. They look forward to the companionship and the sense of belonging that can accompany marriage, but they have no pressing need to prefigure much about it. In the words of one such woman, "I was prepared to go more than half way to keep things on an even keel."

People with Open Agendas can most readily leave behind the marital paradigms modeled by their parents. They do not necessarily need to do so,

and indeed, they often embrace or at least fall into that paradigm precisely because it seems so easy, comfortable, and desirable. Nevertheless, education or a particular line of self-development may lead such a person into a very different life-style than his or her parents had, and that life-style may require considerable marital changes, relative to what the parents did. Then too, people may often need to transform their parents' marital paradigm just because their partner's needs and interests make it impossible to comfortably maintain it.

As we shall see when we get to the subject of marital dynamics, people with Open Agendas can more readily bend and adapt to the new directions carved out by their partners. They can even encourage their partners to move into these new territories, and prod them into taking a few risks, sometimes at the cost of some considerable discomfort to themselves. Moreover, they can persevere much longer than most people could with an intractable partner who puts severe tension on the marriage, and they can typically do so without accumulating a lot of unexpressed resentments. A young professional, married thirteen years, quickly discovered that his wife often lacked the easygoing temperament that he was used to in his parents:

Louise is probably not as stable a person as I would have expected myself to marry, in the sense that she can get very upset about something really quickly. It became a tension in terms of adjusting to her being upset over a long period of time about things like the kids' education and the particular problems the kids have had in their classes. She tends to blow up immediately when something upsets her, and then calm down a couple of days after the fact. Experience just taught me that there was no point in trying to discuss it until she calmed down and kept the whole thing in perspective. If I'm upset about something I always ask myself, "Is this an important issue? Is it going to matter next week? A month from now? Well, certainly it won't. Then why get upset about it?"

Most things are not worth getting upset about. But she gets upset first and only later realizes it isn't the most important thing. Sometimes I get tired of having to say to myself, "Let's wait till she cools down." Like this fall, she would carry on from the time I got home until eight or nine o'clock about something the principal did. There's no profit in letting yourself stay worked up for three or four hours about something that is beyond your control.

This man clearly does not like this tendency that his wife has, particularly at those times when he himself becomes its target. Yet, true to his own philosophy, he tends to minimize the importance of anything unseemly and he focusses on the positive.

The only thing that I can think of that's been an aggravation is that tendency of hers to blow up. It's been a source of—well, "disappointment" is a little strong—perhaps "unease" that she persists in being that way. But I'm more mild-mannered than most.

84 • *Three Corners*

Because of their fundamentally positive outlook and their considerable fund of good feelings about marriage, people with Open Agendas do not buckle under in times of stress. They can wait it out, even rise to the occasion, and use adversity as an opportunity for greater self-development and self-discovery. A minister, who saw his parents' marriage as positive and his own home life as good and comfortable, married a woman whose family history had left her with a lot of insecurities. He told me, "Carol had to deal with having been made to feel inferior by her mother and father, and she still struggles with this feeling a bit. Her coming out of her dependence on her mother and realizing she's an important person—that's been great to watch." But this man perhaps understates not only his own contribution to his wife's process but also his accomplishment in coaxing the most he could out of a difficult situation. Here is Carol's account:

> When our daughter was about three, I had a depression-type nervous breakdown—not bad enough to be in the hospital, but I was on medication, and I'd have moments of complete panic and depression. A lot of it was caused by my mother's hold on me. She used to say things like, "If you don't do thus and such, your father will drink more and it will be your fault." This was always held over my head. When I left home I felt like I was deserting her and a sinking ship. But I didn't realize this until it suddenly came out, and then it took me about five or six years to really snap out of it. It was a very difficult time for me and it was tough on Mark, I'm sure. I think if it hadn't been for Mark it would have been far worse than it was. He really stood by me, and I'm sure it wasn't easy for him. And it took a long time. I've heard him say that it's been a good experience for him because it helped him, in his work, to understand the things people go through, having witnessed it in his own family. Looking back on it some twenty years later, it was a growing thing for both of us. I think it was good that it happened.

People with Open Agendas are also best equipped to fill in whatever gaps are left by their partner, in terms of the whole array of tasks associated with making a life and family together. They can more readily interchange roles and take over the tasks left undone, should the occasion call upon them to do so. This occurred when a female respondent brought suit against a potential employer for denying her a job on the basis of sex. Her husband spoke of the repercussions of that court battle on their marriage:

> I really did have to face the question, "Are you all mouth, or are you ever going to do what you say you do?" What I did was to take over what I had been doing part-time. It started originally with lunches in Ohio. I was home writing my dissertation and she was working in a nursery school, so I began to do the lunch so that she could come home to a good meal. It's a relatively easy thing to extend that to another meal if you're there at home. And it just grew that way. I don't remember any real negotiation about it. . . . When the

four of us were home all the time, I probably devoted three to four hours a day to it. I get up first, I do breakfast, start the fire, and do all that stuff. I'd go home and prepare the noontime meal, usually did most of the dishes. . . . I like to try new recipes. I want to write a cookbook someday on nineteenth century food. I'm hopeful that that will be a joint publication. I've always thought that she'd be a very good scholar. She's a methodical, dedicated, creative researcher.

Notice how this man not only took over the traditionally female role of cooking and dishwashing, but did so with a keen, creative flair that could culminate in a new venture together as a couple. Compare his account to that of another man who exclaimed, "We were brought up in an era when the man went out and earned a living and the wife took care of the house, and it stayed that way. I wouldn't under any circumstances have anything to do with keeping house, for instance. She's far superior in that field." Here we see the difference between an open marriage agenda and a closed one. People with Open Agendas can most readily blur the traditional distinctions between male and female. They are more androgynous, to use the technical term for this tendency. The women are not afraid to show their strength and self-assertion, and the men need not hide any tendencies toward gentleness, timidity, and vulnerability. A woman spoke of some areas in which she willingly fills in for her shy husband:

I realize some things are very difficult for him to do, so I take over and help him. He's not a weak man; he's just very shy, because of the way he was raised. My parents always made me feel I was the greatest. They always praised me, whereas he could never seem to please his parents. He's so shy about some things. I've mothered him, and I think he needed that badly. And I've taken over some things like calling the plumber, and giving someone the dickens. And I've done most of the disciplining of the kids. But when it came right down to push, he'll take over. He probably felt I was doing a good enough job. And lots of times he left it up to me because he was afraid he'd get too angry. I do think I've given him more confidence in himself. But I've also taken responsibilities which, if I were a weaker person, he'd have shouldered.

Notice how she herself sees the connection between coming from a secure home in which esteem was amply given, and developing the strength and flexibility to rise to any occasion, even if that means doing some of the things which, in her world, men typically do.

Of course, insecure homes, or homes with parents who were quite stingy in handing out praise and approval, do not necessarily produce children who remain forever inflexible, unyielding, and fixed in their vision of what a marriage must be. As we shall see, the transformations that some marriages undergo can dramatically reverse the tide of tendencies flowing from one's earlier

86 • *Three Corners*

family history. People who bring rather closed agendas to their marriages may find it possible, desirable, or perhaps just necessary to open them up later. It depends, first, on their standpoint and feeling toward the marital paradigm modeled by their parents, and then on the dynamics triggered by the particular collision of paradigms and agendas that any marriage involves.

Some general remarks are now in order. First, the fit between the different agenda types presented here and any actual marriage should be understood as a loose one. These agendas are not meant to exhaustively describe any marriage. An agenda is merely a single cluster of intentions, and no such cluster can embrace the full wealth of desires and intentions or the fears that anyone seeks their marriage to address. There could be no pure cases of any of these agenda types, no one whose only purpose in marriage is to rear children, or to avoid some demon, or to turn marriage into an Economic Calling, a Safe Return Home, a Religious Calling, a Safe Haven or a Hedged Bet. Anyone's design for marriage is a composite of myriad purposes, and even those respondents who were selected to illustrate a particular agenda often have many of the strivings that make up the other agendas as well. All people have some demons they wish to avoid, hedge their bets on marriage in at least some minor way, and want their marriages to be Safe Havens. The very concept of marriage is often metaphoric; it may represent our grandest hopes and our fondest ambitions, even our most vague and indefinite yearnings, so it is hardly surprising that no single model or type of marriage could exhaust the totality of anyone's imagery about it. That said, the fact remains that marriage agendas do point to real phenomena because images and intentions are perfectly real. People act on them, see their partners in terms of them, and often seek to maneuver their partners into more closely approximating them. Marriage agendas, then, are real tendencies and not just fictional abstractions or distorted caricatures.

Before leaving part I and the subject of marital statics, it is worth casting a summary glance at its thrust, as part II will build on it. We have been surveying some of the images that people bring to their marriages as well as some agendas that flow out of these images. While I have carved up the diversity of images in terms of all three corners of marriage (the inner-corner, the partnership-corner and the variety of third-corners), I want to make it clear that these images can only accumulate, get stored in, and to a large extent constitute the inner-corner alone, and they do so long before a marriage or even a courtship is formed. The inner-corner should be understood as the master organizer, the supervisor, and director of our marital projects, the unseen choreographer of our partnership dance. The partnership- and third-corners do not themselves organize or direct anything; they are outward manifestations of the inner drama. Since the human self cannot contain itself, it spills outward, seeking and creating the second- and third-corner channels for its

further expansion and development. As it does so, the inner self is guided by all the paradigmatic images that linger on as the traces of earlier experience. This is the process that we have been noting in part I, as we watch courtships and marriages begin to unfold.

To put the matter starkly, the inner-corner is filled with all the noise and clutter from the past. We can neither avoid having that clutter nor do anything to erase it; it is there, impressed and imprinted in the vault of our permanent record. Experience may be a good teacher, but it keeps on collecting trinkets which take up room. Even positive, joyful experience is clutter in this sense; it leaves an imprint, which then profiles our future expectations and inhibits us from remaining open to all possibilities.

What we can do, given the futility of attempting to erase the clutter, is learn how to live with it, as we develop the eyes to save us from blindly stumbling into it and the legs to move around it. Marriage sometimes coaxes us to gain this facility, but it can just as easily fail to do so in either of two ways. On one hand, we have seen throughout part I how tempting it is for people to create the very circumstances of partnership that will lead them to bump into their familiar clutter all over again. On the other hand, some of the marriage agendas that people create in their eagerness to avoid their inner clutter are no less confining. It is as if the old clutter in the room appears so formidable that we cordon off a tiny little section to move around in, ignoring the fact that we are usually bringing new clutter into this section, and forgetting that there is far more spaciousness to be found in using the entire room if we could only learn to navigate amidst the old clutter.

In partnership lies the chance to learn some new navigations. Just because marriage brings two cluttered rooms together (to put it rather unkindly), creative forces can be freed. Even if I want to recreate my familiar clutter in my marriage, my partner may feel too confined within the limited territory I have mapped out, resist it, and once more exhort me to move around in whatever wider space I have access to. Needless to say, both the old and new clutter that my partner brings to the marriage may also have to contend with my own resistance. There are limits to marital statics given by the reality of partnership. Marital dynamics can break through the inertia of statics as soon as two personal histories come out of their respective encapsulation and stand revealed to each other.

Notes

1. See Abraham Maslow, *Motivation and Personality*, 2d ed. (New York: Harper and Row, 1970).

2. Marvin Goodman, "Expressed Self-Acceptance and Interpersonal Needs," in *Family Roles and Interaction: An Anthology*, ed. Jerold Heiss (Chicago: Rand McNally, 1968), pp. 107–115.

88 • *Three Corners*

3. Elizabeth Bott, *Family and Social Network*, 2d ed. (New York: Free Press, 1971), p. 60.

4. Lillian Rubin, *Worlds of Pain* (New York: Harper and Row, 1976).

5. Both Lila Balch and Bob Milardo have reminded me in personal communications that once children do leave, some couples with a For the Children agenda may be able to refocus their relationship around the grandparent role.

Part II
Marital Dynamics and Development

4

Introduction to Marital Dynamics

Marital statics is the study of individuals' images about marriage, how these images typically arise before partners ever meet, and how they attain some measure of inertia. Once people do meet and marry, the inertia of these images may sometimes persist unchanged for many years, and it could then appear that the field of statics is sufficient to explain what has been going on. I did interview a number of persons who claimed that nothing essentially new, surprising, or unpredictable had ever transpired in their marriage, neither in the early period nor at any time later on. They claimed, further, that they could not identify any differences in themselves or their partner as a result of living together, not a single new insight, discovery, or understanding about each other, as if their marriage were nothing more than a series of external events that have come and gone without seriously affecting what they know and feel about one another. These are relationships that are described as if they have no internal history, no development, and no dynamics, everything essential about their connection having been sorted out even before the marriage began. It certainly appears, in these cases, that the inertia of early images can sometimes rule the day indefinitely and filter out any significant change before it can make its impact.

Nevertheless, some continual surveillance, some work of screening out is still required for one partner to resist any serious impact of the other, or to keep protected from the vulnerabilities of change. Insofar as this active maintenance effort is necessary to keep the early inertia rolling as it is, statics alone cannot explain each new change-resisting surge of activity that appears. We thus need a theory of marital dynamics to account for the forces of both maintenance and change in a relationship. Any individual's images and agendas for marriage are not immovable objects, however doggedly persistent they may be. Our partners may offer up some considerable resistance, thereby making it difficult to frictionlessly enter our paradigms and agendas into our marriages. With marital dynamics, we turn to the forces and counterforces created when two people, with two separate life histories that

92 • *Three Corners*

are still emergent, come together to make a long-term relationship. Here are some early recollections of a woman who has been married for fifteen years:

> Living with a person is totally different form dating a person. When we got married I realized that you have to make adjustments. I saw my mother in her pajamas but not my father; he was always dressed. Clyde didn't wear pajamas; that was sort of a rude shock. I went, "Oh, where are your pajamas?" and he said, "I don't wear pajamas," and I went, "Oh, God!" I can remember my reaction to it. I was so embarrassed. I bought him a bathrobe, thinking that would be kind of a subtle hint. He hated it; he never wore it. He doesn't walk around the house naked, but in the bedroom he just gets undressed. Or if he's in the bathroom taking a shower, he's not embarrassed if I walk in there. He just doesn't ever get embarrassed that way. . . . Eating habits drove me nuts too. He ate differently than anyone I ever saw. He could eat a chicken wing, leg, or breast with a knife and fork and never pick the thing up with his fingers. In my house we used to love to pick up the bones and suck on them. With Clyde, I never dared, for the first two or three months, to say, "Do you mind if I pick up this pork chop bone?" I mean, it was driving me nuts. I got out a book of etiquette and it said chicken could be eaten with the fingers, so I showed it to him. I was afraid he'd think I was really gross.

Here we see two very different paradigms coming together—two different products of family history having a minor collision early in a marriage. The collision did not prove to be serious; it touched neither partner at the deeper core of their images and agendas for marriage. The fact is that in any intimate relationship, two different sets of rules or models or at least images of the countless details of everyday living meet face-to-face. Every such partnership is therefore laden with dynamics, some hidden and some of them out in the open. Here I shall deal only with those aspects of connection that have seemed to matter the most to my respondents. Essentially, the meeting of two people's life histories can take three different forms. In *paradigm conflict* there is a head-on collision of some key needs, images, or agendas. His and her life-experiences inspire respective visions that in some way contravene each other. In *paradigm consensus* both partners are in spontaneous agreement about certain core images and expectations. Two life-paths converge together rather than collide. And in *paradigm complementation* each partner's deepest inclinations are different from the other's; yet, in the absence of expressed or felt opposition, the fulfillment of one partner's leanings is compatible with the fulfillment of the other's. Two life-paths diverge without serious conflict.

Paradigm Conflict and Paradigm Consensus

Since every person's marital paradigm contains innumerable elements, I presume that every marriage has in it some paradigm conflict, some consensus,

Introduction to Marital Dynamics • 93

and some complementation—that is, some collisions, some convergences, and some divergences. The balance between these three forces will be crucial in determining just how satisfying or unsatisfying a particular marriage may feel. I find that marriages can easily survive powerful paradigm conflicts, provided that there is also some key paradigm consensus to lend a measure of positive feeling and shared vision of what it means to make a life together.

In a culture of patriarchy the most trying paradigm conflicts in the early period of a marriage often focus on how much a husband should be home, what time he should return from his job or other outside third-corner, and what the rules are for checking in with his wife if he is away for more than a few minutes. Needless to say, as women effectively challenge the culture of patriarchy, the focus of these conflicts often shifts to the wife's third-corner comings and goings, as it is no longer assumed that her place is to provide domestic service for any of her family members who may need or want it. Since virtually all of the men and women in my data inherited patriarchal paradigms, it usually took at least several years of marriage for any concerted challenges of this paradigm to be made. Most of the wives have never been inclined to make such challenges, and thus paradigm conflicts with their husbands take place within the overall patriarchal framework: she focusses on her partnership-corner and clamors for more of his attention; he focusses on his third-corners and clamors for more independence. ✗

Becky Gorman, married fourteen years, recalls how difficult it was to adjust to her husband's work hours:

> One time I had expected Morris home at a certain time. I knew he was painting a car [in his father's auto-body shop], and he told me he would be home for supper, and I waited and waited and waited. Of course the frustration kept building up. When he finally got home I said, "Don't talk to me!" But that didn't last long. I understand things like that now, they don't bother me. Being newly married and being alone—I had *never* been alone! There were always people around where I was. And it was hard to adjust to, it really was. That's the one big thing that I remember. It didn't bother me so much being alone during the day, but the nighttime loneliness was really hard.

After a few months Morris got a sales job, and they moved to a new town several hours away from their familiar setting. Becky told me, "I was used to someone getting up at a certain time and being home at a certain time. When Morris started selling, that was when the real test for me came because he was gone evenings, and I had never been left alone." Two years and two children later, Becky was still struggling with these same issues.

> Now I had *two* children to work with, and Morris was still out selling, and there was still the loneliness that I was trying to adjust to. Lots of times he would say that he'd be home at a particular time, and two or three hours later,

94 • *Three Corners*

he would come home. I understand that now. If he's three or four hours late, I don't worry and I don't get myself all upset, because I understand that's part of his selling.

Morris recalled the same car-painting episode that Becky had remembered from fourteen years back:

> I was painting a Cadillac and I didn't like the way it came out, so I repainted it. I didn't feel like cleaning off my hands to call my wife and tell her I'd be late. I was three or four hours late, and when I got home my wife was all upset and crying. I got cleaned up and went ahead and made the beef stew she was going to make, and she got over it.

Morris also provided some additional background information that clearly reveals the paradigm conflict lurking behind the Gormans' early issues:

> At home, if I was doing some body work and if I got home at midnight, my parents knew what I was doing, and that's all there was to it. I was used to that, and my wife isn't. If my father wasn't there for supper, my mother went ahead and had supper. Right now, Becky's father works in a lumber yard, and if the roof was falling off the building he'd still leave work at 4:30. I'm not built that way. I go home when the work is done. But her father is home at a quarter of five, and her mother is pacing the floor if he's five minutes late. Well, my wife was that way when we first got married, and she's gotten over that now. Last night I got home at 9:15. Now that was early; I sometimes don't get home till midnight. My wife doesn't even plan on me having supper unless I tell her that I will be home for supper.

Despite the Gormans' early paradigm conflict about a husband's schedule and his accessibility to the home, their basic paradigm consensus was far stronger, revolving around a shared agenda to make their marriage a Religious Calling. Becky told me, "After I joined the church my main goal was to marry within the church." Morris, in fact, was one of the few eligible young males in her area who met this requirement. Once married, Becky and Morris were both inclined to see any emotional frustrations as undeserving of much emphasis. As Becky put it:

> Our church teaches us that we can become perfect if we follow the Savior's example, and this is what Morris and I are trying to do. Without the marriage we can't obtain the perfection that we want. And we hope by giving our children the proper training that they too will feel and believe the same way that we do and that it will be a continuing process through the generations.

Morris put it even more strongly:

> My goal was not to get married to be married, but for eternal companionship. If you both believe in the teachings of the church, if you live them,

there's no reason why you shouldn't have a successful marriage. We have
that transcendental goal, and we have more of a common yoke.

Through the Gorman's religious third-corner consensus, potentially grievous
paradigm conflicts thus get shelved, neutralized, or simply discarded.

Agenda Clashes

Even aggravated agenda clashes may be neutralized by some counterbalancing paradigm consensus. An *agenda clash* is any conflict in which the partners' willful marriage intentions, based on their respective paradigms, directly
contradict each other. Agenda clashes are particularly explosive because they
are fueled by a keenly explicit awareness of what should and should not be
occurring in a marriage. When expectations go unmet under these conditions, both partners may feel cheated and betrayed by their marriage, each
determined to induce the other to change his or her ways.

These agenda-clashing dynamics were dramatically illustrated by Mike
and Jill McCarthy, married twelve years. Their responses to their familiar
paradigms set them on an early collision course with each other. For Mike,
the one thing he wanted to avoid in his own marriage was his mother's veto
power over his father's activities.

> I think my mother is more the ruler than my father. Sometimes I didn't par-
> ticularly care for that. Like if I wanted to take him to a ball game she would
> put up a stink, and of course my father would say, "All right, I just won't
> go." I feel that this won't happen with me.

You felt the man should be the head of the household?

> Oh yes, definitely. If I'm going to make a decision, I want her to go along
> with it.

On Jill's side, there was ample training for that compliance which Mike
sought in a wife. Jill's mother married a man who was her senior by more
than twenty years, and his life-style kept him largely inaccessible both to her
and to their family. Despite that, Jill's mother remained dependent and uncomplaining.

> My mother holds a lot of her feelings inside. She's always appreciated my
> father bringing us up, building her a house, taking care of her. Even though
> we never had a lot of money and expensive things, that didn't mean anything
> to Momma as long as she was taken care of and we were taken care of. She
> was passive that way. She wasn't a demanding person.

96 • *Three Corners*

So long as Jill was content to fall into her familiar paradigm, everything with Mike went smoothly. Their implicit contract, starting with their courtship, was that Jill would continue the compliant pattern that her mother had modeled and that Mike wanted, in return for which Mike would give to Jill the male attention she had always lacked: "When we started going together and before we got married, I guess Mike showed me some of the attention and things I had always wanted from my father. My father is not an affectionate man at all, and Mike is very affectionate." In turn, Mike found himself so comfortably in command that it was he who twice initiated courtship breakups because of their age difference: "I felt a sixteen-year old girl shouldn't be going with a twenty-two-year old man." Mike was also the one who controlled their subsequent reconciliations and the general flow of their courtship relationship: "Since I was older, she would want to do whatever I wanted to do. She had this tendency to follow me, at the time."

Even during their courtship, however, some cracks began to appear in the contract the McCarthys had fashioned together, as Mike sometimes wanted more compliance than Jill was ready to deliver, while Jill often craved more of Mike's time and attention than he was comfortable giving. Jill remembers some "fights off and on":

It was usually because I wanted him to spend all his time with me, and he's very athletically inclined and likes to play basketball or any other sport. He still wanted to go with the guys, and yet have a steady girlfriend who's going to be sitting home waiting for him to come over when he wanted to.

In their first year of marriage, the McCarthys' courtship tensions escalated into a full-scale agenda clash. "We used to quarrel quite a bit," Mike remembers:

The first year was hell, really. We have some friends that tell us they're really surprised that we're still together after that first year. I wasn't going to let happen to me what happened to my father. So maybe she didn't want me to do something and I figured, well, I'm just going to do it. I enjoy sports so much that I wanted to go to games every single day, while she wasn't at all interested. And most of my friends hadn't gotten married yet, and I just wanted to be able to go off with them whenever I wanted to. I guess she wanted me to slow down more than I expected I'd have to, so that made me quicker to jump if she said anything.

Jill's account dovetails closely with Mike's:

We fought almost the whole year. Right off the bat I was pregnant with my first child, and I was working, and Mike was out playing sports all the time. I didn't drive. We didn't have a telephone, and I was more or less stuck alone

there in an apartment that had mice in it. On weekends he would sit in front of the TV set. I used to unplug the TV set every day. I'd want to go for a ride, and he'd never be done watching TV until the end of the day because sports would come on the entire afternoon. . . . I didn't think he cared for me as much as I had thought he did, because I saw less of him after we were married than I did before. He didn't feel quite so obligated, I guess, to be there every minute.

Notice how a new marriage, in the McCarthy's example, unfolds through the meeting of paradigm images imported from earlier life-experience. Behaviors that seem innocent and uncluttered to the partner who makes them can trigger alarm signals in the one who receives them. Two partners cast each other as stand-ins for all the significant partners they have ever had, and any transaction thus gets silently referred to this larger context that neither partner had a hand in shaping for the other. Both Mike and Jill must have felt betrayed by the other. The less accessible Mike became, the more he reminded Jill of her inaccessible and inattentive father, while the more Jill protested and demanded, the more she seemed to Mike to resemble his restrictive and domineering mother. Each partner's most feared demon to be avoided was now rearing its ugly head.

Jill's readiness to actively protest Mike's inaccessibility may appear surprising, given her mother's model of uncomplaining passivity. Other women would have remained enmeshed in their familiar paradigm, uncertain about how to contest a husband's overly shadowy presence. But Jill had gained some direct experience with confrontation as an adolescent, when she learned to ward off her father's constant harangues.

My sister was a tomboy. I was the only one interested in boys, and my father thought about the things he did when he was younger—his mind is warped that way. When I dated anyone, he wouldn't speak to them. In high school I hated my father and we were always fighting. Some of the things he accused me of that I didn't do—it really hurt.

When things with Mike became difficult, Jill must have borrowed liberally from this conflict experience with her father, especially insofar as Mike's pattern of separateness came more and more to remind her of her frequently absent father. Thus, although Jill began her marriage by falling into her mother's familiar pattern of passive dependency, she also brought with her some suspicions that her mother's path would not adequately meet her needs, as well as some conflict skills that her mother had never developed. All she needed, apparently, was a little experience with frustration to convince herself to agitate for more of Mike's time and attentiveness.

Even though Mike and Jill both found themselves wrestling with the demon they had wanted to avoid—he with a restrictive woman, she with an

98 • *Three Corners*

inaccessible man—this agenda clash was only part of their dynamics. At different periods of any marriage, different paradigm elements become salient. Mike's agenda to safeguard his independent third-corner activity was never more prominent than in his first year of marriage, before Ellen was born. With a new baby, Mike shifted his focus to paradigm elements that inspired very different marriage agendas centering on parenthood. He and Jill then found a strong basis for consensus in marriage For the Children, and their conflicts calmed down. Looking back on her own childhood, Jill complained, "We never did much as kids, doing things familywise, mainly because Dad spent all his time building the house. It wasn't important to him to do things with his kids. I'm trying to let my kids have a chance to do some of the things that I couldn't do." Because Mike's childhood, in contrast, was filled with family outings and activities, he not only could converge with Jill's familistic agenda but could actively lead its implementation. Jill describes the result:

> Children have made our marriage better. I couldn't picture having a marriage without having children. . . . Mike was brought up that they did everything with their parents. I was brought up that we did very little; we didn't go to the beach every weekend. I've had to grow into these things. Now, all the kids have to say is "Can we do this?" and we do it. Because Mike ice-skated, they all talked me into going, and I went along and got on skates, which was something I didn't do as a child that much—I was the one that sat home and read books. So being the type of person he is has helped our marriage that way. I've never been on a pair of roller skates in my whole life until last year. There's a lot of things the kids wouldn't have an opportunity to do if it were up to me. I have a girlfriend whose husband says, "Oh, you go ahead and take the kids ice-skating." Mike's not that way; it's "Come on Mom, let's go," and we all go. I feel I'm lucky that way.

In this way, the McCarthys' early agenda clash became counterbalanced by more consensual agendas, which fixed their attention on their joint third-corner activities with their children.

Varieties of Marital Dynamics

In the remainder of part II, I shall illustrate some overall patterns of marital dynamics, using relationship maps as visual aids. Each partner will be represented as a triangle with three points, as shown in figure 1. The inner-corner will be shown as a dark circle, the partnership-corner as a light circle, and the third-corner as a gray-shaded circle. A solid line between any two corners will signify a strong and active connection between them; a broken line will signify a weak one. Two contiguous circles will represent a fusion of those two corners.

Introduction to Marital Dynamics • 99

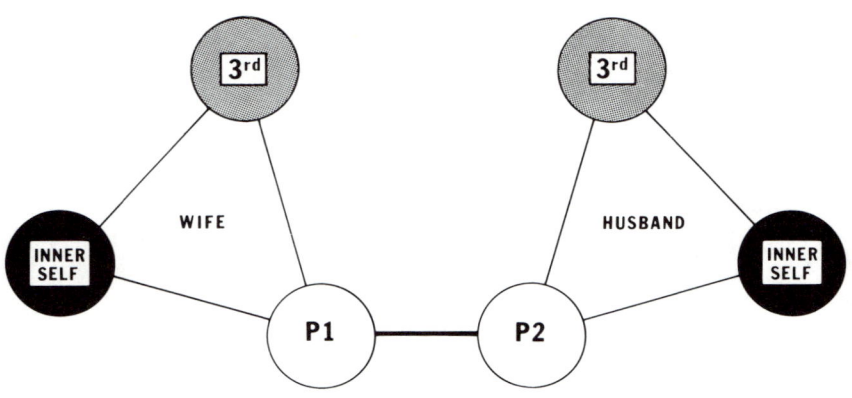

Figure 1. A Partnership Diagram

The two triangles in figure 1 depict two people joined together through their partnership-corners, both having all three of their corners well developed and in balance. Technically speaking, this is a "connected" relationship and will be fully explored in chapter 8. I offer it here only to get the reader used to visualizing any partner as a triangle with three different points of reference.

Separate chapters will describe each of three kinds of marital dynamics— romantic fusion, dependency-distancing, and separateness. Each pattern of dynamics will have its own triangular configuration and will be illustrated accordingly. A fourth pattern of dynamics, connection, will be explored in part III, as it has four different subtypes. We shall see that all four subtypes of connection can be extremely durable and highly satisfying to those who live them. For that matter, the separateness pattern of relationship can likewise be durable and satisfying, depending on the familiar paradigms that each partner brings to the marriage. "Good marriage" is one of the most relative concepts in the world, resting overwhelmingly on an implicit comparison with whatever one has previously seen or experienced. Two people who both rate their marriages as "very happy" are not necessarily referring to even roughly equivalent realities, and each of their happinesses could easily feel like misery, if it were possible for them to trade places.

5
Romantic Fusion

Some spouses initially begin their relationship with a romantic upheaval. The partnership itself becomes each partner's all-consuming passion and interest. As shown in figure 2, there are two different fusions involved: not only are each spouse's partnership-corners (P1 and P2) fused together, but each of their inner selves (the dark circle) is fused with their own partnership-corner as well. It is as if the inner self does not stand in its own light but becomes an appendage of the partnership, as the latter alone provides self-definition and focus. Given that the inner self is an energizer, notice how all the energy of these two spouses hovers around their partnership. Hence we have the incredible intensity, drama, and excitement that surrounds the couple, as well as the tendency to elaborate the partnership and its meaning through constantly being together, talking together, and, when separated, thinking about each other. Notice, too, how insignificant both partners' third-corners have become in their respective personal space. Appropriately, Philip Slater has referred to this situation as a "dyadic withdrawal," a withdrawal into the twosome and away from all the involvements and commitments maintained before the relationship came into prominence.[1] Figure 2 shows as broken lines the connection from each person's third-corner to his or her inner- and partnership-corners, thus indicating how marginal the third-corner has become for both partners.

A Case Study

All of the typical dynamics of romantic fusion were present in the courtship of Mark and Pat Tyler, married ten years when I interviewed them. In Mark's words, "It was intense and passionate and exciting and also confusing. We thought we were two parts of the same brain. I'd start a sentence and she'd finish it. Later we discovered we were talking about two different things! But we didn't know that at the time." Pat speaks in much the same way:

102 • *Three Corners*

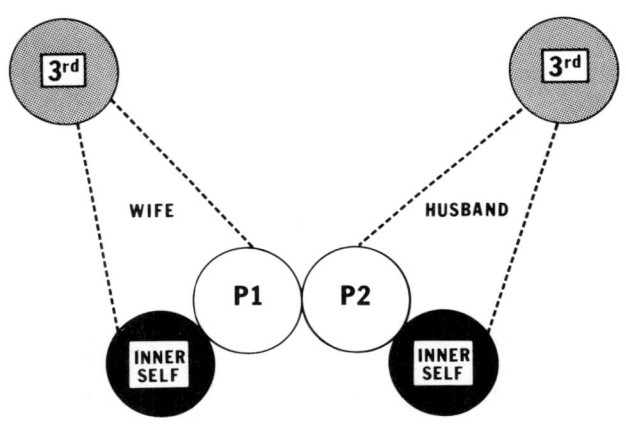

Figure 2. Romantic Fusion

It was very intense. Mark never went to class, and I had quit my job the day before I met him. We spent all our time together, all day and all night. It was a great time. In our first acid trip we got totally immersed in each other and decided we were really one person, and we spent three years thinking that's how it was. After three years we began separating out more. At first it was great having someone to be totally open with, but then there came a point when it became a little stifling.

Why should the blissful intensity of romantic fusion become "stifling"? One would imagine little incentive to be delivered from that ecstatic state. Yet, despite the symmetry of each person's triangle with the other's, despite the reciprocity, romantic fusion is fundamentally unstable because it rests on two illusions. The first illusion is that two people are really only one, "two parts of the same brain," as Mark put it. The illusion, here, is that each partner's inner self is nothing but the common denominator, the unity of the partnership. In reality, no partnership could ever express or exhaust the full richness of a person's inner self. To assume that it could is to ignore a vast range of inner impulses that have nothing to do with the partnership. Pat provides a clear summary description of the rise and fall of this illusion:

In the very beginning it was idyllic bliss. It took a long time to realize that we were coming from two different places and didn't need to be in total agreement. We had assumed that everything had to be worked out together because of all this "us-ness." That was romantic and beautiful, but it didn't work. We tried for a long time to make it work, but it became clear that that wasn't us. We've decided that most of the problems we have to deal with now are "me-to-me" problems and "Mark-to-Mark" problems.

The second illusion is that in the unity of partnership, each partner is the equal of the other. While both partners may indeed take turns being the leading edge of their one "brain," one partner typically gravitates to the full-time position of leader and definer. Almost invariably in my data this partner is the male. With the benefit of hindsight, Mark sums up their situation:

We thought of ourselves as equals, but in fact I was the dominant one. I was financially responsible, and that was fine with Pat. Pat did all the cooking and the housework, and that was the way it was supposed to be. When it was time to move, it was my decision, but I always felt she had the option to disagree with my decisions, though she didn't exercise it. At that time I provided her definition of herself. When I first knew her she didn't know how to talk, to open up to someone, because she never felt she was a person someone could be interested in. Her being able to open up to me was crucial to our relationship. At the time I had no conception of how shaky she was about her own identity. But I did kind of understand and pry a lot of stuff out of her. For the first part of our marriage, she was completely devoted to me and our daughter, and there was no reason for conflict. She didn't think of herself as a separate person, and that was fine for me. I'd go to work, I'd come home to delicious food and loving company. I could have gone on like that forever.

Mark was clearly in a position of great power and benign domination, yet they defined themselves as a communion of equals. Mark not only made all the major decisions but formed the major opinions for both of them. ("I did become aware," Pat recalls, "that in discussing current events, for instance, all my opinions came from Mark. I did respect his opinions, but a lot of it was that his opinion was automatically the family opinion".) Mark was also the emotional supervisor and director of their common identity. Her identity was defined as shaky, his as stable and secure. She was closed and taciturn; he was the lever that would pry her open and let "a lot of stuff out of her." It was not that he was the bad guy in this drama. Willingly as Mark gobbled up the power to define and direct their fusion together, Pat handed it over to him just as eagerly. In her words, "I thought in the beginning that Mark was a total wonder-child, a veritable God. That was the way I'd chosen to see him. It was disillusioning to find out he wasn't."

Romantic fusion usually breaks down because the male partner is less fused with his partnership-corner than the female is, and he does less of the support work to keep the fusion primary. Eventually, he cannot help but betray her because his attractions to his various third-corners leave her in the lurch. Mark and Pat were no exception to the rule. They were able to ignore the growing bundle of little betrayals and feed their image of total unity for about three years. Between the third and fifth year, that image came under increasingly serious questioning. Mark was busy finishing his college degree

104 • *Three Corners*

and working at jobs that were either low-paying or unappealing to him, or both. No longer defining himself in terms of the early fusion with Pat, he began to crave more and more outside (third-corner) confirmation of his personal power and identity, so that a lot of his energy was shifting away from her. In the meantime, with the help of a women's group, Pat had become more cognizant and assertive of her own (first-corner) needs, and she began to challenge Mark around the issue of household tasks and responsibilities. Mark, who had started out as the all-powerful lever who would open her up and "pry a lot of stuff out of her," now found that much of her "stuff" was emerging from an unwanted part of the barrel:

> I did feel a distance from Pat. She was suddenly having experiences that I wasn't part of. I thought it was great that she had friends of her own and some definition of her own, but she was also all of a sudden after me to cook and wash dishes, and I didn't know how to do any of that.

The culmination of this development came when Pat became pregnant with thier second child and also got herself a full-time job. Mark recalls the confusion he felt around the time the baby was born:

> I was feeling apprehensive about everything. Everything was going to change, and I didn't know how. I didn't feel great about myself and my ability to handle things. I wasn't making much money and we had this extra kid. I wasn't sure I wanted another kid. It meant financial commitment; it meant a longer period of having little kids around. I felt backed into a corner. There'd been a lot of conflict and hostility between us, and I was unsure of what was going on.

When Mark became attracted to a woman he met at a party a few days before the baby came, a series of events unfolded that would permanently darken the already-tarnished image of unity. The details are unimportant, and the attraction waned as soon as Pat sniffed it out, even before any sexual consummation had occurred. ("This was supposed to be a great love affair," Mark muses. "Instead, I caught all this shit and never got laid!") What matters was the symbolic significance of the would-be affair. Feeling displaced, Mark stood ready to attach the full force of his private drama to the most dangerous of all third-corners—a lover—precisely at the time that Pat most wanted his undivided support:

> Even going into this, Pat had been feeling that I wasn't very attuned to her. And I wasn't. Again, when things were getting heavy I had a tendency to space out, and if something made me feel more positive about myself, I'd go with it. This relationship now was a boost to my ego. Here was this nice person who thought I was great, and I needed that reinforcement.

Romantic Fusion • 105

Pat's account reveals how tenaciously she must have been holding on to the illusion of unity, despite two years of its gradual undoing. In reality, Mark's attraction to someone else was only the coup de grace for their fusion, but for Pat it stood in a class by itself as ultimate devastation:

I felt isolated and abandoned and uncared-for, and that Mark's responsibilities were not fulfilled and he knew it. I was incredibly angry. . . . Things will always be somewhat different as a result of that incident. I had allowed myself to be so vulnerable to it. I had been defining myself in terms of Mark. I couldn't believe what an incredible impact what he was doing could have on me. . . . My vulnerability was in terms of the fact that his presence with me was called into question at the only time when I could not afford to question it. I had just had a baby, I was exhausted and sick, and all I wanted was to curl up in bed and sleep, and Mark was dumping this shit on me. This is the time when a woman is the most vulnerable; too much energy is tied up in other things. I really resented that I couldn't have this time to be taken care of.

There followed a brief period of separation, and then a reconciliation and gradual rebuilding of the relationship. I asked Pat if the re-establishment of trust is still going on, some five years later:

Yes, I think it always will be. Which is preferable to how it was before. It was very nice, but it was not real. You cannot have that kind of trust in somebody and not expect to fall on your face at some point. We *weren't* the same person. But it was totally nice while it lasted. We both really seemed to need to be able to do that, so I don't regret it. It just was hard coming down from it.

The Origin of Marital Disturbances and the Demise of Romantic Fusion

One reason why romantic fusion is so unstable is because the gender differences that precede it can only be suspended for so long before they once more overtake the couple. The fact is, males' and females' basic triangling tendencies are often alien to each other. Following Nancy Chodorow's analysis, we have seen that women come to marriage with a strong need to recover the kind of intimate connection they knew with their mothers. Their very security of female gender is bound up with a lively sense of intimate blending and continuity, first with their mothers and later with husbands or other significant intimates. Men, in contrast, come to marriage with a need to find themselves through pursuits in which they can stand as separate, independent beings. Security of male gender seems to entail, first, a wrenching

106 • *Three Corners*

free of their connection with their mother, a female, and then a continued independence from that world of emotionally charged bondage that males seem to feel females represent.

In terms of triangulation, what all this means is that married females and males will have rather different needs. Women's triangulation will most often widen their sphere of intimate, personal relationships, building compatibly on their previous bonds rather than replacing, sidestepping, or overriding them. Men's triangulation more often will detach them from their ongoing emotional bonds, bringing them into settings in which they can display their achievements, skills, conquests, or other tokens of individual distinction and prowess. In historical practice, men have tended to triangulate into work or leisure pursuits, women into child rearing or female kin networks, if such are available. Thus, male triangulation tends to separate husbands from their wives, while female triangulation either fills up the spaces left when husbands are unavailable, or it is accompanied by overtures that invite husbands to participate in it jointly with them.

Two factors intertwine to create disturbances in a twosome when one of the partners initiates a separative triangling move. One factor is the situation of asymmetry—that is, the second partner has no strong third-corner of his or her own to compensate for the first one's declining accessibility. This is the factor that most often triggers some disturbance for the twosome. The disturbance emerges first as an inner discomfort. It is a malaise, a sense of unease, and it is usually felt first by the partner of the spouse who has broken some of the fused-togetherness through initiating strong triangling moves. In the conventional situation, it is the wife who first feels the disturbance, as the husband is the one to triangulate away from the marriage. For him, marriage is often something of a Pyrrhic victory: he wins back something archaic, something primitive—the chance to recover with finality the total nurturance and connection which he knew as an infant in the protective arms of his mother. But the victory is fraught with peril, as Dorothy Dinnerstein has so well taught us. It harkens back to that time when he could not yet begin to emerge as a male identity, an identity that later came to be measured by his distance from that "female" world of dependent submersion, and by his capacity to stand away from it, alone. For new husbands, therefore, strong moves toward third-corners signal their continued independence from "feminine" confinement, and their suspicion that from marital bonding it is but a short step into insufferable bondage.

The second important factor in marital disturbances is responsible for their remarkable variety of expression, as they manifest and proceed to unravel. Again, I refer to the familiar paradigm to which each partner silently refers in order to interpret what any triangling move means for their relationship together. Each spouse's familiar paradigm includes a unique perception of triangulation—a vision of the kind and intensity of triangling moves that

might be undertaken as well as the kind of responses a partner might be expected to make to these moves. Furthermore, every such paradigm offers two sets of imagery and prescription, one for how a husband's triangulation might be dispatched and responded to, and the other for how a wife's might be handled. Needless to say, the images directed to a wife's triangulation may be rather different from those directed to a husband's. With this background established, we can begin to look at marital dynamics more closely.

Note

1. Philip Slater, "On Social Regression," *American Sociological Review* 28 (1963):339–364.

6
Dependency-Distancing

Often it takes new husbands very little time to make strong moves toward their third-corners. Danny Gardner, married to Sheila for twenty-six years, reflects back on the first year of their marriage, which followed a brief whirlwind courtship in their junior year at college. He had been "quite a man about campus," he told me:

> I was no virgin, and hadn't been for about four years. And I had a car in college. I also had some habits that got me into certain circles where behavior wasn't very prim. For example, I played poker a lot. I was president of my fraternity, I was a student senator, and yet I made a B + average. . . . I think a lot of the problems in our first year had to do with old habits I had trouble breaking. The fraternity boys weren't really very supportive of a marriage, and I was vulnerable. For example, they'd get a card game going at the fraternity house and I wouldn't make it home for dinner. . . . There seemed to be a little drifting back to precourtship behavior on my part. While we were dating I didn't have time to play poker, to go with the boys. But after we were married I found time often. Maybe at this point, she was mine; I didn't have to worry about her anymore. So now I was free. I think there was some of that in it.

Meanwhile, Sheila dropped out of college to make a home for them in a small apartment, and within two months she was pregnant. How did she feel about these quick moves her husband was making into a separate third-corner?

> It was not a good year. He was still president of his fraternity and not ready to settle down. . . . He was going to prove to his friends that being married didn't change him that much. I was fixing up the apartment and getting things ready for the baby, and I was busy really spoiling Danny badly. I wanted to be everything to him. If he wanted a sandwich I would hop up and fix him a sandwich. In some ways it was a welcome change. I didn't wish I was still in my sorority; I was ready to be through with that. I didn't mind getting into something new and playing house. I was content and happy doing what I was doing, and felt that he should have been content and happy to

be the father and so forth. I was being a mother before the baby came, and he wasn't particularly being a father.

Notice the two different approaches to triangulation. Sheila stood ready to pull out of any third-corner (such as college or her sorority) that might interfere with her new marriage bond. In this respect she fell right into the groove of her familiar paradigm, as her mother had likewise forsaken her education and training to marry, stay home, and raise four children. In contrast, Danny withdrew from his third-corners only long enough to permanently secure his new marriage bond, and then he drifted back to them with redoubled vigor. In so doing, he too was following the implicit instruction given by his familiar paradigm. He had spoken unsympathetically about his mother's "extreme jealousy" and the fact that his father "was so easy to get along with, I couldn't understand why in the world she couldn't get along with him." But Danny's paradigm was at least as much informed by his home-town environment as it was by his own parents. I asked him what qualities he wanted in a mate around the time when he met Sheila:

> I thought the husband was boss and the wife should behave herself while the husband was not under any such constraints or rules. . . . I don't know if you're familiar with these small coal-mining towns, but they can be kind of rough. There's a lot of drinking and gambling and womanizing. A successful womanizer was kind of a man about town. It was so obvious and blatant that it made an impression on me.

Apparently Danny had been resourceful enough to successfully transpose some of his home town's behavioral code onto his college round of life, and he did not want marriage to seriously interrupt that pattern. He told me, "I knew she was home, and she would be there when I got there."

Clearly, at the very outset there was little symmetry between Sheila and Danny in the way they handled their bonding and their triangulation. Like other women, Sheila's need for active, personal bonding was straightforward and direct. Having never had any strong experience of herself as separate, she innocently assumed that being married would keep her in secure connection. Everything in her familiar paradigm pointed toward a marriage at the center of her bonding needs. Though she faulted her mother with "nagging" her father, she was inspired by the model of marriage her parents presented:

> They were just total support for one another. It wasn't that they were each other's only support, but it was always there. And they had a loving, affectionate kind of relationship. And I used to think, "One of these days I want someone with whom I can be loving and affectionate." I was probably jealous of it, of having someone constantly there to make a fuss over you and to be loving toward you. I admired that. When we first got married, I think I expected that to happen immediately, because that's what marriage was.

The pattern of marital dynamics that began to unfold in the Gardners' relationship may be termed *dependency-distancing:* one partner remains fused with the partnership-corner and is hence dependent on it for self-definition; the other partner distances into one or more independent third-corners, away from the partnership-corner. Figure 3 illustrates the pattern. Unlike romantic fusion, in which P1 and P2 are reciprocally fused together, there is now a gap between the partners. The two triangles are positioned in an asymmetrical relationship. While P1's energy is still focussed on her partnership-corner, P2's private drama is now focussed on his third-corner, which begins to receive the lion's share of his energy. To P1, this shifting away of her partner's energy can easily feel like a betrayal of the earlier romantic mutuality between them. Though this pattern can persist for a long time, its basic asymmetry and lack of balance make it highly unstable, and the more P2 distances away from P1, the more vulnerable P1 will feel.

Again, it is more often the female partner who in the early period of the marriage remains fused with and dependent on the relationship, and therefore she will be the one to feel the disturbance. The marital dynamics will then unfold according to how she responds to that disturbance. Once again, the familiar paradigm is called upon for instruction, as marital paradigms provide not only the basis for experiencing conflict and disturbance but also some well-travelled pathways for dealing with it. In Sheila and Danny's case the outcome is predictable. Both came to marriage with a strong sense that any disturbances in their respective parents' marriages were due to their mothers being overly reactive, complaining, or jealous, while their fathers were blameless. For Sheila, her mother's inappropriate response to whatever disturbed her was not to be emulated:

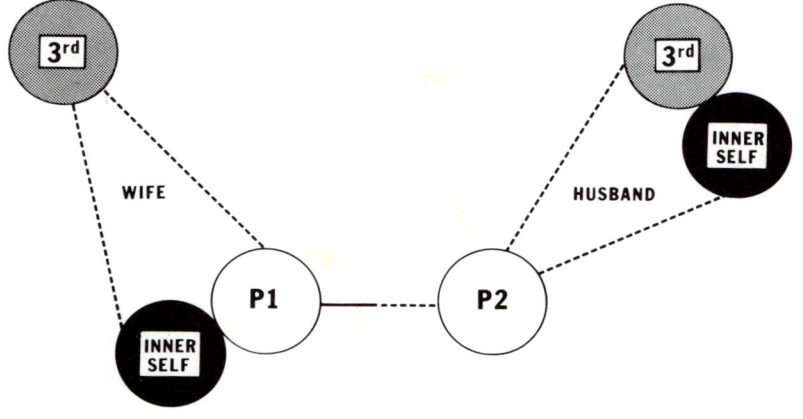

Figure 3. Dependency-Distancing

112 • *Three Corners*

I remember hating my mom at one point because I felt she wasn't good enough for Dad. At that age—I was seventeen or eighteen at that time, the last one left at home—I thought that Dad was so wonderful he deserved anything she could do for him. I felt she was a nag and spoiled, just a lot of whining. Nothing ever seemed to suit her. She was never in a good mood. It was a passive kind of reaction to whatever he did; she would react negatively to it.

The stage is thus set. Since, in Sheila's feelings about her familiar paradigm, husbands are the blameless ones when things go wrong in a marriage, all she can do is internalize the disturbance and fall into bewilderment, immobilized to launch any kind of serious confrontation. She mused, "I think I felt more fear than resentment, because I was afraid that I was inadequate, and that was the reason why Danny did not seem to love me in the same way that my dad loved my mom."

With a new baby near the end of their first year together, Sheila acquired a third-corner of her own. The disturbance stabilized somewhat, as now there was more symmetry between Danny and her in their respective triangulations. The underlying tensions remained, however. The greater symmetry perhaps kept them contained, but since, in Sheila's familiar paradigm, marriage fundamentally means a close bonding with a spouse, the sense of discomfort lingered on for her. When Danny "quit the playboy routine," to use Sheila's words, and started graduate school, the now-established pattern of separative triangulation continued. The only difference was that Danny's third-corner shifted from his fraternity and other extracurricular activities to his studies. He told me:

> I just did not want to hang around in graduate school for three years and then come out without a degree, so I just did the whole thing, and Sheila was a brick through all that. On occasion she was unhappy and it would get her down. We hardly ever went anywhere, and I had so little time for her. She knew where I was—I was in the office typing or in the library. But she went through several years of my concentration and interest being rather heavily directed somewhere else.

In fact, "it would get her down" more than "occasionally," but Danny never knew just how much. Instead of expressing her discontent, Sheila tended to stifle it and try harder to make their marriage work, as if she alone were responsible for success or failure. She reflected:

> You might say graduate school was a turning point in a kind of bad direction in many ways. We formed habits there that took years for us to get by. I got into the attitude of, "I must always keep the children quiet so he can work." And so we got into the idea that they were my kids, it was his work. And it became a kind of protective sort of thing. I protected him from them, them from him, and consequently the three of us were kind of stood off against him as he worked

Dependency-Distancing • 113

and finished. He was doing one thing; we were doing something else. We might as well have been two different families. And I thought I was doing what I should be doing because I was allowing him to work, and he of course was doing what he should be doing, which was to get done what had to be done. Our communications were rotten.

Once Danny began his professional career, nothing essentially changed for quite a few years. By now there were more children plus a move to a different region of the country, but the marital dynamics remained as they were. Danny easily shifted his cherished third-corner from his studies to his work. Sheila's third-corner had grown from one to three children, and with a new house she had opportunities to expand her domain:

I was busy getting the house fixed up and being den mother and Girl Scout leader and doing my motherly thing and loving Danny. I was determined to be a fantastic mother, have fun with the kids, enjoy every minute of it, and be a fantastic wife. The kids were easy to fit into that pattern and that worked wonderfully well. As for Danny, my idea of a fantastic wife and his might have been two different things! He just didn't seem to have time for whatever I was being!

Despite her dissatisfaction with Danny's inaccessibility, Sheila did not yet actively struggle with him about it. There was nothing in her familiar paradigm about frank and honest confrontation with a spouse. Indeed, her lingering images of her mother's "picking" at her father must have led her to equate any expression of challenge with inappropriate negativity. She exclaimed:

I was not good at expressing it. But don't forget that I had heard my mother bitching and griping, and I was not going to do that, right? So it just had to come out behind my kneecaps! That was really a motivating force in what I did or did not do. And it was probably a really dumb thing. But I had to play it that way.

The marital dynamics illustrated by Sheila and Danny Gardner are repeated over and over in my data. The basic theme is that wives want first and foremost to bond through a marriage and then to have their husbands eagerly join them in building a nest that will include children. Husbands' designs seem more elusive and even downright paradoxical. They can throw great zeal into bonding at the outset of a relationship, but once secured, the bond seems only to provide them with more confidence to distance themselves from it. This combination builds into marriages a fundamental lack of symmetry between husbands and wives in their styles of triangulation. The greater that asymmetry, the more disturbed is the marriage. The Gardners' marriage is clearly a disturbed one, despite the fact that their arrangement persisted essentially

114 • *Three Corners*

unchanged for about fifteen years, and it could have gone on that way in-definitely. Disturbed marriages are not necessarily short-lived ones. People can become so good at managing disturbance that they almost forget that the problem is there. In Sheila's words, "I did sense that there was something lacking between the two of us. But I was so busy, and he was so busy that we didn't pay that much attention to it."

Notice how familar paradigms are complex enough to help generate dis-turbances, and then help mask them or hide them. The Gardners had a basic paradigm conflict concerning the limits of a husband's triangulation. When Danny's triangling moves left him inaccessible to Sheila, her familiar paradigm inspired her first to feel some disturbance and then to live with it rather than to openly "bitch and gripe" like her mother.

Marital Paradigms and the Management of Disturbances

Paradigm conflicts do not necessarily mean open confrontation or expressed conflict. The conflict is in the foundational structure of two sets of marital beliefs; it inheres in the difference in background assumptions that each part-ner brings to the marriage, and in the asymmetrical triangling moves that may result from them. Whether these differences get vocally expressed or hide under a silent cover of resentment or frustration; whether those who have them are fully aware that they do so or simply feel some vague and uncertain discontent—these are separate issues. The underlying structure of marital disturbance is a different matter than its manifestation. Other women in Sheila's situation might have grown inexplicably depressed or physically ill. Some would have angrily lashed out at their husbands, and still others would have firmly expressed their grievance but without any overlay of anger and resentment. Clearly, the type of response to a paradigm conflict—the way we manage a marital disturbance—is itself determined in no small measure by additional paradigmatic images drawn from our earlier life-experience. And injury may get compounded by insult, if grievous paradigm conflicts about the limits of one partner's triangulation are further aggravated by fundamental differences about how to express (or keep silent about) those grievances. That is, double trouble emerges when people have conflicts about how to have conflicts.

A woman named Angela found herself in the thick of such double trou-ble. Her familiar paradigm was filled with uncomfortable images revolving around her father's alcoholism, her parents' continual conflict and eventual divorce, and her pervasive sense of aloneness and abandonment. When her mother went to work following her divorce, Angela had felt even more alone: "I used to come home from school and there was nobody there, which I swore

would never happen to my kids. Whenever I seemed to need somebody or wanted somebody, they were never there. I had nobody to really turn to." Soon after Angela got married to Joe, he wound up in the army, and she fell back into her familiar sense of abandonment. Returning home after a two-year stint, Joe began to triangulate in precisely the ways that Angela's familiar framework had led her to fear most. Hence the conflict:

> He used to go out with these guys—they were married too—and I didn't like the way their marriages were and I did not want my marriage like it. These guys drank a lot, and that used to infuriate me. Or like he'd go with them hunting and camping and I'd be home, and that used to make me "ugly." It brought back a lot of my childhood. I was alone, I was frightened, and here he was drinking. I didn't want him to be like my father.

Having fallen back into the paradigmatic patterns she feared most, she reacted by selecting from her familiar paradigm the type of response to that situation she knew best, explosive and angry outbursts: "I used to fly right off the handle. He didn't like it at all; he was brought up differently. His parents didn't yell and scream and cuss, and my mother did. I take after that. He can't stand that." Note how this paradigm conflict about time at home versus time away, about the rules governing a husband's triangulation, escalates further through an additional paradigm conflict about what to do or not to do about grievances. Her parents yelled and screamed; his parents never expressed grievances even if they had them. Her yelling and screaming was just a normal release to Angie, but to Joe it must have felt monumental. He told me, "If the kids weren't around, I don't think we'd be together, just because I think we would have parted over something small." Angela would never have said this, because in her world angry outbursts are stock-in-trade; they are not the stuff of marital breakups.

Marital Disturbances and the Problem of Fusion

Let us assume that a fully functioning adult could closely bond with a partner and remain an autonomous, individuated self. Traditionally, then, males and females are only half complete, each gender having the capacity the other lacks. For females, who find that the bonding capacity comes naturally, the path toward a better-rounded self is to learn the skill of individuation—to become independent centers of movement, activity, and initiative. For males, who find it necessary to individuate with such vigor early on, the path toward better-roundedness is to acquire skill at bonding—to form intimate partnerships in which they can warm up, become expressively sensitive, and partake of the many-layered delicacy of another's personality. Because bonding and individuation are such opposite capacities, one having to do with being together

116 • *Three Corners*

and the other with being alone, any extreme development in one direction can best be tempered by some parallel development in the other. But this well-tempered blend is easier said than done. When excesses in either direction get challenged by an intimate partner or become simply too unworkable, the tendency is often to redouble rather than to relax one's efforts in the troublesome direction, as if there alone lies the pathway to security and comfort.

Both individuation and bonding, then, have their shadow sides. Individuated purpose and activity can turn into exaggerated self-containment, into a reclusive distancing from any warm, nurturing, softening human connection. We have seen that men often throw themselves headlong into work or some other arena of achievement that enables them to prove their worth as males, particularly in the eyes of other males. Danny Gardner exemplifies this common pattern of male triangulation away from the home along with the seeming incapacity to function actively within an intimate bond, with all the emotional give and take that this entails. Individuation thus jumps into its shadow—a distanced self-containment.

But bonding also has its shadow side. It is one thing to have an active connection with someone who enriches and nurtures one's self; it is another to require that connection to define or *constitute* one's self, for then one has no independent center of existence with which to bond. In the latter instance I shall use the term *fusion* to call attention to bonding's shadow. While emotional distancing is most often a male tendency in modern western culture, fusion typically appears as a female countertendency. We shall see that these respective shadows of bonding and individuation tend, when they come together in a marriage, to aggravate each other in an ever-tightening vicious circle.

Chodorow will once again provide us with our point of departure. In her analysis, female fusion or "merging," as she sometimes calls it, has its roots in the long attachment that a girl has to her mother, unlike a boy. Being of the same gender as her mother, a girl finds it easier to experience herself "as a continuation or extension of her mother,"[1] and her mother will treat her daughter likewise as an extension of herself. In contrast, a boy's early differentiation of himself from his mother (and his consequent facility for early individuation, often lapsing into emotional distancing) is rooted in his oppositeness from her, in the fact that he must break his identification with her in order to establish his male identity. Women and not men, therefore, come to "define and experience themselves relationally," and "they retain capacities for primary identification," enabling them "to experience the empathy and lack of reality sense needed by a cared-for infant".[2] Chodorow thus concludes that women rather than men "mother" children because women have the requisite relational capacities built into the very structure of their psyches.

Chodorow implies that women's relational capacities are general, extending beyond child-caring aptitudes, and this is where her analysis is both weaker and incomplete. At times she seems to be arguing that married women

turn to their children to express their capacities for love and affection because their husbands have repressed their own needs for love and are thus incapable of meeting their wives half way. In other words, women turn to children by default. Given that men "find it difficult and threatening to meet women's emotional needs,"[3] children become the only solution to women's "wanting intense primary relationships".[4]

But nowhere in Chodorow's analysis do we find a developmental basis for adult women being any better equipped than men to sustain an adult style of primary relationship. What we do learn is that a female's development in western families fosters a continuing attachment and primary identification with her mother well into adolescence and beyond, and that this experience may leave her with an insufficiently individuated sense of self[5] and with tendencies toward boundary confusion[6]—that is, with inadequate differentiation of herself and her own needs from those of others. This development may prepare a woman for an intense and sometimes symbiotic connection with her child, but it leaves her ill-equipped to bond with an adult man in a manner that preserves her own integrity as a differentiated self, as a person with needs, drives, interests, and impulses that she can press forward as her own, regardless of whether or not her husband or lover happens to share them.

Among my respondents, the tendency of wives to fuse rather than bond with their husbands is as prominent as the tendency of husbands to emotionally distance from their wives. Indeed, marriage often seems like a dance in which the husband urgently tries to get away while the wife tries to climb on the husband's feet. We have already seen husbands' evasive maneuvers appear in their separative triangling moves away from the home. Now we will look more closely at wives' tendencies toward female fusion.

I shall start with one of my divorced respondents, whose brief experience in a marriage and subsequent dealings with two new suitors will illustrate the struggle women often have to bond without fusion. Mary was twenty-eight when I saw her. Divorced for nearly four years after having been married for five, she was functioning competently as a single person and mother of a four-year-old daughter. She had resisted several offers of marriage, not wanting, she said, "to grab at the first straw that comes along." She had a good job, enabling her to buy a house and a car, and she had done a lot of the repairing and renovating of the house herself. As a divorcee, she apparently resumed her premarital pattern of independence. Even as a child she recalls being "a very introspective person" who "used to go in my room a lot and read and think. I was very content there. I had what I wanted. I had my books and my studying, and I was very interested in that."

Though well-individuated and autonomous as a single person, Mary found it all too easy to get herself swallowed up in the service of any man with whom she was involved, perhaps falling into her childhood pattern of "giving in" to her two brothers, of whom she spoke with genuine fondness.

118 • *Three Corners*

Her marriage to Bobby was a disaster from start to finish. Initially, she was attracted to his robust personality: "He had a great deal of charisma. He used it in the wrong ways, but I've always been very attracted to people who are not followers, and he definitely was a leader. People did things his way, and there was not any question about it." Unfortunately, Bobby could never turn his forceful personality and his imaginative flair into a productive adult life-style. He spent the money he earned on extravagant boats, guns, cars, and golf clubs. It was Mary's salary which actually supported their home and her organizational and domestic skills that ran and maintained it.

Mary kept hoping that everything would come together if she waited it out: "I had this feeling all the time that he was not grown up and that eventually he would come to his senses. I think probably I tried too hard. I felt that if I worked extra hard I could make up for his immaturity. I always felt that the whole responsibility for the marriage was on my shoulders." Essentially, the more eager a functioner Mary became, maintaining the partnership-corner for both of them, the more of an under-functioner Bobby became, distancing into various third-corners. In the first year or so of marriage, the pattern was not yet extreme, and their relationship had its satisfactions. "I felt needed," Mary said:

> And I felt that I had a purpose in life. Before the baby came, he needed me a great deal. I was the only stabilizing force he had in his life. I took care of him. That part was nice in a way, to feel that needed, but yet it would be very irritating because it was always up to me to figure out solutions and get answers.

Once the baby came, things quickly deteriorated further. Bobby resented the baby and stayed out later and later, sometimes going away on hunting and camping trips with his cousins for several days at a time. Before long he began seeing other women, including one who eventually became his second wife. Mary herself took no steps to end the marriage, having steeled herself to stick it out indefinitely. When she went back east to show her baby to her parents, Bobby kept putting off her return home, until finally—presumably having solidified his relationship with the other woman—he told her that he did not want her to come back, and thus ended the marriage.

As victimized as Mary seems to have been, the fact remains that she did not bring to her marriage a workably adult pattern of bonding. Her formula seems to have been: Find a strong man to lead you and define you, to whom you can totally give yourself, and when that fails because of his ineptitude, content yourself with his needing your care and your stabilizing influence. In the first case she fuses with a strong man's guidance and initiative; in the second his lack of strength and guidance creates such a management problem that her entire life is given over to doing the remedial work necessitated by his chronic and chaotic childishness, in which case she is still defining herself

only in reaction to someone else. In both instances she forfeits her individuation as well as her capacity to be a differentiated self with autonomous needs and wants that she will press forward as her own. Her tendencies toward fusion, then, inhere in her readiness to reshape herself to fit whatever the man in her life wants or needs her to be. In her own words, "I had let things happen rather than make things happen."

Again, Mary's fusion tendencies are shared by many if not most of the women in my sample. What is unique about her is how well developed her autonomy has always been as a single person, how easy she nevertheless finds it to abandon that autonomy, and how remarkably articulate she has become about her own tendencies. About a year after her divorce, she met Bruce:

> Again, he had a wild charisma and tended to overshadow me. But he was very aware of what my capabilities were and he never put me down, and he appreciated my independence and the way I felt. But he did overshadow me, because he was a much stronger personality; people do what he wants them to do, the same way with Bobby, only Bruce was much more developed. . . . We saw each other for a while, and then we decided that we would get married. But I didn't want to get married right away, and I don't think he did either. And we lived together for about eight months, and I could see that it was happening again, that I was just being overshadowed completely. I was not doing what I wanted to do. I was letting the other person run my life. He was never demanding, but I never would express my desires. He expressed a desire; that became my desire. And a lot of times it really wasn't what I wanted to do, but I would make sure that he would get what he wanted. It's very hard to explain why I do that. It's not that I stop being myself, but I start living completely for another person.

Since Bruce moved out, Mary still sees him periodically, and she obviously cares for him. Yet she told me, "I don't think I want to live with him for the rest of my life, because I love him so much that I would give him anything. I want to be a person on my own." I asked her if she ever would want to marry again, and her answer was consistent with what she had learned about herself:

> I would like to, yes. What I want now is quite different from what I wanted before. I want the compatibility and all that, but I'm looking for a different person. I'm not looking for the person with charisma. I'm looking for someone with simple tastes and simple desires, who I can be with and still be myself.

She then described a recent suitor whom she could conceive of marrying:

> He's pleasant, he's warm, he tries to be very helpful with people, but he doesn't have that kind of a drive [like Bobby or Bruce]. With a dominant person, I just let him have his way. I will do it because I want that person to be happy. Someone who's not quite as strong, I do things for them, I want

120 • *Three Corners*

them to be happy, but I know that they're doing the same for me. But I don't want to be the dominant one, either. And I don't believe that I could ever dominate this person, and that makes me happy. I want it to be a 50–50 thing.

At this point in the interview, I wondered aloud to Mary whether trading a strong, "charismatic" person for one not so charismatic meant also trading away greater feelings of love and attraction for lesser ones. "You might never," I suggested, "feel that heightened intensity for this new person." Mary agreed:

There would not be that kind of a feeling, but I would be happier, because I'm not having to submerge myself. And in the long run I think that I'll be happier. It's just very hard to forget that one attraction [to Bruce]. I think growing up is a very strange process; I think you learn sometimes that the things that you really like are not always the things that are best for you. I stop and I think where I was, to where I've come, from being very submissive to the strong, dominating type, to standing on my own two feet and being very independent, and also quite successful—now that's a big step. And knowing that you can do it on your own, you don't have to be afraid. I would never get married now to make it easier for me. When I become submissive, I am not contributing anything to a relationship; I am becoming a mirror image of the other person.

Female Fusion and Male Distancing: The Vicious Circle

Chodorow suggests that for a girl to establish a sufficiently individuated sense of self, her mother must not overinvest in her. For this, a mother should have help with child-care and some companionship with other adults, as well as meaningful work that offers a sense of self-definition not restricted to her mother-identity. In addition, a girl should have a father who is present enough to counteract her tendencies toward fusion with her mother.[7] Chodorow claims that these are all conditions which modern industrial societies have tended to rule out. Still, even when these conditions appear to be at least moderately in evidence in my data, they do not always seem to save a daughter from boundary confusion, from lack of differentiation of self from others, from problems of establishing autonomy, and hence from problems of fusion with a husband. We shall follow the case of Jenny and Sam Olson closely in search of some clarity on this issue.

Born in 1943, Jenny grew up on a small farm in rural Maine. Long before Jenny's birth, her father had raised (initially with his grandfather's help) his five younger siblings after their parents had died. Jenny's mother thus "took on a whole houseful" when she married Jenny's father, as these five younger

siblings and also his grandfather were part of the territory. I have no information concerning what needs of her own, if any, this woman was serving by starting a marriage under these circumstances. Perhaps economic security had much to do with it. Already widowed herself and the mother of a young daughter, her traditional values left her with little alternative but marriage to meet her economic needs, and perhaps at age twenty-seven in a rural, underpopulated region, she did not find many eligible males around. In any case, she lived essentially a preindustrial round of existence in this farmhouse.

Whether this existence qualifies as the sort of "meaningful work" that Chodorow says will protect a mother from overly identifying with her children is not clear. Surely there was hard work with this houseful from the very beginning. Within the first six years of her marriage to Jenny's father, Jenny's mother had three more daughters, Jenny being the last. Matters were further complicated by the fact that Jenny's mother's sister lived on some neighboring land, having married Jenny's father's brother—that is, two brothers had married two sisters.

Since all of these people were accessible to one another and probably had daily contact, the triangular dynamics must have been complex. The two brothers continued to work the farm together after their respective marriages, and Jenny remembers her mother sometimes bringing lunch to them out in the fields. There, she would often catch wind of some detail about the business aspect of the farm, and soon she would be discussing that detail with her neighboring sister. The two brothers were to some extent allied with each other against their wives, as Jenny remembers her father and uncle "joking" that the farm would work just fine if not for the two sisters' meddling.

With her sister so close at hand, Jenny's mother could have had an ally of her own and a source of ongoing adult companionship. The two sisters did in fact talk every day, but Jenny says that they were often quarrelsome together, and it is unlikely that either woman was a comfortable emotional support for the other.

As for Jenny's father, Jenny remembers him as "always there". She and her sisters were actively involved in doing farmwork with him: "I think some of the memories of childhood were being out in the fields with Dad. He made it a fun time rather than a work time. He always got one more row to hoe out of us." While it sounds like there may have been some meaningful bonding between father and daughters, and some basis, therefore, for the latter to individuate away from any fusion with their mother, it is doubtful that the father was a very active presence in the house, in the earlier years of their childhood. In any case, Jenny did not ultimately use her father as leverage to break her fusion with her mother. She remained symbiotically connected to her for many years, unable to begin to individuate until after nearly two decades of marriage. We need, then, to learn all we can about Jenny's relationship with her mother.

122 • *Three Corners*

"A very domineering lady," was Jenny's summary description of her mother. Apparently, Jenny saw virtually no conflict in her family because no one, including Jenny's father, wanted to challenge this outspoken woman. Whenever tensions arose, her father was more inclined to go out and stew in the barn than to stand his ground with his wife. Jenny herself learned habits of compliance early on. She told me, "I never had a fight or a harsh word with my mother until recently." She added that she and her next older sister, with whom she was close, "never discussed anything with our mother. Perhaps we were afraid. Her approval was hard to get, and none of us wanted a loud speech if we didn't do things her way." Nevertheless, as most children will, Jenny must have readily adopted much of her mother's view of the world:

> I think when we were brought up we were geared to marriage and having a family. I never questioned it at that particular time, although I have since. Our mother and father felt that going to college wasn't necessary for a girl, and I believed that. When I was in high school I once had a chance to be an exchange student in France, and I turned it down because my mother assumed I was going to get married and raise kids and that would be my life.

When I asked Jenny if she had ever thought about what qualities she wanted in a mate, she again remembers deferring to her mother's views:

> Mother was one of the largest influences. She told you some of the qualities that would be needed in a husband. Once you were on your own and you were married, you would need this certain amount of income. You would need a fine Catholic boy. If mother approved, it was okay; if she disapproved, you were really in trouble. Rather than go through the troubles, you said, "This one's okay but that one isn't," and you never looked any further.

While Jenny's relationship with her stern, puritanical mother was anything but warm and nurturing, she surely enjoyed many offsetting sources of close, empathic emotional support. She and her one-year-older sister always "stuck together like glue," she told me, and to this day they remain each other's closest confidantes. Perhaps this sister bond could not really become an active force in Jenny's emotional life until long after her infancy, but there were other sources that must have been accessible from the beginning. Her two paternal aunts had essentially grown up in Jenny's house. By the time Jenny was born, they were almost old enough to be her mother, and they continued to live with her throughout most of her childhood. Jenny remembers them fondly:

> They had a great deal to do with our lives as children. They took care of us, literally. I don't see my mother in that position as much as I see them—taking care of our needs like curling the hair, taking you to bed. Many times my mother was too busy for us.

Even after these aunts married and moved out, they remained accessible, and Jenny recalls several years as a teenager when she and her sister would stay with one of these aunts for several weeks at a time in the summer months.

During these summer visits Jenny enjoyed going with her sister to weekly dances at the Grange hall. There, at age fifteen, she met Sam, the man who in three years was to become her husband. By then, Jenny was already oriented to marriage. Like her close sister, who also married at eighteen, she "wanted to get out from mother's control," and it mattered little that she had had no experience with adult intimacy:

> We all had the Cinderella story, where everything is cute and perfect. I saw the dating days of all my sisters and their marriages. And I liked the romance part, and the rest I sort of just pushed aside and didn't even want to see. You never saw my mother and father kiss each other or even touch. That was just not there. And when I saw my sisters with their boyfriends, I think it was this Cinderella dream I was holding on to: Hey, that's what it was all about! In looking back on my courtship with Sam, I think I was in love with love. Sam was great hearts and flowers, which fit in with my picture perfectly. I felt I knew him completely, he knew me completely, and we were on that merry little road that goes off into the sunset. Now, it was all that light, romantic thing. I tell my children now I would not want them to go in with the attitudes that I had with marriage. I was blind; I never even bothered with issues. It was just going to be perfect, period.

The fact is that none of Jenny's premarital life-experience had equipped her to differentiate herself and her needs from her social surround. She complained that her fate as the youngest of the family was to have "too many bosses to tell you what to do." And what might she, in a free world, have wanted to do? Apparently she never found out, because no one ever encouraged her to have her own needs, to cultivate her own inner sense of direction and initiative. For this, she would have required nurturers who could diffusely identify with her, empathizing enough with her to acknowledge and sometimes honor her individual needs as they naturally emerged.

Unfortunately Jenny had no such nurturers. Not her mother, whose approval was too difficult to get and who professed to know her daughters' real needs better than they did themselves. Not her father, who may have made the outside work a "fun time" but who was too segmentally involved with her to make much of a difference. Her close sister? Her two paternal aunts? From them came empathy in abundance, but it was not the kind that fostered any self-assertive personhood in Jenny. It was the empathy of coconspirators who needed allies to ward off boss-mother. (Jenny told me that the aunts, too, felt resentment toward their older sister-in-law, Jenny's mother, who became their functional stepmother some years after their own mother had died.) Together, they all plotted their great escape into marriage. Aided by the Cinderella story,

in which a girl is rescued from her everyday oppression by a windfall marriage to a prince, all their primal hopes of unconditional love, approval, and security get projected into a glorious fantasy. Marriage spells the first freedom to be yourself.

Unfortunately, because "yourself"—Jenny's self—had arisen only as a fantasy underlife carved out in secret with her sister, she lacked the personal power to translate that abstract fantasy into a living, practical reality. Having deep-rooted suspicions about her own competence to initiate action, and still fused with her mother's all-knowing direction, she all too easily slipped back into the safe illusion that other people—this time her husband—would know what is best for her.

Even during the courtship, Jenny's shift from her mother's to Sam's direction became quickly established. He was five years older than she, which perhaps lent to his judgments a greater ring of authority: "We did not fight all the time that we were dating. We had that going for us for those three years. We didn't fight because I agreed with everything Sam said. As far as I was concerned, Sam knew how things should be." Jenny's compliant attitude fit together perfectly with Sam's expectations. He told me:

> I always thought marriage would be very glamorous. The honeymoon would never end. I would always be the boss; I remember that distinctly. I could always picture my wife running around [he pauses to laugh]—a clean house, dressed in a starched apron. Mrs. Perfect, the perfect homemaker. And I would come home from work and my slippers and pipe would be out—that type of thing. . . . I always judged we had a very good courting. We seemed at the time very compatible. Whatever I wanted to do, we did. There was never any bickering. I thought we were so compatible that this pattern would just continue and never end.

Plainly, Sam came to both courtship and marriage needing to be in charge, to prove his masculine mettle. One reason was that his two brothers were both exceptional athletes, but Sam was not:

> My older brother was the star athlete of the county. I wasn't. I think the first year I went out for football, it was because it was expected of me. But I liked horses, and I used to—not really take out my revenge, but I used to love to get my brothers on the horse, because none of them knew what they were doing, and that was my cup of tea.

Sam's father was likewise a hard act to follow. He was something of a god-father–patriarch for the whole extended family, the one to whom all the uncles, aunts, cousins, and nephews would come for advice about their problems:

> I thought I really had to emulate my father, because I knew Jenny had a great deal of respect for my dad, and I tried to put myself on a power level with

him and act like him. I don't know whether it lasted a day. I am not my father; I'll never be my father. I just couldn't carry through with it. I didn't have his patience and his understanding.

For Sam, marriage must have offered the promise of that leadership and lime-light that had so far eluded him. "Jenny was always very agreeable to what-ever I wanted to do, which was fine with me. I most always had my way." Sam led, Jenny followed, both travelling the pathway they hoped would de-liver their fondest fantasy-self—Jenny the Cinderella girl, Sam the potent prince who came to rescue and then lead her happily ever after.

It did not take long for both of their fantasies to show themselves un-workable. By the time their second anniversary came around, they had already had two children. They had left Maine to go live in a suburb of Boston, near Sam's parents but far away from Jenny's familiar surroundings. Sam's eager-ness to be the sole authority often resulted in arbitrariness, in decisions that quickly jolted Jenny's fantasy that Sam would want nothing more than to take care of her in a spirit of knightly nurturance. It was Sam who had made the decision for Jenny to get a job when their first child was not yet a year old. They could use the money, he told her, and his mother was willing to babysit. Sam likewise made the decision for Jenny to quit the job when she started having severe nervous symptoms. Says Jenny with obvious irony:

> The choices were made because Sam was the all-knowing one. In looking back on it now, I can see that I should have had a say in my going to work or my quitting work, but as far as really expressing my feelings, I think that was totally inside. I didn't know my feelings then, either.

Not only were Sam's decisions arbitrary, but he seemed to have little in-clination to be with her and their child. Jenny recalls an occasion during her difficult second pregnancy when Sam's partying inclinations became too de-manding for her to sustain:

> We had moved in with Sam's parents for three months, because the doctor told me I had a pending miscarriage unless I took it easy. We were wrapped up in this go-go-go all the time. And I didn't feel good, and it was really get-ting to me. I remember one particular incident. We were at his cousin's house, and everyone was going to go to a party, and I said no. And he said "Okay, we'll go home." Well, he got in the car and drove like mad—it scared the dickens out of me—because I did not say, "Yes, we'll go" when he wanted to go. Again I went into tears. We went back to his father's house, and Sam left again immediately with great squealing of tires. I was totally done in. I was devastated. . . . Neither of us ever told the other what we had felt. And in my mind, Sam's feelings were still right, and if I didn't feel like Sam did, I was wrong, and I judged myself wrong for not having the same feelings so that this marriage could be that Cinderella idea that I had from the beginning.

126 • *Three Corners*

With two children arriving so quickly, Sam's fantasy of the perfect home-maker devoted only to serving his needs was soon shattered. "She was tending the youngsters. I was rather resentful that I didn't have all the time, but I kept it inside. I would busy myself with other things." Those "other things" started with a bowling league and late-night partying at his cousin's house. A few years later, when Sam and Jenny bought a farmhouse and moved back to Maine, these were followed by a Jaycees club (which Sam helped to establish), by a successful venture in town politics, and by a consuming passion for buying horses and taking them to weekend horse shows—a throwback, perhaps, to that one adolescent pursuit in which Sam had been able to outdo his brothers. He recalls: "I would come home from work, eat, get dressed, and go to a town council meeting, or I would come home and go out in the barn and spend the night fooling around with a nag. We lived in the same house, but the communications were really nothing to behold."

By now there were four children, and the pattern of Sam feeling excluded from Jenny's total attention was now compounded by his realization that he was anything but that paternalistic family patriarch that his father had modeled: "Jenny always had a terrific relationship with the kids, and I think I was a little jealous, especially when they got older. I always wanted them to confide in me, especially my oldest daughter, and I was a little hurt that they didn't. As I look back, I don't really blame them. If they did confide in me I'd just tell them they're wrong and that's it!"

For her part, Jenny's life revolved around the children. She was still fused in principle to Sam's guidance and direction, but in practice she no longer trusted or believed in it. In Massachusetts there was a period just before her second child came when they moved into a house some fifteen miles from Sam's mother and father. She recalls coming home from the hospital with the new baby:

> I thought everybody was inconsiderate because they left me with my little five-pound baby that had to stay in the same room all the time and a nineteen-month-old demon. All the relatives disappeared and I was totally alone in the house with those two babies, and I was scared.

As Sam became less and less accessible, Jenny's nervous symptoms grew worse and worse, sometimes getting so out of control that she had to call one of Sam's relatives to come and be with her. When they moved back to Maine the pattern continued. Though her mother was once more available for direction, Jenny never appealed for her help unless she fell into an extreme panic and no one else was around. ("Mother always left it that once you were married you never went back home to Mother with any of your problems.") Jenny's close sister once again helped to drain some of the tensions, but since they now lived with their own families in separate houses in neighboring towns, Jenny could not be actively fused with her in the way that she yearned to be.

For many years her life-pattern remained the same. There were short-lived interruptions of the nervous symptoms, as when she went back to work for a year until her third child was born:

> I was very secure in that job; it was the one thing I knew I could do well. Lots of times I was in charge, and that felt good. And it didn't involve Sam questioning my abilities.

Once out of the job and back at home, the symptoms returned, but her children increasingly helped to stave off her terror of being alone. As she grew more fused with them over the years, she craved less fusion with Sam:

> My children had replaced Sam in an awful lot of areas. I would replace the feelings that I wanted from him with the children. . . . They confide everything in me; I never would with my mother. But I have to be a real person to them too. I'm very open to them about everything, and it has brought a very special closness. If Allison [her oldest child] has any problem at all, the deepest, darkest secrets come out to me. And I find that I'm accepting and allowing her free choice a whole lot more than her father is. He comes off as the authoritarian father figure a lot. But when the children start disappearing because Dad's going to give them a speech, I can say, "I don't want that for my children."

We have seen this classic pattern before. He triangulates away from the marriage to launch a campaign on behalf of masculine individuation and distinction; she finds her third-corner through fusing with the children. Now, which came first? Did Jenny play the children off against Sam and thus unwittingly drive him more and more outside the home in search of recognition? Or did Sam's need for outside recognition precede any measure of support he might have gotten from Jenny, in which case his inaccessibility became the factor which drove Jenny to seek more and more solace in the children? Was Jenny replaying her old alliance with her sister against boss-mother's power, with Sam now substituting for boss-mother and the children standing in for Jenny's sister? Or was Sam's distancing a mere function of his old campaign to be the conquering hero outside the home that all the males in his family of origin seemed to be except him?

As usual with vicious circles, the question of origins is irrelevant because once in gear, any such circle is fueled by inputs from every point around it and not from any point in particular. In this case, what is clear is that the more Sam distances, the more Jenny feels betrayed in her need to fuse with him. The more she tries to render him more accessible or turns to her children for substitutes, the more he feels the need to distance from her. In chapter 7, we shall explore a common resolution of this circle.

128 • *Three Corners*

Notes

1. Nancy Chodorow, *The Reproduction of Mothering* (Berkeley: University of California Press, 1978), p. 103.

2. Ibid., p. 207.

3. Ibid., p. 199.

4. Ibid., p. 203.

5. Ibid., p. 140.

6. Ibid., p. 110.

7. Ibid., pp. 140, 211–213.

7
Marital Separateness

Thus far we have looked at two patterns of marital dynamics. The first, romantic fusion, is balanced and reciprocal, with each partner's inner self fused with the partnership. Though symmetrical, romantic fusion is unstable and usually short-lived as a vision of expanded wholeness. Its overwhelming intensity soon consumes the couple in their own flames. Without new and fresh materials drawn from outside the bond, the partners quickly exhaust each others' resources and burn each other out. Then there are several possibilities. Sometimes both partners renew their respective third-corner commitments, in which case they can make a comfortable and orderly retreat from their fusion and rebuild their relationship on a more realistic foundation. That is, they begin to integrate their relationship with their total life-space, and each of their inner selves is again set free to the variegated richness that any self possesses.

But the retreat from extreme fusion is not easy, and we have seen that it is usually uneven. Males like Danny Gardner and Sam Olson not only begin to seek fresh materials from third-corners away from the partnership but they do so with a zeal and alacrity that becomes truly alarming to their wives. Females like Sheila Gardner and Jenny Olson, in turn, find little incentive to individuate into any third-corners other than their own children, and they either remain fused to their husband's direction or they fuse with their children to compensate for their unmet bonding needs. Hence the second pattern, dependency-distancing, emerges.

Though frequent, dependency-distancing is not an inevitable sequel to romantic fusion. The pathways through marriage show enormous variety, and partners' inventiveness keeps on confounding the attempt to nail down any monolithic analysis of developmental phases. Many marriages begin without any romantic fusion at all, and with scarcely any romance. Some relationships seem to settle into the dependency-distancing mode almost from the very beginning, starting with the courtship. In my data this is most likely when the wife marries young (under age twenty), when she has led a sheltered premarital existence, when she suspends her education and/or training shortly

130 • *Three Corners*

before or after marriage, and when the husband is several years older than she. Sheila and Danny Gardner typify most of these conditions, while Sam and Jenny Olson satisfy all of them.

In no case did I find a marriage that began with the husband in the dependent position and the wife in the distancing one. Murray Bowen describes a "dominant-adaptive" marital pattern that is similar to what I have called dependency-distancing (the dominant partner distances, the adaptive partner is dependent), and he claims that females are as often found in the dominant position as males, while males are as often seen in the adaptive position as females.[1] Perhaps in making this statement, Bowen was not taking into account the overall developmental history of relationships. In my data, some wives who began their marriages in the dependent position do become more distancing later on, presumably as a response to a long history of their fusion needs having been frustrated. Their husbands may then feel somewhat threatened and displaced, and while a wave of insecurity may lead them to lessen some of their own distancing in an attempt to regain their favor with their wives, these men do not often trade places with them and assume the extremely dependent positions their wives held earlier. Rather, what usually emerges is a distancing–distancing pattern, in which he remains essentially as he was before, and she now becomes more like him in seeking her major life satisfactions outside the marital bond. I shall use the term *separateness* as a less cumbersome name for this distancing–distancing phenomenon.

As shown in figure 4, separateness restores some symmetry into the marital relationship. It is balanced and symmetrical. To be sure, the spouses' partnership-corners—P1 and P2—are pulled even farther apart than they were in the dependency–distancing pattern, but the fact remains that separateness is often more comfortable for both partners. For example, it frees a

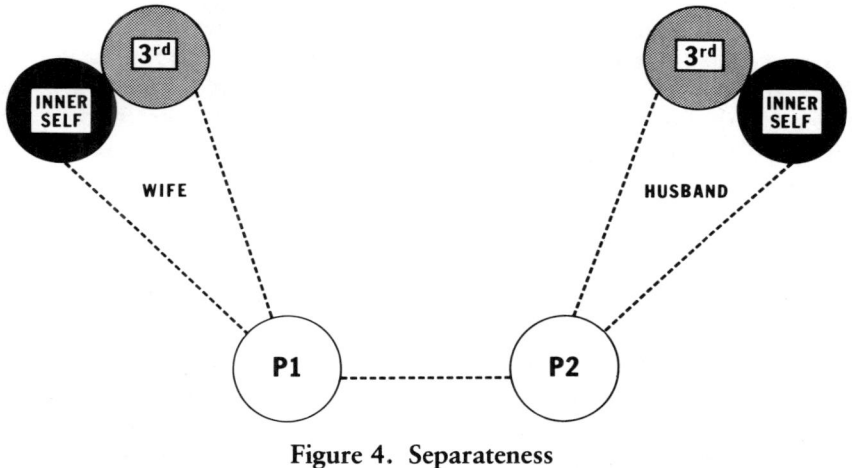

Figure 4. Separateness

Marital Separateness • 131

dependent wife from her unrelenting emotional hunger and gives her a sense of personal power, while it frees a distancing husband to engage his cherished third-corner with more singlemindedness than ever, no longer called upon to explain his inaccessibility. Separateness may be stable and durable so long as it remains symmetrical. This means that both partners' third-corners must retain their centrality for their respective inner selves.

Both the Gardners and the Olsons, who were cited as examples of dependency-distancing, eventually shifted into the separateness pattern. When we left Sheila Gardner, her third-corner had recently expanded to three children, a new house, and various child-centered activities like Girl Scouts. While virtually all of this was carried on with no more than token involvement on Danny's part, Sheila had not yet moved from her position of dependency on him. It was as if he was her silent, unseen partner as she went about her third-corner business. What finally brought her to begin to pull back from her fusion with Danny was the entrance of their last child into the first grade, some fifteen years into the marriage:

My last chicken was out of the nest, and I had a depression which was so overwhelming that I didn't think I was ever going to get up from it. It was time for me to get out and do all the things I'd always said I was going to do when the kids grew up. And what was it? I just didn't know where I was.

A supportive counselor helped her through her depression and got her interested in some volunteer work as an outlet for her enormous energy.

While I was doing the volunteer work I began to get a sense of me again. . . . I'm talking about my ego having been totally zilchoed when I got into this depression, and I really thought I couldn't do anything but be a housewife and a mother, and gosh, they didn't need me any more, and what am I going to do, and so forth. I just began to realize, hey, I have resources of my own. I'm relatively bright, I'm this, I'm that. People began to pay attention to what I could do.

Before long, the volunteer work was succeeded by a job and by the resumption of her college education, which she had long ago traded for marriage and children.

I'd gotten used to him going on being Danny and working really hard and doing all that nasty stuff, and now I was going to go on and do what I wanted to do and have fun while I was doing it. I was busy at this thing and at that thing. And then I had friends outside our relationship, meaningful friendships, both male and female. And it began to become clear to me that I had more meaningful relationships outside of our marriage than I did with him. And I began to make an unfavorable comparison. . . . It was as if I was a teenager. I was beginning to leave home! And I'm sure I played that for all

132 • *Three Corners*

it was worth, not really knowing the devastating effect it was having on him. I had been feeling rotten, I had been blaming him for it, and now I was feeling better, no-thanks-to-him type of thing.

For the first time in her married life, Sheila was now involved in a number of third-corners that were not simply extensions of her home and family. No longer fused with her partnership-corner, her inner self (the first corner) became more autonomous, more capable of conceiving and initiating actions rooted in her own needs and strivings. Triangulation is the mover and shaker of all marital dynamics, as mentioned earlier, and Sheila's strong triangling moves (to job, to school, and to friends) proved to be no exception.

The resulting separateness could have felt more comfortable to both partners. The greater symmetry of third-corner commitments might have taken the heat off the relationship and thereby stabilized it. The rule is, however, that marital dynamics unfold in accord with the partner's response to the spouse who makes the strong new triangling moves. This response is governed by paradigmatic images that may instruct a partner either that these moves are to be regarded as dangerous and should therefore be suppressed, or that they are safe and sensible and deserve to be accommodated in a spirit of uncomplaining equanimity. In Danny Gardner's familiar paradigm, "the wife should behave herself while the husband was not under any such constraints or rules." A wife outside of the home is surely up to no good:

> I didn't ask her to work, I didn't think about it. I assumed, why would she work? And then she got a job, she had a couple of jobs that got her into the outside world. And I began to revive the old jealousy thing. . . . She told me once she was going to go fishing, some fellow had asked her to go fishing, one of these former Maine guide types who knows everything about the woods. I didn't say anything about it, so one morning she left and went fishing and came back around noon. The whole thing was innocent, really, but as the morning went on, I started getting mad. I thought, "What in the hell is she doing, going fishing?" That kind of put me on to this thing of, "She's been home all this time, now she's out in the world, who knows what might happen?"

Danny's fears of someone "making a cuckold of me," as he put it, were further inflamed by his own secret yearnings, which he must have projected onto Sheila:

> There was about a two-year period when I had a very regular recurring desire to be free. I didn't do anything about it, but I thought often about it. Free of Sheila and of the children. Just leave—why don't I go to California or something? I didn't have a girlfriend I was going to run off to California with, but I'm sure that part of the freedom would be freedom to do my own thing with women. Maybe I was tired of responsibility—the damned work every year. I'd come home, what in hell am I doing all this for? There was that.

These kind of images led Danny to fear the worst, and as Sheila escalated her triangling moves, he became more angry, irrational, and resistant. Then the marriage entered a period of extreme disturbance, as Sheila would not back down.

> The more jealous he became, the more angry I got. I felt, "I have never done anything for you not to trust, nor do I intend to do something, yet you're not trusting me." Then my honor really did get at stake, and I got very upset and angry with him for not knowing me any better than that. I was feeling like we weren't very good friends at all.

Dependent partners who begin to break their fusion are fighting for their lives, as the choice is between continued oblivion or emergent, autonomous identity. The more fused a wife has been, the more frustration she has endured while fused and dependent, and the more internalized (instead of expressed) the frustration has remained, then the more explosively a wife will react to a husband's attempt to block her moves toward independence. Sheila said:

> He was continuing to fuss and fume and go on, and I just hit the ceiling. I remember getting really violent about it and throwing a chair at him or something. I was really mad, and acted it out. I couldn't do anything else, I just did exactly what I felt like doing, and that was what it was. And I hated his guts. I called a friend of mine and she came and got me and I left. That lasted about forty-eight hours.

I shall not detail the Gardners' aftermath of all this turmoil. Suffice it to say that the relationship was soon rebuilt on a more congenial footing. There was a period of soul-searching and self-disclosure with the help of a Marriage Encounter weekend. Sheila continued to pursue a variety of third-corners outside the home, and Danny became less threatened by them, once it was apparent that his fears were ill-founded. Danny did become a little more emotionally accessible, but in practice it does not appear that he fundamentally altered his work-centered lifestyle. Rather, Sheila too became busier and busier with her third-corners, including an absorbing full-time job. Except for a new commitment to church and some summer travel together, the Gardners did not seem to actively participate a lot more in each others' lives, nor to structure the time to bridge their gaps through talk, for example. They seemed to enter a period of comfortable, settled separateness, which was essentially where they were at the time I interviewed them.

Jenny and Sam Olson's marriage went through a similar development. As with Sheila Gardner's depression, Jenny's uncomfortable dependency began to show up in severe problems of personal incapacity. (Here Murray Bowen's work is again instructive. He writes that a partner who stays in the adaptive

134 • *Three Corners*

position will tend to lose the capacity to think and function independently. Under these circumstances, even a slight increase in stress can throw this partner into dysfunction. Common dysfunctions are "physical illness, emotional illness, or social illness, such as drinking, acting out, and irresponsible behavior.")[2] In Jenny's case, the dysfunction took the form of extreme nervous symptoms, which often intensified at night whenever Jenny was left in the home with only her children. As the symptoms grew out of control, sometimes to the point of keeping her in bed, she grew more and more alarmed.

> I did absolute research into my symptoms after a while. I read Dr. Claire Weekes' *Hope and Help for Your Nerves*. Now that helped me a lot. I read it whenever I had physical symptoms and I found out I could override my own. Once I discovered Claire Weekes' book I really went on a search to find myself. There was an awful lot of things that I became aware of in myself, and the more I found, the more secure I got with myself, it seemed like the more insecure Sam was getting. The tides were turning.

While Jenny's search took a much different outer form than Sheila's did, it was structurally the same. Both women intensified their involvement with third-corners that had nothing to do with their husbands. Jenny's equivalent to Sheila's job, school, and friends was her reading, to which she attached the full focus of her inner self.

> I went to the public library, read every psychology book they had in there. I was learning a whole lot about myself and other people. . . . Perhaps in my self-awareness I became more outspoken with my own feelings. We had battles that were rotten, but I did not become so overly devastated anymore. I would fight back a whole lot more, but the more that I fought back, the louder it got.

Sam remembers the same escalation of hostilities: "We had no real communication all those years—my being very domineering and Jenny being very passive. And then when she became very vocal with her objections, I became twice as vocal and twice as domineering." As with Danny Gardner, Sam Olson did not stand ready to yield independence and equality to his wife. In his familiar paradigm, a man is a strong and all-knowing patriarch, and Sam's inner security in fulfilling that image had always been too precarious to risk sharing any power. He recalls:

> I still figured I was boss and I was going to do what I wanted, or I was going to make the final decision on most everything. . . . When Jenny talked me into seeing a counselor with her, I was very threatened, because I had to get into myself, and I didn't want to get into myself. I was fine, she was wrong. . . . And then I have this thing with Jenny and her superior intelligence. I

judged her a very smart person, and she reads all these books, and I'm more apt to read *Playboy*, and this was a threat to me. . . . We saw the counselor for a very short time, and then I actually refused to go back. I did not need a goddamned shrink!

Even without the continued intervention of the counselor, Jenny's fusion with Sam was already breaking down. As her inner-corner shifted away from his direction, she began to initiate more actions that were totally independent of him:

It was almost like it was okay for me to do things. I remember one Sunday when Sam was busy, and there was somewhere I wanted to go, and he was not ready, and he was ready to do battle with me. And I told him, "Do whatever you want to do. It's fine by me. I'll go by myself." And I took that attitude, so that you only became more separated, but I was more secure in that separation. I didn't really care if I was with Sam. I preferred to be by myself.

As with the Gardners, the Olson's new phase of unsettled and volatile separateness was calmed down by a Marriage Encounter weekend which Jenny initiated. In the aftermath, the marriage did become more connected than the Gardner's did. Sam pulled back from most of his separative third-corners, became a little more open and communicative, and joined Jenny in a lot of regular Marriage Encounter functions organized by their church. Nevertheless, an interesting reversal began to emerge. As we shall see, real connectedness in a relationship depends on equality, for which neither Sam nor Jenny seemed prepared. Recall that their dependency-distancing phase had been their solution to the problems in each of their familiar paradigms. For Jenny, marriage meant a chance to be Cinderella, to be taken care of by someone other than her domineering mother, who always failed her. For Sam, marriage was a chance to be a conquering prince like his more accomplished brothers, or a revered patriarch like his father. When these solutions broke down, it became all too easy for both partners to fall back into their familiar paradigms. For Sam this meant once more failing to measure up to those around him, this time to his wife. And for Jenny it meant adopting her all-knowing mother's stance, now that her prince had proven himself no better than her mother in caring for her.

For both partners the path of least resistance is to be either "one-up" or "one-down," with little leeway in between. To be sure, Marriage Encounter has now given them an ideology and a language of marital connectedness, which they both speak with some facility. The fact remains, however, that Jenny is the one who defines their third-corner activities, and she is the leader and the specialist in pursuing them:

136 • *Three Corners*

I read the Bible from cover to cover and was ready to jump on my soapbox about religion. And we found that in our dialogue, if there was a religious question, I kept seeing Sam as down there, and I was getting up here. And I kept resenting the fact that he didn't look any further than he did. Last summer I was devouring every [inspirational] book John Powell wrote, and I urged Sam to read one of them so we could discuss it. He didn't have the time for reading. I resented that he didn't learn the same way I did. . . . I have perhaps become preachy in some of my beliefs. I have a feeling of superiority a lot. And there are days now when I look at Sam and there is nothing in him that I envy. Sometimes I feel sorry for Sam in expecting larger strides when they talk about growth in Marriage Encounter—spiritually, personally and the whole bit. And lots of times when we are dialoguing, I can say, "I feel sorry for you," which I never would have said before. Because there is nothing that he has in his life now that I could not handle, and perhaps handle better.

Jenny's invidious language reveals a keen need to outshine and outdistance her husband, even while she professes to want closeness. She now seeks her life sustenance in her reading and in her church-centered third-corner rather than in her partnership, and though Sam often joins her in this third-corner, he does so with an inner sense of reserve and distance rather than risk competing with her. He struck me as a tired warrior who has succumbed to the power-challenge of his underling and is now resigned to living in a territory ruled by her. A strong show of surface connectedness thus hides a much deeper layer of separateness, which continues to bubble up periodically from underneath.

Comfortable Separateness and Development-Free Marriage

We have seen that the Gardners and the Olsons shifted into separateness only after the women had endured years of frustration in the dependency-distancing pattern. In contrast, some couples ease into a pattern of separateness almost from the very beginning of their marriages. That is, both the wives and the husbands come to marriage with exclusive third-corners that absorb the lion's share of their private dramas. If conditions are such that these respective third-corners remain available, the marriage can go on comfortably for years without any semblance of development at all, and with scarcely any connection between male and female worlds. There are several variants of these development-free marriages.

Many women begin their marriages still actively fused or bonded to their mothers, and they may still depend upon that third-corner for their sense of identity and security. A respondent named Helen Pratt, an only child, lived with her husband Tom in her mother's house for the first five years of her thirty-year marriage, with her mother living in Helen and Tom's house for

the past ten. I tried in vain to get from her some sense of development of her marriage over the thirty-year span. No, there weren't any surprises about married life, she told me, looking back at the early period. Nor could she identify any way that marriage had "added things" to her life. "Has your marriage gone through any phases?", I queried, and she replied that after several years Tom had developed a slowly progressing illness—"a scary time that brought us closer together." Their two children also "made us happier." I probed for anything more specific Helen might tell me about the impact marriage has had on her or Tom's life:

Has there ever been a turning point in your marriage?

No, I don't think so.

Have you ever come to understand something about Tom that you didn't understand as well before?

No, I don't think so.

Have your feelings changed in any way towards him?

No.

Has being married to him changed you in any way?

No.

Do you suppose being married to you has changed him?

No.

At one point I asked her if she has ever wanted to work outside the home. She replied, "No, and it makes me feel guilty that I don't want to. I *like* being a girl. [She is fifty-three years old.] I like being taken care of and waited on." Yet, aside from Tom's income-earning activities, he does not appear to have much of an inclination to "wait on" her. His temper "flares up" when she asks him to do things around the house, like painting or papering, and he is resistant to going out to dinner, which is something that she likes to do. "He'll say, 'For the price it would cost you and I to go out to dinner, we could have the whole family here.' So then I say, 'That's great, but I end up doing all the work!'"

At this point I asked Helen, "Who is the boss?", and without hesitating she replied, "He is. I think we more or less do things that he wants to do when

138 • *Three Corners*

he wants to do them. That doesn't bother me, because they're things I like to do too, usually." I asked, "Suppose you want to do something and he doesn't?" She replied, laughing, "Then we just don't do it. Sometimes he might go along, but he'd sulk all the time, so it's better not to go." At the end of the interview, she added, "He does make me feel appreciated. When he comes home he wants his meals on the table, and when he goes to work he wants to know that his pants are pressed and his shirts are clean, and he lets me know that he appreciates that."

Despite the lopsided power structure in this marriage, there were few signs of any paradigm conflict or disturbance over any generic issues of female bonding versus male separation, or over any of their respective paradigm elements or specific agendas for marriage. Indeed, their paradigms and agendas complement each other like smoothly meshing gears. Tom is free to elaborate an exclusive male world centering around the third-corners of work and hobbies and buttressed by his sharing of his sons' athletic interests. He is free, therefore, to distance as much as he wants from any "female" emotional engagement. Helen can retain her girl-like fusion with her mother, supplement that fusion with the notion of being "supported" and "taken care of" by a husband, reverse the poles of her own fusion by rearing two children, and never have to struggle to apprehend herself as a separate individual with autonomous needs and desires.

As partners they are comfortably worlds apart. For Tom marriage is an Economic Calling and a Safe Haven, an opportunity to quietly get restored and be "king of his home" (the words Helen used to describe what a husband should be), and a chance to daily confirm his masculine worth through the charge of earning the whole family's living. For Helen marriage is a Safe Return Home, a chance to play out the traditional culture's vision of what an adult female should be, without ever having to differentiate from her fusion with her mother. Two paradigms complement one another, and it seems to work out to each partner's satisfaction.

Contrary to how static things may look, there are active dynamics at work to keep their relationship safe from any semblance of development in thirty years. She will comply with virtually anything he wants, and he is therefore free to continue being anything he was before he married her. In turn, she will want nothing from him enough to fight for it, so he will never have to significantly alter his world in order to accommodate hers. In any case she has never individuated enough to have a differentiated outlook or to be enough of a self-mover to require his accommodation. Helen too, then, is free to remain whoever she was before she married Tom. The pattern can continue indefinitely, so long as Helen feels securely enough fused with her mother that she makes no moves toward individuation nor demands greater emotional bonding with Tom, and so long as Tom feels secure enough in his world of separative individuation that he need never cast a backward glance at the part of himself that was once intimately nurtured by a female.

This case perhaps exaggerates the dynamics in which a wife can sustain her "female" bonding needs outside of marriage in some third-corner, and a husband can satisfy his needs for "male" individuation likewise outside of the marriage, all adding up to comfortable separateness. Certainly, not all wives' mothers remain as accessible to their daughters as Helen's mother did. Nevertheless, a mother need not live with her daughter to remain on hand, and in the working class particularly there is a long-standing tendency of married daughters to remain closely linked to their mothers as long as their proximity to each other makes this possible. In such instances, the new family created by the married daughter is not isolated. It is not emotionally self-contained, and it may not be residentially self-contained either. Given the close continuity of the mother–daughter bond, a woman will not crave any great depths of intimacy from her husband, who is in turn free to distance away from emotion-laden relationships with a female as much as he wants to.

As Chodorow points out, a lot will depend on how the married daughter's mother has worked out her own issues of fusion versus autonomy, and whether, accordingly, she continues to turn to her daughter to fill any unmet bonding needs.[3] A lot will also depend on the daughter's experience and perception of her parents' marriage and particularly on her sense from her parents of how much separateness between spouses can be comfortably accommodated in a marriage.

A sixty-four-year-old respondent named Clara Smith grew up in rural Maine in the 1920s with her parents, her older sister, and, until she was twelve, her father's parents. Her mother remained a housewife, and Clara has repeated that pattern. "My mother always made a very comfortable home for us all. She was very loving to us children, and she was a very good housekeeper and cook. She was a good example." Clara's image of her parents' marriage was positive, and she enthusiastically embraced their model for herself. "My folks were very happily married and I grew up thinking that's what I would do some day."

Throughout Clara's youth, her mother and father endured long separations: "There was very little work in my town, and my dad had to go work on a boat on the Great Lakes, which left my mother alone with his parents and us kids. She didn't like having him away." Nonetheless, these absences never seemed to get translated into marital struggles, and Clara contends that everything became far more comfortable once they moved away from her father's parents and her father could find regular work closer to home. "My mother used to say to us kids, 'Don't live with your in-laws if you can help it.' My grandmother gave my mother a hard time. She didn't want her to leave the house for a church meeting or anything."

Perhaps the everyday tensions between Clara's mother and paternal grandmother helped the former to carve out her own autonomous, differentiated self. At the same time, these tensions provided a convenient distraction

140 • *Three Corners*

from any unfulfilled bonding needs Clara's mother may have felt in her husband's absence, thus keeping the marriage safely harbored from any storms of discontent. Most important, throughout these years and beyond them, Clara's mother had her own mother close at hand, and they were apparently quite well bonded to each other.

For Clara Smith, the upshot of all this was positive imagery about marriage and a keen readiness to continue to bond first with her mother and then (following her mother's example) with her own children. Clara married a chemist named Elmer and got pregnant in just a few months. "The day the baby was born, Elmer was drafted. That was in 1942. It was a pretty dramatic experience to wake up in the hospital and realize you had a baby boy and your husband was off to war." Nevertheless, Clara seemed to take it all in stride, and she and the baby lived with her mother for the first eighteen months that Elmer was away, later joining him in the South. Recall, too, that in her familiar paradigm, a husband can be away for long periods of time and the marriage can still be seen as "very happy."

Once settled back in a Maine city, Clara and Elmer lived a separative marital existence by today's standards, although both of them would have said their marriage was a good one. They had their third child in the seventh year of their marriage. Childrearing was "a lot of responsibility all at once," Clara told me.

> But I love my children and it was very satisfying. The only complaint I could have is that Elmer was so involved in church work that it seemed like he was at a committee meeting every other night. I used to complain that I'd like to have him home more. He'd be better for a while, and then he'd be on this committee and that committee and he'd be off again.

Even when Elmer was home, however, there is little evidence of much emotional connection between them, and their respective home-based activities typically separated them from each other. On Clara's side, it is unlikely that she ever craved a lot more marital companionship than she had. For many years she continued to be actively bonded with her mother and sister. Two of her three children, now grown with children of their own, have always remained close-at-hand in Maine. One daughter in particular is a frequent caller at their home. For Clara, marriage clearly means a Safe Return Home and a calling For the Children. When I asked her if her marriage has gone through any phases, she immediately translated my question into considerations about her children and various phases of her involvement with them.

> Yes it has [gone through phases]. When we came back from the South with our two war babies, we decided we'd like to have a peacetime baby, and we had Nancy and we thoroughly enjoyed her. We were settled down and the other two kids were in school. That was a good period. As the kids got older,

there were problems with them, but we worked them out. Then they began to get married and leave home. Some people have a hard time when the kids leave home, but it didn't bother us that way. My son left to go to work, but he kept in touch and came home. Then our oldest girl got married, but she lived in town and we saw her constantly. But when the youngest got married [she pauses to sigh] she met a fellow at the Air Force base who lived in Ohio, and we hated to see her get involved with someone from so far away. But she married him and now she lives in Ohio. We see them once a year, and we phone and write.

In this way Clara refers the question of her marriage to her experiences with her children. Closely bonded to them, she usually found it easier to see the world from their vantage point than from Elmer's, and at times she faulted Elmer with being too strict:

He's very stern, and he's a perfectionist in everything he does. But you can't expect children to be perfect. I used to take the children's side when he expected them to be perfect. It caused a little resentment. But the children laugh about it. They know their father's a perfectionist and we just have to go along with it.

The slightly conspiratorial "we" is revealing here. In both partners' interviews there is indeed a clear sense of this family having been subdivided into two alien subworlds—she and her children, and he alone—with a minimal amount of real bridging between the two. Now the children have long been out of the house, and Elmer is around much more, having recently retired. What was it like for these two separate worlds to get more exposed to each other? Clara told me:

It was quite a change. I've heard people say their husbands drive them crazy. But Elmer is in and out so much. He loves the woods around here, and he's forever doing something—trimming trees, cutting down trees. If he was home steady and under foot, I think he would drive me crazy. But he's got so many projects. He's got enough to keep him busy for the next ten years. He saves newspapers and he subscribes to so many things that he doesn't get a chance to read them all. He needs to go through them and throw things away. [She has always struggled with his being a "clutterer."] I do think he likes his privacy. If we both had to live in this living-room we'd get on each other's nerves, but he can go out to the den, and he's got a phone out there, and we get along very well.

Here and elsewhere, Clara talks of Elmer's world as one that remains largely alien to her. Yet she works hard to accept his differences without having to participate in them, and she is genuinely content with her married lot in life. "We have good security and good companionship. I feel okay."

142 • *Three Corners*

Elmer's account offered much more pointed recognition of some deep gaps between their two worlds, along with some concern that these gaps had been costly to them. He wavered between blaming Clara for remaining too uninvolved with his interests, and faulting himself with being too harshly critical, too detached from their children, too judgmental, and too unkindly to any criticism about himself. He felt that neither he nor Clara had ever "communicated" enough when they needed to: "That's another thing I seem to remember from childhood: You're supposed to internalize it, maybe talk to God, but don't communicate. Talking to each other wasn't the emphasis."

Elmer's other recollections from childhood were revealing. They all suggest a rather puritanical middle-class home-world in which he—an only child —and his mother were thrown closely together: "My father was away from home every other week for a week, because of his job. So I was with my mother a lot more than I was with my father throughout my childhood and teenage years." When his father was home, Elmer remembers some unkindly treatment. "He had a knack with words. I don't remember that he ever struck me, but he could make me feel so debased, because of some little thing that I did. My low self-image may have started then." Thus Elmer may have been driven all the more urgently into the protective arms of his mother:

> I was secluded, protected, more than the average child. I was at home with my mother. I remember the Bible, and morning prayer, and not being allowed to play out on Sunday. Mother read to me a lot. We almost never entertained; kids came to my house very seldom. During preschool years I remember playing with only one neighborhood child, a girl. There were a few years, just before high school, when some of the boys and I had what we called "The Office" in our barn. And we played baseball and flew kites. But even then, one of them almost had to look out for me. I was really a sissy. They called me "Softy."

There is no mention of the influence or presence of any relatives around Elmer's family of origin. Indeed, his account seems to signal the very conditions of family isolation that Chodorow claims will lead a mother to emotionally fuse with her son as a "male opposite" husband-substitute—conditions that will lead a son, in turn, to develop an overwhelming attachment and merging with his mother, and then a need to preoccupy himself with issues of separation and individuation in order to secure a masculine self-identification.

Elmer, "Softy," became so good at separateness and individuation precisely because he felt so vulnerable and insecure at the core of his masculine identity. Yet, the more he stretches his adult life away from that precarious "female" world of connection, the more the rubber band of those intimate foundations snaps back his attention to what he left behind. His backward glance is an uncertain one, however, and it does not carry much energy. His

long-standing cultivation of separate third-corners leaves him ill-equipped to get back to intimate partnership, and Clara has neither the need nor the inclination to try to pull him into it. She still meets her bonding needs more than adequately with her grown children and grandchildren, just as her mother did, and her familiar paradigm never gave her any grand anticipation of intimate marital bonding, which would probably loom somewhat frightening to her too.

Strong centrifugal forces on both sides have therefore spared this marriage from ever having to elaborate itself much, and these dynamics continue to rule out much of an internal relational history. It remains what a number of my respondents referred to as a "stable marriage," and even Elmer averred that "it's at least as good as most."

Both of the couples just described—the Pratts and the Smiths—have relationships with scant internal development. Like Renaissance musical themes, their marriages repeat the same motifs over and over again without anything new getting elaborated. Both couples are abundantly satisfied with what they have. Both embody the traditional gender-styles in which females are good at bonding and males are good at being separate. Despite the fact that these paradigmatic orientations are opposite and alien to each other, there is little conflict or disturbance in evidence. Each partner's third-corner receives the lion's share of their respective emotional investments, and thus their marriages have built-in safety valves. Even before any tension begins to accumulate, each partner has already shifted most of the burden of ongoing emotional sustenance outside the marriage, and neither is then inclined to feel betrayed by the other.

To be sure, there remains an underlying conflict insofar as wives' basic need is to bond and husbands' is to individuate and be separate. But when wives' marital paradigms instruct them to bond with some close person other than a husband, and husbands' paradigms instruct them to bond with work or some other third-corner interest through which they can assert their separate and distinctive existence, no severe marital conflicts tend to erupt.

For Clara Smith, actively bonded first to her mother and then to her own children even long after they married and left her home, married life is essentially what it should be, just as it is for Elmer, whose work, separate leisure pursuits, and interest in current events have always engaged him more than anything else, notwithstanding his periodic rumblings that he may have been missing out on something. Separateness can produce durable marriages even though the emotional intensity of this arrangement may be very subdued.

The key to this brand of stability is balance and symmetry as well as the timing of triangling moves. If a husband triangulates away from the marriage, the force which pulls the wife into her third-corners must be roughly equal to his, and vice versa. Helen Pratt and Clara Smith both remained strongly and actively connected to their mothers at the very outset of their

marriages, so marital separateness was always, therefore, as comfortable an arrangement for them as it was for their husbands.

In contrast, neither Sheila Gardner's nor Jenny Olson's mothers were viable third-corners for these women, and they both came to marriage expecting their husbands to absorb the full burden of their fusion needs. When separateness comes, as it did for them, only as a sequel to a frustrating dependency-distancing pattern of relationships, the transition is often accompanied by profound marital and personal disturbance. The dependent one requires a soul-wrenching effort to break her fusion with her husband, while the distancing one will rarely accede to her separateness without a fight, all of which sets off some emotional fireworks. Both Sheila's and Jenny's moves toward separateness ultimately became stabilizing for their marriages, but it took a monumental readjustment before the gains of greater symmetry could show up as greater marital comfort.

In some instances even the transitional disturbance will be minimal when a wife renounces her long-standing dependency by making a strong triangling move. This will be the case when her third-corner interest does not involve any obvious, outward change from her previous life-pattern. Then, triangulation away from a spouse can calm down a disturbed marriage almost immediately, without any upheaval at all, as we shall now see. From one point of view, such calming or stabilization increases the marital comfort. It "feels" better and is therefore constructive. From another perspective, it is unfortunate insofar as it reduces tensions to a point at which neither partner feels much inclination to agitate for anything new from the other.

Stuart and Faith Dickson, a couple married over fifty years, are both in their eighties. They spent most of their married life on the outskirts of a large city in Delaware. When Stuart retired from his engineering job twelve years ago, they returned to Maine, where Stuart had grown up and gone to college. The long-ago move to Delaware after two years of marriage had taken Faith far away from the New York farm family in which she had grown up. No Safe Return Home could then define her everyday round of activity as a married person, unlike the worlds of Helen Pratt and Clara Smith. Though Faith had already done some teaching, she apparently maintained the traditional notion that a married woman's place is in the home: "I married because I loved Stuart, and I wanted a home, and I wanted children. I didn't want to teach school all my life" [she laughs]. Apparently, Faith's domestic inclinations met Stuart's needs as well. He exclaimed tersely, "We were brought up in an era when the man went out and earned a living and the wife took care of the house, and it stayed that way."

So far, what we see is a closely matched consensus of marital paradigms, and this consensus was further augmented by the strongly puritanical background in which both Faith and Stuart grew up. Asked what qualities she had wanted in a mate, Faith replies:

I certainly wanted a good man, a moral man. My mother was very much against smoking and drinking, and I never had the slightest desire to do either of them myself, so naturally I expected my husband not to smoke or drink either. And we always considered it a disgrace to get a divorce. God's will was for people to live together for better or for worse.

Despite Stuart's agreement with these notions, the first few years of marriage were not easy. Even though Faith was home raising children and doing what she had wanted to do, while Stuart was out earning a living and thus fulfilling his expressed purpose in life, Faith remembers tensions. I asked her about the first year:

> It didn't go smoothly. I can't remember in just what ways. I just remember we both saying that it was much harder adjusting to each other than we thought it would be. I think I was selfish and immature, and when he didn't do all the little things that I thought he should for me, I felt resentful. I thought he should be ever thinking of little ways to please me. For one thing, I didn't think he was generous enough. He earned a good salary, but he had a different attitude toward money than I did. He was brought up where there was very little money in the family. And my father had always been very generous with me. There was always change in Dad's big pocketbook and we were welcome to it, and I thought that Stuart didn't allow me enough.

Along with this paradigm conflict with Stuart over how to deal with money, Faith was also irritated by his impatient tone, which often seemed to suggest that she was too "slow" and made her feel inferior.

In contrast to Faith, Stuart recalls that his marriage began just as he had expected it would: "Well, it was busy. Actually, very good. She was an excellent cook and an excellent housekeeper, and I managed to bring in enough money to keep us going. There weren't any surprises that I can remember. You just have a job to do, and you walk into that job and you do it." The fact is that after Stuart's father died when Stuart was just eight, he grew up in a house consisting only of females. The engineering job for which he carefully prepared himself became his ticket to individuating and separating from this female-centered world. Work became his most absorbing emotional investment, while, for Faith, raising children did not apparently raise her low self-esteem or compensate for the lack of emotional bonding that she felt with Stuart. Since Stuart's third-corner interest was more compelling than any equivalent pursuit of Faith's, the obvious outcome was that the marriage felt comfortable and congenial to Stuart but rather unsettling to Faith.

Ten years into their marriage and still struggling with a backlog of unexpressed resentments against Stuart, Faith met some women who inspired her to join a "spiritual emphasis" group. Since that time more than four decades ago, Faith's private, hourly "morning devotions" and her feeling

146 • *Three Corners*

close to God have stood at the center of her purpose in life, and her attitude about Stuart became transformed:

> It was not until I read these books that I began to see my faults. See, I was blaming him for everything that happened. My husband is a very bright engineer, and I think he made me feel inferior. Then when I read these books, it made me realize that Jesus loves me even if I'm not as brilliant as Stuart. At first when things didn't go my way I became resentful, and I think that I've been able to overcome that. There were a few things that I would have liked to have changed, but I found out you cannot do that, so I think you have to learn to accept the person as he is and to appreciate him.

Clearly, Faith had now triangled in a third-corner interest—her sense of a direct, personal bonding with God through her devotional practices—that equalled Stuart's work-centered third-corner. Each partner's triangulation was now in greater balance with the other's. Paradoxically, Faith became able to feel calmer and more comfortable with her partner precisely because she moved emotionally farther from him, toward her beloved spiritual corner. For his part, Stuart was never primed to notice the change, as he had been comfortable with his marriage all along, and he lacked the kind of intimate contact with Faith that would have clued him in to her inner struggle and its resolution. She, in turn, had fed his ignorance by internalizing her struggle and resentment, rarely if ever challenging him. Thus Faith's personal transformation never really entered her relationship as an internal marital development whose impact could then become elaborated in their emerging marital history. It remained private to her:

> I don't know as he even knew that I felt better. We never did quarrel much. I would just close up and not say anything. If I'd expressed my feelings, it probably would have helped things out a great deal. But I am not that kind; I keep things inside.

For Faith, then, God came to play the same triangular role that mothers, children, grandchildren, close friends, and lovers sometimes assume for other women whose husbands do not thoroughly satisfy their need for active bonding. Early on, Faith had moved away from her immediate family and her close extended-family ties. Moreover, given her private, solitary nature, she was never inclined to open up to friends in a way that would foster a deep sense of connection:

> When I was in high school I had close friends, and since we've been married we have had close friends, but never any that I shared my deepest feelings with. Maybe one person I did share some of these feelings with, and afterwards I was sorry I had. So after that I was very careful not to express them

again. I feel that I can iron things out with God and I can trust Him, and you can't always trust other people; you really don't know which ones you can and which you can't. Stuart's cousin was married to a lady and she tried to find a psychological reason for everything, but she really was quite often wrong. So I just kept things to myself, and when I have a problem I talk it over with God, and that's where I find my answers.

The Balance between Comfort and Disturbance

It should be added once more that strong triangling moves on the part of a wife, moves that create more balance and symmetry, do not necessarily make for greater marital stability. In the Gardners' and Olsons' marriages we have seen that such moves may instead produce a destabilizing effect, at least temporarily, and may even herald the demise of a marriage. If there is a stability principle at work here, it is that all strong triangling moves must rest on some minimal level of comfort between the twosome. This sense of comfort then remains to undergird the couple, even as they triangulate away from one another. If no such comfort yet exists, the partners must either quickly create it or go through a period of considerable struggle until they can do so.

Both the Gardners and the Olsons credit a Marriage Encounter weekend with having saved their marriages at a time when their growing separateness threatened to break them apart. Both partners believe that their marital interaction changed permanently as a result of that weekend, a belief that I do not share. In my view the change in their actual way of relating to each other was temporary and minimal. What is clear is that a new level of comfort was created between them, and this came not from behavioral changes but from linguistic ones. That is, Marriage Encounter is very effective in creating an intense weekend experience and in teaching couples a language of bonding and feeling. Like a drug effect, the actual intensity of the experience quickly fades, and then only the language of the experience lingers on. But this is no small addition to a couple's repertoire. Couples who can speak that language together, or who simply know the language without bothering to speak it, may then glory in the knowledge that they do, after all, have something in common. Then, even if they continue to live essentially separate lives, their new consensus may bring them enough comfort to set aside the feeling of disturbance.

In many marriages the level of comfortable consensus is not enough to set aside the disturbance brought on by mutual distancing, but is sufficient, nevertheless, to keep the couple together. Even the most disturbing paradigm conflicts and agenda clashes can be softened somewhat by the less contentious paradigm elements that converge in a twosome.

Joe and Angela are one couple whose distance and whose conflicts were almost continual,[4] yet their relationship can persist because their conflict

148 • *Three Corners*

is not all that they have. One of Joe's marriage agendas has always centered on the importance of a wife as a mother to his children. When asked what he had wanted in a mate, he replied, "One that was going to be a good mother, more so than anything," adding that in Angela, he did get a good mother for his kids, and that "The kids have kept us together."

As for Angela, one of her marriage agendas was to Avoid the Demon of children being abandoned by their parents, having herself felt devastated by a broken home and by her mother's subsequent inaccessibility due to working. She told me that a couple's togetherness gets monopolized by children once they arrive, and that she and Joe do not take enough time alone. Yet she remains so protective of her children that there are few babysitters to whom she is willing to entrust them, so the pattern gets perpetuated. For both partners, then, For the Children is the thin threat of consensus supporting this twosome, distracting them from all the disturbances that could otherwise tear them apart and may yet do so. Even partners who no longer feel any spark of affection for one another can thus survive, so long as both remain willing to define their bond in the same general terms.

For some couples, it seems that the mere idea of permanence, the traditional notion that the marriage bond should be indissoluble, defines the only consensus to be found in their relationship, but it is enough consensus to outweigh even their most intractable disturbances. "I feel like we've been in a stalled situation for some time," said Al Clarkson, married for nearly eighteen years. "A series of things have been critical, and I don't know if any of them have been resolved. If it gets bad enough we'll go ahead and fight it through. But I don't see a lot of change in the future. I think we'll continue together, because we both want that. *We're committed to marriage being permanent*" (emphasis added). Al's wife Judy said the same thing, after spending much of the interview detailing how they had grown apart: "We got married with the idea that we'd be together forever. I think that's why I've never seriously contemplated divorce. Even though some things I've said might sound like you should wonder why we're still married, I can't imagine anything else. But I think of things as working through them."

Religion is the traditional champion of "till death do us part" as the cornerstone of marital consensus. Al Clarkson, the son of a minister, spoke of his life as God-centered. In his spiritual framework, marriage can be far less than satisfying and yet indubitably permanent. God, rather than marriage, provides his sustenance. Here he spoke in much the same language as did Faith, who we have seen has easily endured forty more years of marriage without any grievances of her first ten years having so much as been addressed. In similar fashion Al explained, "No matter how much things may be strained between Judy and I, I know God still loves me and I have personal worth that way. It would be a lot better if I sensed that Judy loved me too, but I'm not always centered on her for my value."

Marital Separateness • 149

In this way, a marriage that is fundamentally disturbed can persist indefinitely. The concept of being together permanently takes center stage while the reality of married life becomes so unsatisfying that this twosome can spend little time together. Judy's life revolves around the home and her four children; Al's is taken up by work and by an enormous array of third-corner leisure pursuits in which Judy has no interest. They talk little to each other. "I never know what he's doing unless I ask," Judy told me. She resents his outside activities, and he resents the fact that "Her maternal feelings seem to take priority over everything else." Both indicated that their sexual relationship leaves much to be desired. When they have tried to talk about these and other conflicts, they wind up feeling still worse about each other, so it becomes easier to give up trying to resolve them. Even meals—that venerable bastion of family togetherness in virtually every culture known to us—are taken separately more often than not. He gets up and "gets the kids going"; she sleeps late. Judy added, "He doesn't usually come home for lunch and often isn't home for supper." In this fashion the marriage persists as a disturbed one without either partner seriously considering separation or divorce.

To return once more to Faith and Stuart Dickson, they never needed to struggle with each other's triangling moves and the resulting distance between them, because their respective marital paradigms agreed enough to provide them with a comfortable consensus. Both have always firmly believed that marriage is forever and divorce is a disgrace. Both have always believed marriage means that the husband earns a living and the wife stays home and raises children. Outwardly, nothing very obvious changed about Faith's life following her spiritual conversion. She still stayed home and maintained the domestic front, just as she always had. The only difference was that she felt much happier. Thus, even though Faith's religious priorities directed her attention more and more outside her marriage toward transcendental principles and goals, Stuart continued to see her change as acceptable.

On one hand, Faith's morning devotions have always remained alien to him, and he has had no inclination to explore that kind of devotional world. He exclaimed, "I tell my ministers I'm a reluctant skeptic, and I am. I still can't get rid of the skepticism. It's terrible." On the other hand, his own Christian upbringing and his continuing strong commitment to Christianity in principle lead him to remain in sympathy with Faith's purpose. Had Faith's third-corner moved her toward some form different than home-centered Christianity, the ensuing development for the marriage might have been anything but stabilizing and calming.

In general, marital changes, the sense of something new having unfolded or developed in a twosome, the feeling of an internal couple history replete with different phases and periods—all these are due not to issues isolated within the couple relationship alone but to changes in their patterns of triangulation, to new triangling moves or to intensifications or defusings of old

150 • *Three Corners*

ones. Such changes invariably trigger new issues for the couple relationship itself, and any internal marital development tends to usher forth from the couple's attempts to deal with them.[5] Faith's new spiritual devotions could have prompted new issues, but the change was simply interpreted as compatible with their earlier consensus, and therefore this couple was spared the need for new relational developments.

Joint Triangulation as Separateness

Another pattern that keeps relationships safe from change and development involves joint triangulation—that is, both partners move toward the same third-corner. While this process can often unleash some vigorous new dynamics for the twosome, here I shall consider only those instances in which joint triangulation seems to rule out any new development in the marriage itself. These couples depend upon their joint triangulation alone to provide their comfortable consensus, to delineate their common goals, and to affirm their reason for being together. Their emotional energy gets directed away from their own bond and its qualities, and into their shared third-corner, and the history of their marriage may thus be written as the history of interests that lie outside it. When matters relating to the third-corner are going well, then the marriage itself is seen to be going well, by definition.

Two of the marriage agendas discussed in chapter 3 particularly lend themselves to this form of joint triangulation—marriage For the Children, and marriage as a Religious Calling. Regarding children, almost all couples have or adopt them sooner or later, with the children then becoming the focus of at least some joint triangulation, as the partners move to incorporate them into their lives. Often, however, the jointness of this triangulation is minimal, insofar as husbands' involvement with their children becomes negligible. In these cases, husbands are typically triangling away from their marriage and family and into their work or separate recreational pursuits. Children then fill a gap for wives and help bring the couple's triangling forces into symmetry, as both partners now have a third-corner of their own. Such marriages may calmly persist indefinitely, without any important internal development, but if they are short on any comfortable basis of togetherness, the marriage is vulnerable to getting pulled apart by the first significant triangulating force that comes along.

It is rare for partners to share a marriage agenda For the Children just because men's identity is so often fought for in separative activities away from the family nexus, for reasons already discussed. It takes unusual circumstances for a man to join his wife in giving primacy to child rearing. Jake and Louise Miller exemplify these conditions. Jake came to marriage with a rather Open Agenda, having all the typical flexibility of a middle sibling and

a positive anticipation of married life from watching his parents' "stable, happy, quiet relationship." When he married Louise he discovered that she did not quite fit his familiar paradigm of what a wife would be: "Both of my parents are very stable. Louise is probably not as stable a person as I would have expected myself to marry, in the sense that she gets upset about things very easily." Both Jake and Louise remember tensions in their first year of marriage. Louise said, "We struggled," but she was rather vague about the details. Jake was more specific: "The rough adjustment was surprising. The essence of it was having to deal with one person, on a day to day basis—how to adjust expectations. I can remember the tension. I don't remember being unhappy being married, other than thinking, 'This is rough,' at times."

Jake felt some disillusionment when his assumption "that sex would be something you'd want to do everyday" turned out to be ill-founded, but the biggest tensions revolved around pressure from Louise over Jake's slow progress toward financial security. In keeping with both their familiar paradigms, neither partner wanted Louise "to have to work," as Jake put it, and Louise's considerable anxieties over Jake's career development came into conflict with Jake's more casual, things-will-turn-out-all-right attitude. Early on, then, Jake's lack of any model for dealing with confrontation and his essentially Open Agenda for marriage led him to bend in those matters that seemed to count the most to Louise, and to do nothing to provoke or prolong her outbursts of "upsetness." He told me:

I do get tired of having to say to myself, "Let's wait till she cools down." You take it without defending yourself because if you defend yourself she gets even more upset. But a couple of times I have not taken it—just shouted it out. It doesn't seem to resolve itself any differently from the times when I just take the quiet approach.

For the first three years, though there was little open conflict, Jake and Louise struggled with only partial success to find a comfortable consensus for their marriage. Then For the Children came to the rescue, with the birth of their first child. For the Children had been Louise's marriage agenda all along, as it seemed to her the most prudent pathway for correcting the difficulties of her parents' marriage.[6] In her framing of this agenda, however, Louise's focus was not so much on her own child-centered inclinations, which she took for granted, but on the crucial importance of a husband feeling and acting the same way, because then she could have the active male involvement in the family that both she and her mother had lacked in her own father.

For his part, despite some initial ambivalence about having children, Jake was malleable enough to make Louise's agenda his own. Besides, he had already learned habits of compliance in matters that were of signal importance to her. He told me:

152 • *Three Corners*

Louise was the one who said, "Let's start having kids," and I said "Okay, but I don't want the kids to become the center of the family." By George, it happens, and you don't gripe at it. But it's kind of a change from what I expected my attitude would be when they were born.

The Millers' joint triangulation into a child-centered third-corner calmed down their marriage by providing a comfortable, overriding consensus. In Louise's words:

What I think is the critical factor in our marriage in terms of how happy we are right now is our children. Two things intertwine here. One is that Jake feels as strongly about the kids and spending time with them as I do, and the other is that Jake is a very unusual fellow. He has no preconceived notions of what he should or should not do around this house. He would never come in from the office and sit down and read the newspaper unless the table were all set and he asked me first if there was anything he could do. And it's never been a situation where I'm the wife at home who thinks we should be spending more time with the children, or I'm sick of the kids and I want to get away from them. We don't have those kinds of incompatibilities, which I see among some friends we have. We put our children first. We do it together.

Jake's account squared closely with Louise's:

Neither of us have strong outside friendships anywhere close to being as important as husband and wife and kids. And my profession is not at all crucial to the way I live. The way we live really is just family-centered. The family's our life. I wouldn't have expected that when I was being married. . . . Once the kids came, there's been a different phase in terms of the way we interact, because obviously you don't give yourselves the same attention until after the kids go to bed, and even now she's so busy until midnight catching up on all the things to do around the house that we don't spend the kinds of time together alone, obviously, that we did before the kids came along.

When two partners triangulate in this way into the same third-corner, their own relationship can, in fact, undergo significant new development. For example, a power struggle could ensue over who gets to control the third-corner, and both partners could learn something more about each other in the process. Or couple interaction could intensify as a natural spin-off of having this new corner of comfort and solidarity. For many partners children can be unwitting contributors to the unity between them, providing them issues to discuss, such as a child's problems, or material they can use to celebrate their own coupleness, such as a child's triumphs. In Louise and Jake's case, their newly won consensus did have a stabilizing influence on their relationship, and both came to discover and appreciate each other's child-rearing talents. But because both were so single-minded in translating their own bond into a child-rearing venture, their marriage all but ceased to have an independent existence with a history and development of its own. In Louise's words:

Marital Separateness • 153

Jake and I have very little time, and we both opt to share our lives with our children. We'll be here to share our lives with each other more when there is more time. He does his thing, I do my thing. We'll communicate, but we do not spend a significant amount of time heart-to-hearting. You've got three kids, and you're as busy as we are from 7:00 in the morning until 9:30 at night when everybody's tucked in and the dishes are done, and he works in the living room and I iron downstairs just to get it done so the next day will be free to do whatever is on the agenda. . . . We understand each other without saying a lot.

Jake expressed a lot more disappointment about their lack of more intensive couple bonding:

She's an incredibly organized person, and yet I wish she could say to herself, "It is not always crucial that the house is organized," and I'd rather have her do something she'd like to do for herself, rather than the laundry, kids. . . . She'll be up doing housework at 11:00 at night, where to my way of thinking she should be relaxing and doing something she'd like to do—maybe sit down and chat for a while. Before the children were born, I said to her, "I hope that when children come, it doesn't mean that you'll pay less attention to me." We both really care about the kids, and yet I wish she could step back from the kids a little bit more than she does.

Clearly, Jake is the more ambivalent partner about structuring their marriage For the Children, while Louise feels unequivocal and uncompromising about its importance. Louise's agenda easily wins out, however. The principle at work here is that whenever one partner has a fairly open marriage agenda and the other partner is tightly riveted to any of the more determinate agendas for the twosome, the path of least resistance is for the marriage to take the latter direction. Thus Louise can easily pull Jake into the service of her essential purpose, because Jake is the more flexible one. Meanwhile, their own bond tends to fade away into their jointly created third-corner, where they find and know each other principally as parents of each other's children. Such a pattern can produce a stable couple bond, but its development is restricted to the further elaboration of parenting qualities. Beyond that, the relationship itself will have no development unless some major new triangling (or detriangling) move forces a renegotiation.

Figure 5 provides an illustration of the Millers' marital situation and the typical pattern of joint triangulation as separateness. Louise's triangle is shown on the lower left-hand side of the figure; Jake's is on the upper right. All the dynamics of this marriage revolve around their joint third-corner in the center of the figure—their children. Louise's inner-corner is fused with the children, while the solid line from Jake's inner-corner to the children shows his strong connection but not fusion with them. All of Louise's focus zooms in on the children, while Jake is more free to focus elsewhere if he wants to,

154 • *Three Corners*

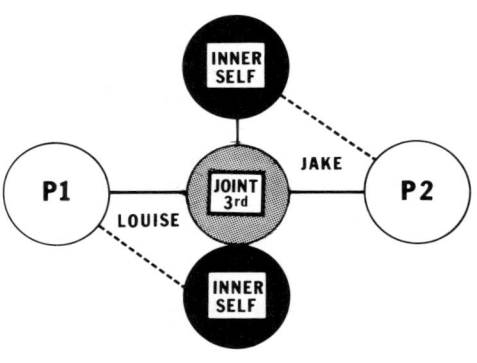

Figure 5. Joint Triangulation as Separateness

an imbalance which results in Louise having the lion's share of control over their joint third-corner. If he were fused with the children as Louise is, there would be continual competition and a power struggle over who gets to control them. Instead, he yields to her sensibilities about them, and little conflict emerges. As he put it, "Because she's so strong, I let her carry the ball."

Notice how the Millers' partnership-corners are connected only through their joint interest in their children, and they are too far apart to get to each other in any other way. The broken lines between each spouse's inner-corner and their partnership-corners show the scant energy focussed on their own bond. The partnership is pretty much subsumed and exhausted by parenting, and the couple bond thus ceases to have an independent history.

We begin to glean what a delicate and fragile balance any marriage is. In the Millers' example, any triangling move that Jake might make away from the home could easily upset the applecart of the Millers' marital stability. As it is now, Jake's level of career-involvement is much less than most male professionals, and beyond his necessary time at the office, he remains a homebody. Routinely, he comes home for lunch, which he calls "a nice break in the day" providing some special alone-time for his preschool son and himself. Unlike many men, he has no third-corner pursuits outside the home that remove him from his family. As Louise put it, "He won't go out and play racquetball three nights of the week, because he doesn't think that's fair. And I don't either. And he knows it."

Such notions of "fairness" are not arrived at lightly. How one partner responds to the other's possible (or actual) triangling moves is governed in large part by paradigmatic images and the feelings that are connected to them. In Louise's familiar paradigm, her father's one-sided career absorption had been a major factor in her mother's succession of physical and nervous illnesses, and in her own consequent neglect. Any triangulation away from the home

on the part of a husband hence loomed dangerous to her, and For the Children was the marriage agenda that seemed to best protect her from the scenario she feared most. Fortunately for her, Jake's familiar paradigm included strong images of a family-oriented father, so he was amenable to confining his own triangulation to child-centered activities with Louise.

Before closing this chapter, a few summary conclusions are worth making. We have considered two different variants of marital separateness. In one, the partners each fuse their inner-corners with their independent third-corners. In the other, joint triangulation, both fuse with the same third-corner. While children were the focus of the Miller's joint triangulation, there are endless other possibilities too. Couples who run a business together may find that their partnership gets totally defined by their common work absorption. Other couples may jointly focus on some all-important spiritual or religious third-corner, or some social cause or movement, or "the party," or the house they are building. Obviously, there is nothing inherently wrong with a couple being deeply engrossed in some joint third-corner; joint triangulation does not cause separateness. What separates in these instances is to *fuse* one's inner-corner with some joint third-corner, for then one is saying to one's partner, "This interest represents who I am, and here alone I will meet you." In that event, or in the case of each partner fusing with independent third-corners, the couple may cease to have any relational history or development, and their fundamental noncontact can easily get mistaken for vitality.

It should not be thought that separateness is an unmitigated misfortune. We have seen that separative triangling moves can calm down marital disturbances considerably, if such moves on the part of one spouse result in greater symmetry with the other spouse's triangular configuration. It is also noteworthy that a period of separateness may be a developmental prelude to greater connection later on. Particularly when a spouse has been fused with his or her partnership-corner, it may be necessary to dwell in a space that is totally independent of the partner for a time in order to recover that sense of one's own center that has been abandoned. Unfortunately, it may then be as easy to abandon one's inner self to some third-corner as it was to the second-corner. In part III we shall sort out the variety of ways that couples can remain connected without sacrificing their autonomy in the process.

Notes

1. Murray Bowen, "Theory in the Practice of Psychotherapy," in *Family Therapy*, ed. Philip Guerin (New York: Gardner Press, 1976), p. 79.
2. Ibid., p. 80.
3. Nancy Chodorow, *The Reproduction of Mothering* (Berkeley: University of California Press, 1978), pp. 211–213.
4. For a brief account of these conflicts, see pp. 114–115.

156 • *Three Corners*

5. As useful as the concept of "family life-cycle phases" is, I do not think it is an adequate device for capturing the issues and phases of a couple relationship. Duvall (the scholar who most popularized this concept), sees couple phases and development as revolving around the presence or absence of children, and, if present, the issues that children create at different age levels. The problem with this approach is that it arrives at phases through a logical device and then plugs families into this a priori logic on the faith that it can apply to them. Of course, children do often create new issues and phases in a marriage, but this is only because children are often important third-corners in one or both partners' triangles. The point here is that marital development proceeds in accord with *any* new triangling (or detriangling) moves, and the phases in a couple's history will reflect the most significant such moves. A new job, an extra-marital affair, the loss of a close family member—these third-corner developments can often make as big an impact on a couple's history as the age progression of their children. For a review of Duvall's phases, see Evelyn Duvall and Brent Miller, *Marriage and Family Development*, 6th ed. (New York: Harper and Row, 1985), p. 26.

6. For more specifics about Louise's background, see p. 66.

Part III
The Dynamics of
Marital Connection

8
Balanced Connection

Few couples I interviewed appeared, at first glance, to have such different temperaments and so little in common as Roger and Betty Hill. Yet, few couples taught me nearly as much about the expansive intricacies of *balanced connection.*

In this chapter I shall start with the Hills' story, and finish with some general statements about the balanced type of connection that the Hills represent.

Married for fifty-three years, Roger and Betty have utterly transformed the familiar marital paradigms that both had brought to their partnership, and for that matter they have moved far away from the fundamentalist Christian paradigm in which both had been steeped. Perhaps they were flexible enough to transform into something new because they had rather Open Agendas for marriage, no doubt in part through the security they enjoyed in their families of origin and the comfort their parents had modeled in their respective marriages. Although both of their familiar paradigms portrayed the husband as the dominant figure in the household and the wife as a housekeeper and mother, the Hills evolved a dual-career pattern of marriage in which Betty pressed forward her pursuits as a writer far more vigorously than Roger ever cultivated his own accomplishments as a minister.

The Hills could so radically transform their familiar paradigms with scarcely any upheaval and conflict because of their gradual approach to the process. They grew into their changes slowly rather than abruptly springing them on one another. Betty describes her evolution as a writer:

> I didn't have much idea of having a career, and it would have been difficult for me to have one because of my stammering. It would have been hard to teach. I started writing when I was ten and continued all through school, but never sold anything until after we were married. I began writing religious plays to produce in our first church, and found they sold very well, so I did this for about twenty years. Writing then was incidental to being a minister's wife, but it was fortunate that I could do it, because I'd have been unhappy without some way to express myself. It wasn't until later that I earned enough to support myself.

160 • *Three Corners*

Keeping her writing "incidental" for so long never felt like a concession to Betty. The daughter of a minister, she wanted to do church work, and her outgoing temperament gave her much to do that Roger would have found too burdensome. He relates, "She's made all the difference imaginable in my pastorates, working with me with the young people and with the women." Betty's enormous energies thus found a ready-made outlet in Roger's professional third-corner. Roger delighted in all her input, neither demanding it nor resenting it as some unwelcome intrusion. Each brought uniquely individual contributions to Roger's pastorates, which provided the focal point for a constantly evolving partnership. They shared the same goals and ideals, and somehow, without any conflict or even a need to negotiate the process, they both grew away from their fundamentalist ideological origins and settled on a more liberal, social justice-oriented religious philosophy. Neither partner can quite understand why their ideological shifts were so effortlessly convergent, but both are convinced that their spontaneous agreement on such matters has been central to the solidity of their partnership. As Betty puts it, "I don't know what would have happened if he'd kept the conservative outlook we began with, because I wouldn't have kept it. Fortunately we moved in the same direction." Roger echoes Betty's sentiments, providing more detail:

> We were unified in our beliefs earlier, and we are now. We were brought up to accept the Bible without criticism as the basis of our faith. That kind of authoritarian religion didn't satisfy either of us. We couldn't picture what God would have to be like to fit into that kind of religion, so there was a great deal of questioning and uncertainty.
>
> In the early 30s I attended a conference at a Quaker college on war and peace, and was impressed with the possibilities of changing things for the better with a Gandhian sort of nonviolence. Betty had always been thinking somewhat along those lines. Our questioning continued, and we discussed things together, things like the future life. We felt religion had to fit with scientific beliefs. . . .
>
> From the fundamentalist viewpoint, we're not religious today, but life has more meaning to us. We're both concerned with human welfare— physical as well as mental welfare of people of all kinds, everywhere. Our interest in recent years has been mainly in the variety of needs people have in addition to their religious needs. Politically, our ideas have verged on socialism: we feel more people ought to be in control of the material things in life. . . .
>
> We've faced everything from the same point of view. We've both been disappointed by the same [historical] events and pleased by the same events. I don't know why, but we've been very unified in our outlook on different things. We've never had much intellectual and political harmony with the people in our churches. We feel more advanced than they are [he laughs at himself], but we've been together on it, all through the years. . . .

We've been especially close. Our marriage has had more of an intellectual relationship than most of our friends have. Our marriage isn't very involved in domestic, family matters, but more in intellectual matters. [Unable to bear children, they adopted two, starting in the seventh year of their marriage. Children were enjoyed, but they were never the basis of married life, and sometimes they were a divisive influence.] We're quite communicative with each other. We read many of the same things and share many of the same points of view. There's a respect for the other person. We each feel the other is quite wonderful. It's a very good ingredient for any marriage.

So far, the Hills' marriage looks like a picture of perfect harmony, both partners having independent third-corners that are blended by their common focus in church work, their convergent philosophies, and their mutual respect and admiration. Here, however, the utopian-sounding consensus ends, and as soon as we look a little closer, the differences and divergences loom so enormous that the feat of somehow harmonizing them is almost inconceivable. The fact is, it would be difficult to find two people with temperaments as radically opposite as the Hills', and with interests so different. By nature, he is a homebody and an introvert; she is an extrovert and would be "miserable," Roger says, "if she were limited to home relationships." He adds:

Being away from home and among other people drains my energy. Having to converse in a small group for an hour or more causes me to wilt. The less contact I have with people, in general, the better I like it. When I was small we were rather poor. When someone came to visit, my mother tended to keep us out of sight, partly because we were a bit ragged. That may have formed part of my feeling. By the time I went to high school I was quite shy. Now Betty is pushy. In a crowd she gets through, whereas I stand aside and wait.

The catalogue of differences is much lengthier than the issue of outgoingness. Betty is highly cultured and attuned to the fine arts; he has no interest in these things whatsoever. She likes to travel; he has never been in an airplane. She likes to eat meals out; he prefers to stay home. She is extremely ambitious; he is timid and hates to call attention to himself. She likes active recreation; he would be content to sit in a boat and fish all day. Their energies even diverge around sleeping habits:

He's always had to take a nap in the afternoon. He sleeps ten or eleven hours every day, and I sleep about five; I'm a poor sleeper. We have separate bedrooms, because I have to read after I go to bed. My mind is restless, and goes from one thing to another. We're completely different from that standpoint. He doesn't have nearly as much energy as I.

162 • *Three Corners*

As is obvious from this description, Betty's inner-corner is richly variegated and complex. Even as a child she was ambitious and competitive: "My greatest desire was to get high ranks in school." Indeed she graduated at the top of her class in both high school and college. Roger speaks of "her constant drive to accomplish." From the beginning of marriage, he adds,

> She was ambitious for herself. She would practice the piano six hours a day; she would study into the night. It's hurt her when her books haven't sold well. She would like to have made a big book club. She always likes to be first. She gets despondent once in a while when her books only sell fifteen or twenty thousand copies, and thinks she's a failure.

Despite all of this inner striving and no inclination to deny or suppress it, there was little room for Betty to elaborate these qualities in her partnership-corner, because Roger had neither the talent nor the interest to develop them. The only solution was for Betty to channel some of her energies into independent third-corners, where she could cultivate and nourish her ambitions and her aesthetic sensibilities to her heart's content, away from the partnership. Fortunately for Betty, her hard-driving inner self was uncluttered by ambivalence, and she was sufficiently single-minded and free of emotional conflicts and worries to come out openly as who she was. Indeed, she stood ready not simply to reveal her inner nature to Roger, but she would have gloried in showing it to the whole world! In turn, Roger had more than ample opportunity to learn about his partner's inner nature because she had no need to hide it from him. He knew full well what her needs and talents were, and benefited from her turning them to the service of his pastorates. When she began to branch more and more outward into independent third-corners, he encouraged her to do whatever she needed to do. "He's a wonderful person to live with—very unselfish, understanding, cooperative. I'm the selfish one, the ambitious one."

Plainly, Betty's inner-corner was too extroverted and expansive to be contained within her partnership-corner with Roger, who says:

> We try to emphasize mutual interests. On the other hand, she's always been interested in music and drama, and we've had an understanding that she goes [to concerts, plays and films] with her friends and I don't have to go, just to be together. She drives, and when she lectures it's understood that I'm not responsible for getting her there. If I'm needed I go with her; if not she goes alone.

Betty has no objections to going out alone or with friends: "I'm independent enough that I don't mind at all. I might if I hadn't built a life for myself as I have." This independence took a giant leap when Betty shifted from writing religious plays and began publishing biographies, for then she began to travel in order to make contact with the people about whom she was writing:

We've adjusted to that pretty well. I've been gone for long periods all over the world, even as long as six months at a time. If I hadn't been able to do this I wouldn't have been happy. I love to travel and he doesn't like travel at all. I've been to India, Egypt, and England four times. He's always been very supportive and cooperative about my going, even though he doesn't like it.

Is Roger truly supportive of all this, in the innermost corner of his being? Laughing, he tells me, "I don't know as I could live with her if I met her now, for the first time. For one thing, she's too famous!" But he clearly says this with tongue in cheek, and he obviously delights in Betty's accomplishments. His inner self is devoid of clutter and conflicts about supremacy, control, and dominance:

Part of the time I'm Betty Hill's husband, and part of the time she's Roger Hill's wife. At religious conferences and in church work she's my wife, but in other situations where she is known for her writing, I'm her husband. She has many admirers for her writing and has done over nine hundred lectures about the lives of people she's written about. In that area I'm her husband. We haven't quarrelled about it; it's just natural.

One reason why Roger finds Betty's independence so natural is that she is not a distancer; she has no need to discover herself in opposition to her husband or anyone else. She may need many outlets for her unbounded storehouse of expressive urges, but aside from the private space that she requires for writing, she would prefer to vent these urges in the company of Roger. She would truly delight in his travelling with her, accompanying her to concerts and plays, and going out to more social functions with her. As highly individuated as she is, she retains prominent relational needs. She has enough balance to nurture her partnership-corner every bit as much as her third-corners. Roger speaks of the "daily attitude of concern" that each of them has for the other:

If there were something Betty wanted to do very much which she felt might injure me, I'm sure she wouldn't do it, and that's been true from very early days. And I would do the same. It's hard to define love, but it could be partly a good will, a desire of the best for the other person—two people going along feeling that there's someone definitely interested in them. There's a growing sense of unity and understanding that comes with this.

Another reason why Roger can so readily accept his wife's distinction is that he has not had to compete with her. He has received many honors himself and has been elected to high positions in the church's social organization, and Betty has always cheered him on. He has never lived in her shadow. He knows full well who he is without needing to make her less or to disempower her. Notwithstanding his inherent modesty and humility, Roger is a strong

164 • *Three Corners*

character with all the three-cornered balance that Betty has. He enjoys the same comfort and security in their partnership, and he has created a variety of third-corner vehicles to express and develop himself, vehicles that are often quite different from hers but no less important and gratifying to him. His inner-corner is perhaps simpler and less complicated than Betty's. Serene and sedentary, thoroughly at home in his immediate and natural surroundings, he engages his quiet world from a remarkably open and receptive center:

> It's a sense of unity, being in harmony with everything in the universe, and belonging. I have no harsh feeling against any person that I know. There are some people that I dislike and some that I think are horrible, but in general I've come to the point where I can rest in harmony with nature and with my home, and certainly with my wife, and with members of my family and neighbors. It's a sense of being where I want to be. That goes into a religious sense of belonging in the whole cosmic situation, being part of it and having one little spot in which my interest centers.

Finally, it should not be thought that the Hills only "tolerate" each other, or that in view of their different qualities they have agreed merely to live in peaceful coexistence. Rather, there is something creative about this convergence of opposite qualities. When both partners seem to say, "You be everything you need to be, and I will be happy with it," when both have the temerity to then go out and *become* everything they need to be, and when that becoming produces such strongly developed yet utterly different characters, something new is bound to emerge from their exchange of energies. Roger and Betty have needed to stretch, expand, and redefine their respective partnership-corners just to actively mingle with such alien creatures as one another.

Roger has learned all about accomplishment and achievement from Betty. He reads all her books and loves to hear the letters she gets from friends, publishers, and admirers of her work. He goes to some of her lectures and slide shows. Somehow, a few of her ambitious qualities insinuate themselves into his own inner-corner, for he winds up accepting some high positions that would have been too overwhelming for him to imagine holding without her influence and encouragement. Likewise, her gregarious, outgoing nature affects him, subtly transforms him probably more than he knows, although he has an inkling: "I'd have a hard time relating to the community without Betty. I'd tend to become more or less of a hermit." Perhaps so, but he agreed to spend three hours alone with me, a total stranger, interviewing him about some of the most intimate details of his long life, and he appeared utterly comfortable as he proceeded to give me one of the most articulate and thoughtful accounts I heard. Roger the hermit-like recluse must have stayed in his cave that day, for this was a vibrant personality who showed anything but awkwardness in meeting the world.

Balanced Connection • 165

Similarly, I don't quite believe Betty when she tells me, "I'm afraid I'm just as selfish a person as I've always been, despite Roger's good qualities." Perhaps this self-judgment is a legacy of the cultural climate of the 1920s, when it was thought that a woman who wants to make a name for herself is selfish, regardless of how she goes about it and what else she happens to do. The fact is, this is a woman who has probably devoted herself to as much service as any three people combined. Roger feels that her involvement in his individual churches has added an "intimate, human touch in her life," though he is too modest to suggest that some of that "touch" might have rubbed off from him. And Roger is fully aware of how Betty has expanded her partnership-corner to play more on his turf:

> She's modified her aggressiveness and drive to accommodate me. She'll take time off to do things like read detective stories to me in the evening or play cribbage. She's acquired some relaxed qualities from me. She's tense ordinarily, and her sense of duty is strong. I've been the relaxing quality in her life. She does relax now. She'll play bridge, and she likes to go to the cottage. We clear trails there together. She'll go fishing with me in the boat. She's not interested in my garden, but she enjoys the vegetables I produce, and takes an interest because it's my interest. And she cooperates with things I want to do.

In quiet ways through the years, both partners have allowed the other's third-corners to become part of themselves. They have modified their own partnership-corners to move more easily in the kinds of worlds that were originally alien to them, and in the process, some of their respective inner-corners have had to expand and reshape themselves. Small wonder that Betty can say, "We don't do anything very exciting, but there's a feeling of companionship and understanding, much more than we used to have." And Roger can add:

> Our relationship is more satisfactory than it was in the first two or three years of our marriage. As time has gone on, we've understood each other better and been more considerate of each other. The later years have been some of our happiest, with less conflict. What may have been a simple romantic interest in the beginning developed into more than that. Your lives become so intertwined that one wouldn't be entire without the other. But why? There's something in two lives interacting day by day, by words, by coming to know the attitudes of the other person, that changes over time.

Roger is surely right, and the "why" of it all is not terribly mysterious. What "changes over time" is, literally, an *interchanging*. Each has grown more comfortable with the other because each has expanded to include more of the other. Being with a partner under these conditions comes to feel more and more like being with oneself.

166 • *Three Corners*

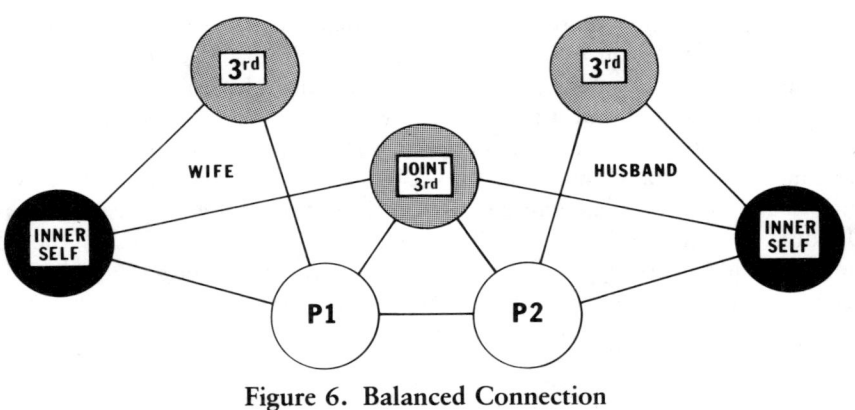

Figure 6. Balanced Connection

Figure 6 provides a graphic illustration of a marriage in which the partners' triangles are in a state of balanced connection, as are the Hills'. The partnership-corners stand close to each other, but they are not fused. Each partner's inner-corner enjoys autonomy by standing in its own space, free of dependency on any of its points of focus, and yet centrally located. Solid lines show the strong connection between the inner-corner and its various outward foci, which are all active parts of its private drama and receive its energy. Both partners in the figure have at least one independent third-corner as well as a third-corner interest they share.

A common example of this pattern is a two-career couple who have children, or who share a recreational passion, although many couples who have the two-career arrangement do not have connected marriages. The literature indicates that in most such couples, the wife continues to do most of the housework[1] and child-care,[2] while the husband fuses his inner self with his work-based third-corner. He distances, somewhat, from all his other third-corners and from his partnership-corner as well. Marital separateness is thus the fate of many two-career couples. In the connected situation, both partners' inner selves are solidly linked to their joint third-corner and share an active involvement in it. Notice, too, how their inner-corners and their independent third-corners are solidly connected to their partnership-corners. Both partners thus stand ready to bring some of their inner drama as well as some of their outside life into the partnership.

The even-handed "balance" in this type of connection is not easy to maintain. More often, spouses find reasons to favor one of their outward foci more than the others. In the next three chapters we shall explore three different arrangements that result from this selective attention. We shall see that triangles can shift their shape while still retaining their connectedness, as long as the inner-corner does not fuse with the corner that it favors.

Notes

1. See Philip Blumstein and Pepper Schwartz, *American Couples* (New York: William Morrow, 1983), pp. 144ff.

2. See C. Holahan and C. Gilbert, "Conflict between Major Life Roles: The Women and Men in Dual-Career Couples," *Human Relations* 32 (1979):451–467.

9
Couple-Centered Connection

Unlike Roger and Betty Hill, some spouses are unable to forge active connections among their three corners until years of married life have gone by. In certain respects these people do not have this connection because they do not want it. Inwardly, it makes more sense to them to fuse with one corner and distance from the others than to attempt any other life-pattern. Drawing on their familiar paradigms, they assume that what they carve out for themselves will bring them the most possible comfort.

If separateness has such great inertia, for example, it is because the partners in this arrangement can feel more or less content with their symmetry of third-corner commitments. Especially when separateness comes as a sequel to a frustrating dependency-distancing arrangement, the greater comfort may seem like such an improvement over the previous pattern that there is scarcely any incentive to opt for something different. To the spouse whose dependency needs have been continually thwarted and who now has a source of gratification away from the marriage, the thought of making a move closer to the partner may feel like a backward step into insufferable vulnerability and frustration.

Nevertheless, there are circumstances that may prompt a couple to risk taking that step. Third-corners that were seductive, exciting, or satisfying may become inaccessible or simply lose their lustre. Life-crises and unpredictable events may intrude into business-as-usual, forcing people to challenge their cherished strongholds of everyday existence. In this chapter Paul and Marian Carter will illustrate one such transformation from extreme separateness to extreme connection.

From Separateness to Connection: The Carters

Married for twenty years at the time of the interview, Paul was an electronics instructor following a recent career change, and Marian had recently taken a job working thirty hours per week as a sales clerk, after having stayed home

170 • *Three Corners*

to raise five children. At the time they met, Paul was getting a college degree and was well established in a navy career that was to span twenty years including his first seventeen years of marriage. Marian was a lab technician until shortly after their first child was born.

For Paul, evolving into marital separateness was a matter of falling into his familiar paradigm. His father was a railroad brakeman:

> He spent a lot of time on the railroad. My mother hired on as a secretary about the same year I left. They sort of seemed to grow apart, because he spent a lot of time at one end of the line and she spent a lot of time at the store doing her secretarial work. When they were together they still weren't together. When he was on vacation he was commony off doing his thing. Even when they took simultaneous vacations, he was on the lake waterskiing, and she was on the shore watching. As we kids left, our parents found their own niches that usually didn't overlap, and when they did overlap there was more irritation than enjoyment.

Paul's pointed analysis here is by hindsight, because at the time of his own marriage, he assumed that his parents' model was both natural and viable.

> I assumed that whatever was necessary for the man to get ahead and be happy was supposed to be the standard by which the family functioned. And the woman basically supported that. I perceived my parents as being basically happily married with a relatively good marriage. There were very few arguments in my youth. My expectations were not in the line of having a "great" marriage and therefore being completely different from them. I think I pretty much accepted where they were at at that time.

Marian's familiar paradigm was rather different from Paul's. Though her father had periodic problems with alcohol, he was otherwise accessible and companionable, and Marian had strong images of a close and affectionate marriage partnership, with a high priority given to family activities. In view of this basic paradigm conflict, perhaps it is surprising that these two, especially Marian, could drift so frictionlessly into a pattern of marital separateness. In retrospect, Marian concludes that it seemed normal because everyone around them was living the same kind of life.

> He went off to sea, and I'm afraid I became extremely independent. I almost didn't need him sometimes. I was kind of absorbed by the children and he was absorbed in his work. Everybody else was living that way too. We were all navy wives and our husbands were all gone. Like a family, we stuck together when we needed something. We used to play cards together and do things together. We weren't sitting around pining because our husbands were gone. We worked around it, we were adjusting to it, and it didn't seem queer

Couple-Centered Connection • 171

because everybody was that way. That just seemed to be a way of life that he had to do. We'd had enough years then to where we both wanted that twenty-year retirement. Once again we were working for the future [a reference back to their earlier college days].

For Paul, the pattern of their separate life was acceptable because it was consistent with his familiar paradigm: "I largely saw the situation as quite similar to what I recall from home, which was, my father was gone to the other end of the line; when he was gone Mother took over." Paul provides an incisive analysis of Marian's growing independence:

She had no choice. To survive she had to become independent. I on occasion judged myself to be an intruder in the world of the Carter family. When I would return I could see that my part was upsetting. The daily routine was totally screwed up because I was there. I did fight for space, but I always lost. The reason I lost wasn't because she wasn't willing to give or that I wasn't strong enough to win. It's that about the time I finally got space, I got pulled out. There was a vacuum, and she'd have to move back in. So over a period of having done this a number of different times, we finally came to a treaty that said, "You've got your area of functioning and I've got my area of functioning. If I can help you over here when I'm around, that's what I'll do."

In this way the pattern of separateness continued for over ten years, through the birth of five children. Around this time, something happened that was so shocking to Paul that it shook the foundations of everything he assumed to be true about marriage. His parents got a divorce:

It was a very big surprise. We had been clued to the fact that it was coming because of the irritation that had been announced between them. But when the divorce proceedings started I felt personally involved. I felt like I had been abandoned. That's stupid, but that's how I felt. I felt my parents had really let me down. It took several years to get over that.

Of course Paul's parents *had* let him down in his mind's eye. He had built ten years of marriage on the model that they had provided him, on the faith that separate life-styles can still make for a solid marriage. "I thought marriage was a one-to-one, forever type situation, which was probably why I lost my cool when they finally did divorce." With all his assumptions thus shattered, Paul was now forced to consider that his own marriage might be resting on a more precarious footing than he had ever yet imagined.

It is worth digressing here a moment to consider the general principle at work: As powerful as familiar paradigms are in shaping our initial stance toward marriage, they go on being just that powerful. And if the key *source* of our paradigm takes a dramatic turn even years later, the aftershocks may

172 • *Three Corners*

be enough to throw our own marriage into profound upheaval and prod us into utterly transforming the paradigm into something quite new. Paul was not the only respondent whose marital transformation was in part propelled by a new development in the paradigm source. Jill McCarthy provides another illustration. She and her husband Mike were cited earlier as an example of an agenda clash. Jill's agenda was to get more husbandly attention than her mother ever got from her father; Mike's was to avoid what he saw as his mother's needless restricting of his father's third-corner activities.

The combination had thrown the McCarthy's into a vicious circle of increasing dependency on Jill's side and increasing distancing on Mike's. Eventually, the circle was broken by Jill getting a driver's license and cultivating some third-corner involvements of her own. The relationship then shifted from a disturbed dependency-distancing arrangement to a more comfortable and symmetrical pattern of separateness. Jill describes the process of transformation with remarkable clarity:

> I think we had been in an argument about something, and I looked at him one day and I said, "It's my turn now! You're going to be the mouse in the corner and you're going to watch me. It's going to be my turn to do things!" I didn't really mean it was going to be my turn and he was going to be home all the time, but it was more or less a turning point when I decided that I was going to join the League and I was going to have an outside activity. I just decided that if I didn't start now, I wouldn't start. That was probably the first time I did anything. I think he was glad that I did it; I know that he was. It didn't take him long to accept it. I had to fight for awhile, fight for my own freedom, I guess, because when we were first married, I didn't fight for freedom to do anything. I fought to have him with me every minute. At first I'd wanted him to stay home and sit with me all the time, but I finally decided, I guess, that if you can't beat 'em, join 'em. If he's going to go out, then you go out and do your thing.

Reflecting on the early period of her marriage, Jill contrasts her own unwillingness to remain dependent with her mother's long-standing frustration:

> My mother grew up not driving, and she never worked outside. I think when I was first married, things would have gone on that way for twelve whole years if I hadn't decided that I was going to be different. Momma just relied on my father. I guess I realized that she loved him and she was satisfied, but I wouldn't have been.

The fact is, however, that Jill's threshold of frustration was apparently influenced by what her mother was doing with her own frustration at every step of the way, for we learn that the older woman had herself gone through a recent marital transformation of the same sort: "She's changed now. He's

retired, she works, and she drives, and she does just as she pleases." Jill does not seem to realize that she herself was simply keeping in stride with these new developments in her paradigm source. When her mother was dependent in her marriage, Jill was dependent in her own. Later, as her mother shifted to a more separate style of partnership, Jill likewise found such a transition to be more and more plausible for herself.

To return to the Carters, the new development in Paul's paradigm source—his parents' divorce—threw Paul into a crisis that Jill McCarthy was spared. To travel through marriage in the groove of his familiar paradigm now seemed to spell divorce, and this realization eventually led Paul to reexamine his entire approach to partnership:

> At that point there was only a beginning perception in my mind of the need for change. There wasn't much I could actually do to protect the marriage from the onslaughts that were happening at the time. I was sent to Vietnam on combat duty. While I was away our last child was born, and this was when I decided that I was only going to stay in the navy if I could get a decent job that would allow me to establish some family bonds.

When he got back, Paul entered a three-year postgraduate program, and he began trying, as he says, "to balance time off":

> I'd schedule my time so that I had sufficient time to study but I also had time left over to do things with the family and with Marian. This was something that was totally new to me. She wasn't ready to quite give up that space yet. She had opened up and gotten hurt so many times that she would be damned if she was going to open up and try it again, even though I could say "I'm no longer going to be scheduled for sea." But my credibility wasn't very good.

Following his three years in graduate school, Paul decided to stay in the navy and got a job in a shipyard. At this point his old, separative pattern resurfaced at full steam. He recalls:

> What we found next was that I really was a workaholic and the job that I was given to do at the shipyard could consume twenty hours a day and commonly did.
>
> In my mind I judged that they see me—I'm home for lunch, I'm home for supper, I can spend a couple of hours here and a couple of hours there, and that's sufficient. My job was providing me with more enjoyment and more fun, more whatever-it-was that I needed to feel good about myself, than I got at home, so I funneled myself very largely into my work. It was a prestigious position. I had a thousand men a day working for me. It was a heady trip.
>
> The kids were starting to get bigger. Marian started playing bridge to survive. I started finding relatively soon that I couldn't play bridge with her

174 • *Three Corners*

because she was much better than I was, so she started playing bridge a lot with other people. And after a while she started going off to tournaments. I never worried at all about her moral standards, but what I started detecting was my very strong irritation at the fact that something else was more important to her than I was. I was angry. She said, "Well, you give me some reason to do differently and I'll do differently!" And at that time I really wasn't in a position to do much differently; I was locked very heavily into the job.

The reader must not miss the elegant symbolism in this new development. She wants to "bridge" and he tries to bridge with her. He finds, however, that he is not very good at it, so he gives up, whereupon she goes off to bridge elsewhere. Paul fails initially at bridging not so much because of the external (job-related) obstacles to his success but because of internal, paradigmatic ones, the paradigm in question being the image of marriage as a Safe Haven for a man's career success. True enough, familiar paradigms are like hard and icy grooves, and rising up out of them may be restricted by the depth of the groove itself. But these paradigms are also like savings accounts, repositories for our life investments, and seeing them as such brings into sharper focus our own responsibility in continuing to make the deposits. Paul became scared enough to close out his "occupational haven" account altogether, because the same kind of account led to his parents' marriage's "bankruptcy." That development was particularly haunting because it was his mother who had initiated the divorce, following a period of her building up some third-corner involvements away from the home. Now, Marian herself was carving out such outside corners. On some level of inner apprehension, Paul must have feared that the outcome would be the same.

The result of this turmoil was Paul's early retirement from the navy, his taking a teaching position three years ago, and his new determination to become more involved on the home front. Since this career change, Paul has typically been able to come home from work around two in the afternoon, and one day per week he does not go in at all. At first, there were still some enormous tensions. Paul recalls his feelings at the time:

I had an ideal, I had a hope. Marian calls me the great optimist. I guess I figured, "If I set things up right, it will work out right," and so that's the direction I went. There were times when it didn't look like it was going to work out right, even after I got the job. Temporarily there was more time and the pressures were off a bit, but Marian still played a lot of bridge, and any time she wanted to rile me, all she had to do was say, "Well, I'll be going to a tournament." Vesuvius! It got the automatic eruption. I'd get uptight enough to kick furniture and doors. She'd go off a couple of days, sometimes four or five days, or it could be an overnighter or just an evening.

Notice the reversal that has emerged: Paul was staying home more than ever before in seventeen years of marriage, while Marian was more involved

in an outside corner. The power dynamics were thus changing along the lines of Willard Waller's principle of less interest: the partner who has less interest in the relationship has the most power; the partner who is more accessible and "interested" is the most vulnerable and least powerul.

Recalling the basic principle of "resource theory" that power depends on resources, it now becomes possible to recast both of these principles in terms of the dynamics of triangulation: A partner has less interest in the partnership because of a greater interest in one or more third-corners; that greater interest is fed by the promise of greater resources, such as money, influence, honors, knowledge, and other scarce rewards that third-corners alone can provide. Paul had retreated from the lure of these third-corner rewards to move closer to his partnership-corner. Since Marian was not yet ready to trust Paul's move toward her, she still held on to her outside corner, so for a while Paul became the more vulnerable one, as he had neither an all-important third-corner nor a comfortable partnership. He referred to this period as "probably the low point of our marriage, the most disillusioning."

Nevertheless, the seed of connection had already been sown, and by the time of the interviews three years later, the Carters were reaping the harvest. Marian had wanted a more connected marriage all along, and she was more than willing to give up the constant bridge trips once she saw that Paul's new commitment was real, since, in her words, playing bridge had really only been a "refuge" for her. They now had stable roots in a single community for the first time in their married life. They got deeply involved in their church, where they led the forming of a musical group. In the midst of this new burst of energy, Marian had a profound religious experience relating to some conflict she had been having with one of their foster children, and she is certain that she received some divine guidance that eased her out of the conflict. Crying while recalling the incident, she tells me of the lasting effects it has had: "I had a whole new purpose to my life. And I could feel changes taking place in me. I could feel myself being more loving, open."

A year before I interviewed them, the Carters went to a weekend Marriage Encounter, and both see this experience as having given them the tools for a lasting connection. Paul tells me, "Openness with our love and affection is one of the major things that is different now, openness with each other and with the kids." Marian says much the same thing: "We were more open as far as what we appreciated. We had some beautiful sex! Things you just assumed each other knew, but we really didn't know, they were revelations. Little things that bugged us: we weren't aware of how the other really felt about it, what it really did to them." Pointing to the difficulties of knowing one's own daily undercurrent of feelings, Marian speaks of Marriage Encounter's strategy of writing daily letters to each other, asking how the other feels about something very current, telling them how you feel (or felt) about it, and then getting together to talk about it.

It's hard to know how you really feel. That's why we slow down enough some time in our day to get in touch with our feelings. That's as much of a revelation as how *he* feels. Sometimes I can't believe that I felt that way. I've never slowed down enough to really get in touch with how I felt, I'm so caught up with what I thought needed to be done.

The Carters' new pathway between each of their inner-corners and partnership-corners has made the difference in their solidity of connection. Marian's statement signals both the importance and the difficulty of uncovering one's inner-corner feelings about the ongoing partnership. Paul offers an appreciation of what it means to allow these feelings and their energy, once uncovered, to flow freely into the partnership-corner. His account deserves to be quoted at length:

I've always sort of known her head and what her ideals are and where she was going with them. I now get to participate in her feelings: her happiness, her joys, her disappointments, disillusionments. I can make those a part of what I am today, and I wasn't previously able to do that. What she is today with her feelings, those are fleeting, but that's who she is today, and I either experience who she is today, or I've lost that day forever, because she's never going to repeat those particular things. We've always talked about our problems, or our kids, or our money, but we never talked about who we really were inside and how we felt about things. We're more into that now. I can experience her on a more intimate basis therefore. . . .

There are feelings which people on the outside would say are bad in that it's not nice to be angry. Anger is a feeling which we allow ourselves to experience. We don't grovel in it. We try not to act on it. But if I'm angry, that's a reaction to a specific situation. I have no control over the fact that I have become angry. But I don't put my fist through the wall now. That's something else—I've kicked doors and that sort of thing in the past. . . .

It's not garbage-dumping, in that I don't blame her for me feeling bad. I'll tell her about the fact that I do feel a certain way and what I think set up the situation that's got me there. I'll try to explain what that feeling is like. It's up to us in the rest of our feelings to evaluate them: every time this happens we end up feeling this way; can we do something about this—together? I end up going off to Beano to support the Knights of Columbus. It causes irritation. She can express to me that irritation and tell me what it feels like. I then have to deal with, do I continue to allow her to feel the irritation, or do I do something about my dealings with Beano? I had to deal with that. She had to deal with the fact that I felt rejected and left alone when she went traipsing off to play bridge by herself. I'm not in a position to tell her, "You don't go play bridge," but I am in a position to tell her how I feel when she does. If she understands how I feel then we can deal with what the situation is that's causing that feeling. So in loving each other and being open enough to each other to express our reactions and our feelings, we're able now to communicate in a condition that does not involve bashing walls and fighting. We still end up with arguments and fights, but it certainly hasn't been what it was years ago.

The Carters illustrate a variant of marital connection that may be called *couple-centered*. The basic principle of this type of connection is that the partnership-corner itself is the source of ultimate fulfillment in life. Still, figure 7 shows that while both spouses' inner-corners lean closest to their partnerships, they do not fuse with them. The autonomy of both partners is thus saved by enabling each inner self to stand in its own space, remaining an independent center of initiative and activity, close though the partners may be. Energy can thus flow out freely to various independent third-corners, although there is a tendency to structure such corners so as to least intrude on the primacy of the couple's space together. There should be no separate recreational third-corners; discretionary time should be spent jointly if at all possible. If children are present, the home will naturally become the center of life, and both partners will devote abundant time to third-corner activities with the children, again often jointly. Nevertheless, a clear distinction is maintained between the family and partnership itself: a "good" family is possible only on the basis of an independently nurtured partnership. As Marian puts it, "Every single day of our lives we're saying 'I do' to each other. We realize how important it is that we do this. It has priority over everything, even our children. Paul and I—that's our sacrament; that's what we're living for now." Paul agrees:

> Nothing outside is more important than that commitment to each other. Because we are deeply and actively in love with each other, it allows the children to see that. It's one of the greatest gifts you can give a kid—to allow them to look at stability and love. They can feel, "I can relate to that; I can be a part of that." We've seen the effect. I see it in how they treat Marian, the respect that they show, the things they'll do working for us now that were totally out of the question before.

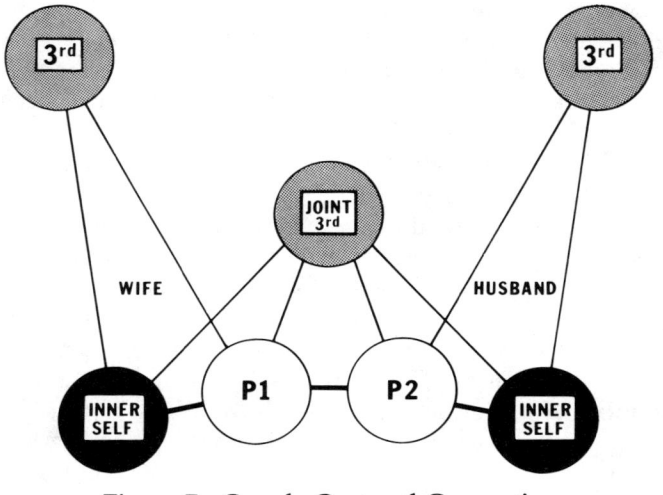

Figure 7. Couple-Centered Connection

Couple-Centered Connection and Marriage Encounter

Though probably not essential, it helps immeasurably if partners who seek a couple-centered connection have some ideological and group support for what they are doing. The Carters believe that their own bond, if perfected, can be an example of God's love: "The only hands that God has on earth are our hands; the only love God has on earth is our love," Paul tells me. He speaks pointedly about American culture's pervasive indifference and hostility to partnership, and the consequent need for group support. Here, he sounds much like a sociologist:

> Part of the system that we find works for marriage is a supportive community, people who also believe in marriage. Because the rest of the world largely doesn't, we're a counterculture in many ways, and to maintain a counterculture you have to remain in communication with other people within that culture. . . . Church groups tend not to be very supportive of married couples either; only the encounter community tends to be largely supportive of married couples. If you take a look at church activities you find the men's group, the women's group. Retreats are largely split: this week's the men's, next week's the ladies'. Though we try to improve those conditions, we recognize that there is very little today that is supportive of couples. The Marriage Encounter community is having a significant effect on what's happening in the religious community because we recognize that this is part of who we are, what we want to be.

In the hands of the Marriage Encounter community, couple-centered connection receives some sophisticated ideological elaboration, and devotees often go about with missionary zeal, recruiting other couples to attend a weekend encounter. There, a couple learns some basic skills in the communication of feelings as well as a general philosophy. Part of the philosophy is essentially a primer on how to protect the couple bond from being undermined by the forces around it. The ideology includes its own version of the devil known as "married singles," people who are married but who conduct their lives as if they were single.

Plainly, this ideology sees little place for independent third-corners unless they are absolutely essential, such as an income-earning job, and it provides a rationale for curtailing all such activities. Marian can say flatly, "We have decided not to take on anything new that we can't do as a couple." Paul relates, "I would love to be able to withdraw from several activities, and yet I'm sort of stuck with them. The church council periodically pulls me out of our being able to function as a pair. We have discussed these things, and when the time comes, that's going out the window." When I asked Paul what is special about his marriage and what he finds lacking in others', it was clear that he sees the spectre of "married singles" haunting everyone around him:

My immediate picture when you asked me that question is, we know this couple—very nice couple, religious, the whole bit. Saturday night there was a football awards dinner. Marian and I sat together. This couple and another couple had paired up wife with wife, husband with husband. There's no coupleness there, there's no togetherness. That's probably the way they are. If they're that way in public, they're probably that way everywhere. I say that because I know what I was in public and what I was at home.

It might be thought that Marriage Encounter's philosophy promotes a fusion of each partner's inner-corner with their partnership-corner, in view of its denigration of all independent third-corners and the encouragement to drop whatever cannot be done jointly. Such is not the case, however. The philosophy counsels an active connection between first- and second-corners, but it retains a prominent view of the inner-corner as a unique center of feelings, reaction, need, and thought, not only standing by itself but in large part constituting the integrity of each person. Marriage Encounter's understanding of autonomy and individuation thus appears much the same as that offered throughout this book, though we differ on the contribution to be made by independent third-corners. Paul Carter told me that even though "the cutting edge of [their] awareness of life" is now in exploring their partnership, there may come a time when he and Marian will have far more time together, as when they quit working, and then "Some of that time is going to have to be devoted to aloneness to do the quiet things, so that togetherness means something."

My own view is that third-corner "aloneness," as Paul calls it, need not be simply a residual "quiet" time to restore oneself for partnership, but an alternate outlet for the inner self to generate and unleash more of its creative energy, with some potentially enlivening effects for partnership. I shall develop the appropriate argument for this position shortly.

As a final comment on Marriage Encounter, it should not be thought that one weekend will magically produce a couple-centered partnership. My data show great variety among the nine couples who attended such a weekend. Essentially, those couples who, like Marian and Paul, were already geared to elevate their own bond to the center of their lives are the ones who carry their newly honed capacities back into their everyday existence together. They continue writing their daily letters and "dialoguing" with each other about their ongoing feelings. They often attend Marriage Encounter follow-up meetings and get involved in the organization. The Carters have turned their relationship into a veritable art form: "I love him in a very exciting way now," Marian tells me; "I like to dream up things that I think might make him happy every day. He has a sparkle about him because I make him feel loved."

For other people, unresolved issues or difficulties in their own development may greatly limit what they can take away from a Marriage Encounter. People who have learned to posture a stance of strength-no-matter-what will

180 • *Three Corners*

not often relax their defenses to disclose their vulnerabilities, just because Marriage Encounter urges them to do so. The price of such "strength" is emotional distance from both themselves and from others, and any real exchange of feelings is ruled out. Similarly, people who fear the inherent defect of their own inner-corner may have difficulty uncovering that corner, much less sharing it with a partner. People with very negative self-images may mistrust the legitimacy of their own feelings and see little to gain from revealing them, despite Encounter leaders' exhortations to the contrary. "We don't fight," Meg Gilman says some four years after an Encounter weekend with her husband Stan in the seventh year of their marriage.

Do you wish you did?

Yes.

What would happen if you did?

I guess that's why I won't fight, because I don't know.

What's your worst fantasy of what would happen?

I guess maybe that he'd see what a shrew I am and leave.

Lacking a strong inner-corner, Meg was unable to create much of a bridge from her private drama to her partnership-corner. Thus when I ask Meg what Stan learned about her through Marriage Encounter, she replies, "Nothing that he didn't already know—that I'm a weak person, that I don't have self-confidence." Such revelations are merely generalized self-judgments; they are not accounts of how one's inner drama is actually responding to specific, ongoing experience.

A couple's current triangular dynamics are probably the best predictor of what they will get from a Marriage Encounter. When Mike and Jill McCarthy went to their weekend, Jill was just twenty-seven and had only recently begun to break out of a dependency-distancing pattern of marriage. For Jill, the cutting edge of her development was to explore her separateness from Mike, not her connection to him. Having been fused to his scant emotional support throughout their marriage, she was now basking in the sunlight of her own third-corner independence: "My whole life has changed. It's changed from a person who never did anything to somebody who is not afraid now to do anything, or to try it. I'm president of my club this year and I don't feel nervous about it. I've gone from a person who never did anything to a person who can accomplish a lot if she wants to." Since Mike had long ago distanced into his sports-centered world and was perfectly comfortable being separate, what

Couple-Centered Connection • 181

remained was to fine-tune their newly symmetrical, separate arrangement. Marriage Encounter opened their lines of communication enough for them to do this. Connection was thus a matter not of bonding more closely but of "checking" with each other so as to better align their separate third-corner activities. Says Jill:

> Without either one of us really realizing it, I think that was a big point when we both thought of checking with each other about doing things. If he's going to get into a softball tournament, he always checks with me first, which is something he didn't used to do—whatever I said didn't mean anything. We discuss things now that we didn't discuss. If I've got an appointment on a night that he's got to do something, I take on the responsibility of getting a babysitter. Or vice versa. He doesn't ask my permission, and I don't ask his permission, but we talk with each other. I can do what I want and he can do what he wants. And he doesn't have to feel guilty about it, and neither do I.

Apparently, neither partner is inclined now to dredge up disappointed or hurt feelings about the other's unavailability, because both are more focussed on safeguarding their freedom to be alone in a variety of third-corners. Again, much of these preferences and tendencies are developmental ones. It may well be that if the McCarthys go to another Marriage Encounter after nineteen years of marriage, as did the Carters, they too will have grown weary of separateness after twelve more years of it, and what they then take home from the weekend could be very revitalizing to their couple bond.

In this chapter we have explored one couple's process of transition from separateness to couple-centered connection. We have also considered the impact of Marriage Encounter on this process and concluded that there is no magic potion to connect the lines from one spouse to the other. Remember that within both partners' inner-corners resides the full force of their respective personal histories, and the weight of these histories may rule out any favoring of the partnership-corner on the part of one or both spouses. Other urgencies may simply be more pressing. In chapter 10 we shall focus on child-centered activity as one such urgency.

10
Family-Centered Connection

This chapter will focus on a type of connection in which the spouses lean more toward joint family activities than their own couple bond. Typically, such people felt comfortably bonded to at least one of their parents and usually to both, and they bear no great burden of unresolved issues vis-à-vis their parents. They look forward to marriage with the certainty that life is most meaningful when the whole family can function together as a close unit. And they have a backlog of positive imagery to make this vision more concrete.

The Turners

Jack and Sandy Turner were one such couple. High school sweethearts, they married after both had finished college. They had recently celebrated their twenty-second anniversary when I interviewed them. While Sandy tells me that she used to be more dependent on Jack, and she "went into marriage as if it were a cocoon," she nevertheless started as a far more autonomous person than did many of the women described earlier. This autonomy was already apparent before they married, when different college choices separated them for two years. There was only an hour of travel time between them, and the close proximity would have led people with more dependent inclinations to bridge the gap through frequent weekend visits, but not Sandy and Jack.

Jack played on various sports teams, which took up parts of weekends, and Sandy was involved in her studies. "We'd see one another perhaps once a month," Jack recalls. "She was a very committed student, more than I was, so she studied hard, and we saw each other infrequently. We'd usually be together for vacations."

After they married, Sandy taught school for a year and then had three children in quick succession. She did not return to work until many years later, when one of the children had already left home and the others were well along in high school. In the eighteen-year interim, her world revolved contentedly

184 • *Three Corners*

around the home. "The family unit became central to both of us," she relates, but this centrality did not define the totality of their marriage, as it did for Louise and Jake Miller, whose partnership got swallowed up in the service of their children and ceased to have any development of its own.[1] Like Louise, Sandy believed that a mother's place is in the home while her children are growing up, but Louise fused to her children whereas Sandy remained connected to hers without forfeiting her own autonomy. Sandy's inner self was thus free to focus both on her partner and on a variety of third-corners. She took courses at the local university, worked at the church, and refined her keen spiritual sensibilities through reading the Bible and through study groups. When home alone, she had a continuous succession of domestic projects that fully engaged her and provided abundant creative outlets. I agree with Jack, who says of Sandy, "I think she was able to further her own personal development. She has a good sense of who she is, what she wants, and where she's going."

Sandy's continued autonomy should be considered side-by-side with Jack's life pattern. Like other men with challenging middle-class careers, Jack has always been devoted to his work, but he never fused with it in a way that would result in distancing either from his partnership-corner or from his familistic third-corner. There were periods when his demanding job pulled him away both on weekends and on weekday evenings, but the fact remains that when he was home, he was fully home. "I'm far from a workaholic," he says. "My first priority is here at home." Accordingly, Sandy never hungered for adult companionship in her home-centered existence, and Jack was no less eager than she to develop a wide array of family activities. He pulled them all into outdoor activities that were new to Sandy and that she lacked the confidence to cultivate on her own. Whitewater canoeing, hiking, camping, and skiing, along with some exciting vacation travelling became the basis of a vigorous familism.

Still, the Turners always managed to nourish their partnership-corner independently of their children. "We are very close," Jack says. "I prefer to be with her more than anybody else. She's my best friend, and I like to be close to her. And I think she feels the same way. That's the way it's always been." When Sandy's father died, her mother became available for child-care relief. "He died the year we were married," Sandy relates:

> So my mother would come to stay with the children whenever we wanted her. She's always been economically self-sufficient. And she's always been eager to come. Maybe one of the strong points in our marriage is that we have had a good deal of time alone. I was not working, and whenever he went to a conference I went with him, always. This was right out from the moment the children were born.

Again, Sandy was far from a dependent wife reduced to tagging after her husband to his conferences. She remained an independent center of initative,

and Jack always encouraged her to pursue anything she wanted on her own. It was he, Sandy recalls, who first suggested that she return to teaching when their children were beginning to leave home. Once she did, she became deeply involved in it, so a lot of the time that was previously available to Jack and the family got pre-empted. Jack tells me, "She is so committed to this teaching that she spends a hell of a lot more time with her work than I do with mine. Sandy has never done anything in a slipshod manner, so it is going to take time to put it into perspective." Though he does not like the situation, Jack remains supportive and he assumes that their relationship can easily endure a holding pattern until she can work out a less consuming stance toward her work. In the meantime, Jack muses, "It's her time, it's her life, and it's her decision how she uses her time. She works much harder than I think she should, but that's her decision." As for Sandy, who has fully savored both domestic- and profession-centered rounds of existence, she looks forward to returning to the home-front:

> I almost feel that I am not a professional person. I was very content at home and content to think of myself as the center of the home. And I probably will not work right up until whatever retirement age is. I probably will work only until our girls are through school, to try to ease the burden. . . . And I don't mind doing it. Teaching is an exciting situation to me, so I do enjoy it. But I also love being at home, and I miss all the things that I used to be able to do and now have no time to do. I like to sew, and I really can't even think of the house anymore; I can't think of what I'd like to do to change here and there. I never cook and bake anymore. I don't have time for any community affairs anymore, which I enjoyed. I've always thought maintaining a home is a career. Being a professional isn't that great. And yet I enjoy it, and I'm glad I'm having an opportunity to be with all the young people. And it has made me more independent, and I like the intellectual stimulation.

The Turners' marriage illustrates a type of connection that may be called *family-centered*. This type is grounded in a clear set of principles: the home is the center of both partners' lives; both partners should devote abundant discretionary time to activities with the children; and couples need enough time by themselves to periodically renew their own bond. In the eyes of moral tradition, family-centered connection is the only wholesome path for a married couple to travel, the path to which churches, the Bible, and U.S. presidents appeal, and the only one that can be talked about in virtually any public circle without risk of incurring someone's disapproval.

The difference between couple-centered and family-centered connection has to do with the different leanings of the partners' inner-corners. In couple-centered connection, the inner-corner leans toward the partnership-corner; in family-centered connection, it leans toward joint third-corner activities with the children, as shown in figure 8.

186 • *Three Corners*

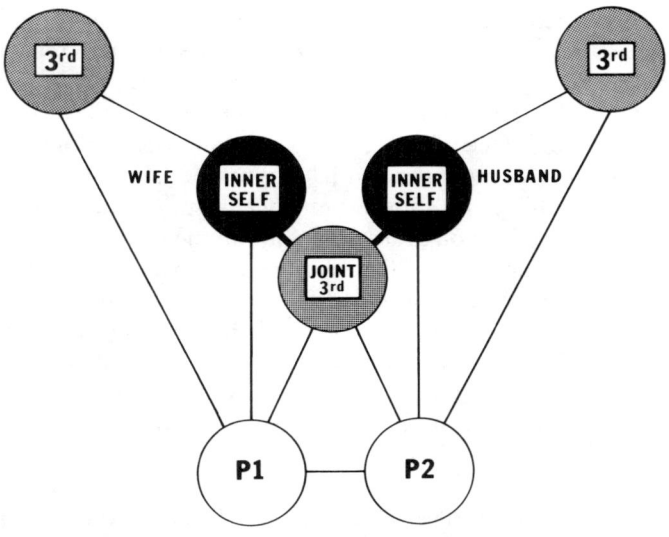

Figure 8. Family-Centered Connection

In family-centered connection, both partners may have independent third-corners, but their activity within them is constrained by an eagerness to preserve the centrality of home and family. The wife becomes the home's true center since her husband almost invariably works away from home. She may have outside third-corners such as volunteer or part-time work, but she will structure them so that whenever any family member—child or husband—is at home, she will usually be on hand. The husband may vigorously pursue his job or career, but not so singlemindedly that it seriously encroaches on his time at home, and in his leisure he will rarely have third-corners that are independent of his wife or family. Here are Sandy Turner's recollections of how she felt when Jack got himself a set of golf clubs:

> We've just seemed to have a lot of similar interests. We both play instruments and sing. We both dance in the couples group, so we do a lot of travelling and rehearsing together. As far as sports go, we canoe and hike together, we ski downhill and cross country—we've always done these things as a family. The only thing that has ever happened that's been disruptive was when Jack got a set of golf clubs and I was afraid I'd develop into a golf widow. That was an upsetting time for me, the only time in our marriage when I really felt uncomfortable. I imagine we talked that out within a week or two. I'd always hoped that we'd develop as a unit.

The rules of family-centered connection can perhaps stretch a little, but Jack's golfing was pushing against their limits, and he backed off. To some,

Family-Centered Connection • 187

this may seem an unreasonable restriction of Jack's space, but not to Jack, who says, "I can enjoy the outdoors alone, but I prefer to share things that refresh me with my wife." The key to family-centered connection is that both partners effortlessly value its principles, and the resulting life-style comes most naturally to them. Only about 10 percent of the couples in my sample meet these requirements. For the remaining couples, this pattern of connection is only occasionally possible because one or both partners do not fully desire it.

Some wives see only their suffocation in the web of family-centeredness, and they seek to extricate themselves from its trappings in any way they can. Other wives are too lacking in autonomy to resist fusing with their children, their husband, or both, and then the unbalanced investments of the different family members in family "togetherness" will increase the likelihood of the dependency-distancing pattern described earlier. Often husbands crave too many independent third-corner leisure activities, are not truly home-centered, are not especially interested in what their wives do in their absence, and/or cannot put aside their work-related concerns enough to settle in with their wives and children. Family-centered connection tends to be especially difficult for men, for reasons elaborated earlier. Women are experienced at sustaining active connection and find it more natural than being separate, while men only feel like men if they can routinely escape from the "clutches" of a woman. "You be at home for me, but don't expect me to be stuck there with you," is their implicit refrain.

Family-Centeredness as a Duty: The Jacobs

Because family-centered connection bears the blessing of moral and religious tradition, many couples are so eager to honor its principles that they may stifle some persistent urges that would lead them in other directions. Especially for those who hold marriage as a Religious Calling or an instrument of "God's will," partnership and family may become serious disciplines, even interior battlegrounds, where the war between the "higher" and "lower" impulses can be fought out within oneself. Externally, these couples do not look and act much differently than couples like the Turners. They are home-centered and family-centered, and their third-corners are mostly joint ones except for the husband's work. The difference is an internal one. Family-centered connection is most vibrant when the battle between the inner impulses need not be fought at all because the partners are doing exactly what they want in their marriage. In contrast, the couples about whom I will now write are more divided within themselves; they do what they think one should, but it may at times require both some effort and some inner denial to carry it off.

188 • *Three Corners*

Peter and Barbara Jacobs both grew up in family-centered, strongly Christian homes in rural Maine. They fondly recall idyllic scenes from their childhoods, and they both came to marriage with familiar paradigms filled only with positive imagery. Born-again Christians, they see their marriage as a Religious Calling. "Church is a very big part of our lives," Barbara states. "We enjoy it. The children enjoy it very much. We are involved as a family. God has set down basic principles for marriage and for bringing up children, and we adhere to those." Peter is very specificc about these principles:

> We look back to the Bible again. It simply says that the man is to be head of the household, and it describes the man's duties and how the wife is to uphold him in his duties. It explains how she is to care for the man and care for the family, and do the housework for the family. It describes where the responsibilities lie.

While Peter's outline may sound unredeemingly sexist in the feminist climate of our times, the Jacobs' accounts reveal a partnership in which both spouses do everything they can to help each other with their appointed tasks. Aside from his engineering job, Peter's life revolves around his family, his home, and the Church. While at home, his first priority is to coordinate with the needs of everyone in his family. Barbara describes some typical daily patterns, indicating a closely interwoven division of household labor. After dinner, "He will get up from a meal and start helping me right in the kitchen; he's always done that. If it's very late I'll suggest that he spend some time with the children, play a game or read a story or something, and get them into bed." Peter's account of daily life is similar. He provides homespun detail about the Sunday ritual:

> On Sunday morning we have the same timetable, because we have to leave at about the same time for church. She will usually come down and get breakfast, and I'll make the beds—the kids each make their own. The little boy has to have a little encouragement, so I'll race with the kids, and they like to tell me they're going to beat me getting the bed made and getting dressed. And then after we've eaten, I'll usually help her clean up the kitchen, and quite often get potatoes and things for dinner and wash them, or cut them, peel and slice them, while she may be doing up the dishes from breakfast. So we do things together, whether it be housework or splitting wood and putting it in the cellar. And I think it's really been like that since the very beginning.

The Jacobs family functions like a well-oiled machine, not only in their home-based activities, but also in their frequent church activities and their seasonal episodes of skating, skiing, snowmobiling, camping, and vacationing together. Peter and Barbara manage to get away alone for dinner once every month or two, and periodically they have some travel time alone that

is prompted by Peter's job. Routinely, their children go to bed early, so they have ample evening time alone together. Nevertheless, both partners provide evidence of two wars of inner urges, perhaps waged only occasionally, as they travel their chosen pathway through marriage. Peter's war, predictably, has to do with an intermittent urge to distance away from the family machine, into some independent, recreational third-corner. "I have very little that I do apart from the family," he tells me:

> Once in a while this has been a secret feeling of mine, that I would like to be able to go do some things alone or with some other guys. It could be like going hunting, or going on a snowmobiling trip. Probably the biggest reason that I don't is not because my wife objects but because I have the feeling within myself that I don't really spend enough time with the kids as it is. It isn't really a restraint that she puts on me, or that the kids put on me. It's probably just an internal one. There just isn't opportunity to do both things.

Later in the interview Peter expands on this theme, providing a remarkable account of his private battle of the urges and how it gets resolved:

> There are things that people [spouses] are better off not to know. Perhaps there have been times that I wished I could do some things and be free to do them and not be tied down. I don't think it would have been helpful to her to have come out and told her how I felt: "You're a drag! I can't go and do this thing that I'd like to do because I know you're not going to want me to do it. You're going to sulk about it or give me a hard time about it and make me feel rotten, and then I'll probably decide not to go and I'll be mad about it." Why should I hurt her feelings, and let that thought come between us, when I know that after I've thought about things like that for a little while, it really is my selfishness that was in the way, not something wrong with her or somehow that she begrudged me an opportunity to go do what I wanted to do? So I don't very often talk about these things. I have those thoughts, and the older I get, the fewer of them I have. After I begin to evaluate them, I feel it's my problem, not hers, and what I would have been doing if I had come right out and said what I felt was make it her problem too.

We shall return to Peter in a moment. Barbara's battle, again following the predictable gender tendencies, has to do with periodic yearnings she has for more intimate contact and connection with Peter. For example, every day both Peter and all the children come home for lunch. "Generally," Barbara tells me, "I try to have the children fed, to make it a little quieter, and the two of us will sit down for lunch, and maybe I'll tell him some little things that went on, and he's just not hearing, because his mind is on what he's got to do that afternoon." I then offer Barbara the chance to wax indignant about it, pointing out that some women would take this "not hearing" to mean that he doesn't really care enough. She replies that "There have been times when I've

190 • *Three Corners*

kind of felt that way, but I think it was out of self-pity. I realize his job responsibilities are very demanding." I prod a little further, asking her if she thinks Peter listens more or less than he used to. "On the whole, less to just everyday talk. If it's anything really of a serious nature, why, he's right there," and she quickly returns to a more positive note, exclaiming how grateful she is for the kind of husband she has. "I feel very fortunate when I hear of other families and the problems they have." She then provides a lengthy critique of a neighboring couple who both work, "live two completely separate lives," have separate finances, even sometimes vacation separately. "It seems like their whole life, they just go in opposite directions. There doesn't seem to be any relationship there at all."

I ask to what extent Peter and she preserve a private dimension in their marriage. Barbara answers, "He's, as I say, quite quiet. If he has problems at work, he never brings them home. I don't know what goes on at work, because he just feels there's no sense in burdening me with his problems there, and he's quite a private person." I ask if she would want to hear about those things. "Sometimes I can understand him not [telling me] because it involves personnel. Then it's not good for him to go around telling things that have happened. But yes, there have been times when I wished he'd just kind of let me know what his day involved."

Perhaps there resides in many of us a parental voice that admonishes, "You can't have it all." If so, the Jacobs reprogram that voice to speak some counterpoint: "What you can't have," they might say, "is not really what you want anyway, and if you give up all your wants to God, you can have far more than you could ever dream of." Unfortunately, it may require some time to make this saintly surrender a fait accompli, and in the meantime, some very real yearnings get indefinitely deferred. Peter must explain away his urges for more private space as "selfishness," and Barbara must dismiss her desire for more intimacy as "self-pity." Together, they keep themselves focussed on the straight and narrow path, and their religious framework provides them with an elaborate assortment of conceptual condiments to make their discontents more palatable. They would argue that I dwell too much here on these wars of the inner urges, that they are not at all major battles, but the most minor of skirmishes, even opportunities to learn valuable lessons that can help them grow and mature spiritually. They may be right, for there is no doubt that their family-centered connection is real, strong, and satisfying. They are surely unaware that they touch each other only lightly and seldom directly because most of their connection is through third-corner intermediaries of church and children. They come precariously close to fusing their inner-corners with their joint third-corners (children and church), and thus falling into a pattern of separateness described earlier.[2]

I have a hunch about the Jacobs. If they gave their inner urges more permission to speak out, they could have far more than they now have of each

other, and still give to God and their children whatever they care to. If Peter could bring out of the closet his secret desire for more independent space, perhaps he would also find it less necessary to cloister his work-life as his own private preserve, and then Barbara might begin to have more of the intimate contact with him that she craves. It may be that as their children get older, the delicate balance of triangular forces will naturally shift to bring them more directly into contact, which is what seems to have happened with the Turners. Spouses who are well-practiced at family teamwork have a strong advantage over those who are not if they want to move their inner selves toward their partnership-corners. A lot will depend on Peter, and on what is really going on in his inner self. Can he bring any of that secret inner energy directly to Barbara's corner, or is his craving for outside excitement a need to protect himself from her influence? Peter himself rules out the latter possibility:

If we didn't have the children, we'd still like to do enough things alike that there would be very little that I would want to change. I like to fly, but she'd go flying with me too if she didn't have the children to take care of. We'd go places together. I would get to do a lot more things I'd like to do. . . . It's because the children have things that they're involved in that have to be considered too.

Independent Third-Corners in Marital Connection: The Murrays

Because flying is such an excellent symbol of independence and freedom from earthly constraints such as spouses, it is worth lingering here to consider another respondent who has the same flying passion, handles it differently than Peter Jacobs, and yet maintains a well-connected marriage with strong elements of family-centeredness. In the process, we shall learn something more about the dynamic interplay between partnership on one hand and individual freedom and autonomy on the other.

Alec and Janet Murray had been married for fourteen years when I interviewed them, and had two boys, eleven and thirteen years old. Unlike both the Turners and the Jacobs, religion played a very minor role in the dynamics of the Murrays' family life. Alec's familiar marital paradigm was a comfortably positive one, but Janet's was decidedly negative, so much so that Janet had formed a Hedged Bet agenda toward marriage, as described in chapter 3. She was the woman who had sought in the world of horses a refuge from her uncomfortable home and her parents' troubled relationship. Her long courtship with Alec was often tailored to this interest in horses, and she thus insulated herself from all the perils of partnership that were so alive in her awareness.[3]

192 • *Three Corners*

Alec became enamored of Janet the first day they met as they chased an errant horse of hers. He was determined to surmount the many obstacles that stood between them. He was from a working-class family, she from a middle-class one; he had a high school degree, she graduated from college; she was Catholic, he was Protestant. Janet's mother, who rarely approved of anything, was not inclined to break her nay-saying pattern on behalf of this upstart oil-truck driver. And Janet herself, Alec told me, "was not in the least interested in boys. She could care less whether I came to see her or not."

Despite all this, Alec persevered. By the time they married, Alec had converted to Catholicism and gotten himself a job that encouraged advancement through the ranks of the company. He had formed a long-standing habit of supporting Janet's interest in horses. Perhaps fearing that their background differences were already a stumbling block, he was eager to do what he could to accommodate her:

> I think the first few years you have a feeling that if you do something that she doesn't really approve of, maybe the whole thing is going to burst. I tried to be stable and not cause a lot of commotion; not do things . . . [like] wild living and raising ructions [sic]. I tried to hold a job and have a steady income and not do things that would get Janet upset.

By the end of the first year-and-a-half of marriage, the Murrays had had their first child and Janet was pregnant with their second. Janet had quit her teaching job, and they moved to New Hampshire. In some respects, home and family became Janet's domain while work became Alec's, as in many of the separative relationships described earlier. Once Alec entered the managerial ranks of his company, there were periods following his promotions to more demanding supervisory positions when his new responsibilities seemed to totally consume him.

Nevertheless, these periods were the exception rather than the rule, and there were some strong countertendencies of connection that steered the Murrays clear of any sustained pattern of separateness. Alec was typically an eager and supportive parent, and he continued to be an accommodating partner. In contrast with Peter Jacobs, he often discussed his personnel and other management problems with his wife, whose support and advice he found invaluable. Unlike Barbara Jacobs, Janet knew what was going on in her husband's world. At home, they often worked together on domestic projects. Even before they married, they had pooled their money to buy a small home and had spent all their free time fixing it up together. Later, after several years in New Hampshire, they bought some land and together did most of the building of a new home, an endeavor which amplified Janet's appreciation of Alec's considerable mechanical and building skills. Through the years, they have maintained a nightly ritual of playing a game of Scrabble or cribbage,

often with the children. And when one of their sons recently got involved in basketball, they started routinely going to his games, always together.

Despite these and other couple- and family-oriented activities, the Murrays have never been as locked into a family-centered existence as the Jacobs. Both Janet and Alec vigorously developed some independent third-corner passions, and each has always supported the other fully in their respective endeavors. People with a Hedged Bet agenda for marriage often begin their married lives with an active, independent third-corner. Janet's horses served this function for her, so much so that her father has chided her on more than one occasion, "You love the horses more than you love him."

For the first six years of their marriage, two children along with numerous community involvements kept Janet occupied, and she had no horse. It was Alec who decided to get her one: "She always had a horse, and not having one must have been hard on her because she thinks the world of horses." Alec has always done the heavy work of hauling hay and putting up fences for the horses preceding their several moves, and with his support, one horse eventually led to others. He often goes to club meetings with her, and he notes, "There's a lot of nice people in the horse circle, and we've made a lot of friends." In Janet's words, "He doesn't mind going with me. He's the type of person that gets along well with everyone. He can make a conversation when everybody else is sitting there with egg on his face." Still, the horses are essentially Janet's third-corner. Alec occasionally rides with her, but "only once in a blue moon," and he is never involved in the trail rides and clinics she attends.

As Alec became more confident about his marriage, he rewarded himself with permission to develop a third-corner of his own—flying.

> You mature as time goes along and you find that you can do these things, that you don't have to be tied right together all the time and yet you still can have a very solid marriage. She can go her way and I can go my way to a certain degree, as much as married life will allow. I'm interested in flying; she has no interest in getting in an airplane. I took her once, scared her damned near to death, and I don't think I'll ever get her into one again. [Janet tells the story of how the plane developed an electrical failure over Mt. Washington. Alec exclaimed, "Oh shit, no flaps," and in his intense concentration he did not bother to add that it would still be possible to land the plane. Janet muses, "I thought we'd have to fly around until it ran out of gas, and then, plunk!"]

While Alec is disappointed about Janet's reluctance to fly with him, he still gets her support for his doing it. He tells her all about his adventures, and on days that he can't fly but still goes over to "hangar-fly" (sit and talk about airplanes and flying), she sometimes goes with him. She knows fully what flying means to him.

194 • *Three Corners*

I knew from the moment Alec and I first went together that he was just madly involved with the idea of flight. And yet when he really got serious I was upset with his doing it because I was concerned for his safety. And when he was studying for his license he did become very involved in it, and evenings there was no Scrabble game. It was just always study, study, study. Nowadays I've kind of gotten over the worry, and all that studying was just a fleeting thing. It didn't really separate us, it just made me sort of jealous at the time.

Both Alec and Janet extol the glories of their respective third-corner passions. Alec says, "When I climb into an airplane, I forget everything else. I enjoy myself. It's an outlet for me, and I can get away from the rat race of the everyday worrying about this, worrying about that." Janet waxes truly eloquent about her horses:

Unless you've got a hobby that you totally enjoy, I don't think you'd understand it. It's a communication between the horse and me and nature and God and the whole world. It's just a very pleasant thing. You go off with problems, you come back without them, because in the meantime you've just encountered so many other things. You're refreshed and you can focus on whatever you need to.

Clearly, the Murrays have a different philosophy than the Jacobs about how to handle independent third-corners. Both Murray partners give themselves and each other the right to indulge those personal inclinations that the Jacobs would override as "selfishness" or "self-pity." Now, is Alex's permitting himself to go off flying better or worse than Peter's refusing himself that permission? Arguments can surely be advanced for each side, but because moral tradition is already on the side of the man who forgoes his private pleasures to devote more time to his family, I shall simply state the case to be made for the other position.

Independent third-corners are neither self-indulgent luxuries nor greedy escapes from adult maturity, at least not necessarily. If they answer to some deep-seated personal needs, and those needs do not add up to a simple reluctance to bond with one's family members, they may strengthen a marriage rather than weaken it. Third-corner passions may help consolidate one's autonomy by providing another outward angle from which one's own energy center and inner impulses can be experienced. Supporting a partner's third-corner is not merely an idle concession, because a partner whose inner self is thus strengthened is one who has more interior resources to give and to bond with.

Both Alec and Janet told me in so many words that by cheerfully letting each other go, they typically get back a rejuvenated and more vibrant partner. "I can feel a difference in him after he's been flying for an hour," Janet

says. "He comes back a happier person, and he's more responsive, just because he's done what he's wanted to do, and it's the same feeling that I have when I go on the horse. We feel better about each other, and perhaps he feels better about himself." Clearly, no worries about selfishness stand in either of these partners' way.

Only connected marriages, however, can reap these benefits. They alone have the mutual, three-cornered balance that can synthesize two opposites—separateness and togetherness. It takes a strong partnership-corner to give a person the security to periodically leave it, and to reaffirm one's sense that to leave it is not to weaken its solidity. It takes a strong inner self to stand in one's own space, and to temporarily separate from the security of togetherness to develop some purely individual capacities or sensibilities. It requires a strong third-corner to lure one away from the cozy confines of partnership or of self-contained complacency. And most important, it requires a strong interconnection between all three corners for a person to use independent activity in an integrated manner—that is, as an opportunity first to build an expanded inner self, and then to stretch the boundaries, limits, and frontiers of partnership so that it might better accommodate this newly transformed self.

The Inner-Corner in Marital Connection

Any inner self is loaded with myriad impulses, urges, wishes, and feelings. Some inner selves are probably more complex than others, and some are more divided against themselves by conflicts than others. An inner self so divided may have difficulty allowing certain impulses to surface for all to see, particularly one's own, dear self. Suppressed, these impulses will likewise remain hidden from one's partner, especially if they involve apprehensions about partnership. What then happens is a spiral effect. A partner who feels vulnerable to partnership cannot let the inner cat and its nine lives out of the bag. The more this suppression goes on, the weaker the partnership actually becomes, because it lacks the intimate materials to energize it. A weakened partnership, in turn, may not feel secure enough to comfortably accommodate departures into individual third-corners, and then the inner impulses that require those third-corner outlets have no way of getting themselves expressed. This may result in more resentments and conflicts about partnership, going on and on in a vicious circle.

Peter Jacobs, with his secret but unexpressed inner urges to get away by himself, and Barbara Jacobs, with her wish for more intimate partnership, may have gotten themselves into this spiral effect. Peter remembers times "when we competed with each other," long before they were married:

We both were in the youth group at the church, and were kind of competitive there for leadership. She was the president in her last year there. So we

196 • *Three Corners*

went through times of being in competition when maybe I would have liked to have been the leader and she got to be it, and still we were boyfriend and girlfriend. So I guess the opportunity for either of us to be upset or feel jealous of the other was there. . . . I can remember that the girls always seemed to want to be in competition with the boys. I think she was a better swimmer than I was. If she beat me at something, then the other kids would all cheer her on, and then they'd tell me she was better at this than I was. . . . Those sorts of things happened all through childhood.

When I ask Peter how he usually dealt with the situation, he replies:

The same way that I deal with it now. I think that two people can't both be the boss; they can't both always be right, and if they both decide that they are right and they're going to argue about it down to the death, then something bad's going to come of it. I felt the same way then as I do now. Although I may have felt hurt at times, I don't think that I ever argued about it or let it bother me that much. Just generally let it pass.

It was shortly after this point in the interview that Peter explains that in adhering to the Bible, the issue of ultimate family power gets definitively resolved in his favor.

Somehow, Peter's presentation spontaneously drifts from stories of being outdone in childhood competitions, to the principle that a relationship should have only one boss, to the assertion that two people cannot both be right, and to the Bible's authority to put the matter to rest. Now, when the matter of being the boss and being "right" becomes a pressing issue in a relationship, it does not lose its salience through simple arbitration—in this case, through the Bible reminding the Jacobs that a husband is indeed the head of the household. Rather, the issue's salience lives on in one or both partner's inner life. Just as a reformed alcoholic may continue to wage an inner struggle despite all outward evidence of its resolution, so a person with insecurities about personal power may still feel the issue unsettled, despite having insinuated the reigns of power into his own hands. Peter's inner self is a self divided. Only the strong, virtuous Peter—the devoted family man and God-loving soul—can surface in his inner life and take outer form and direction. Only the virtuous Peter can likewise find his way into the partnership.

The weaker Peter lurks about in frequent silence. (Actually, he is not really weak; he simply fears that he is.) Especially in the event of differences with Barbara (if, for example, she wants to buy something that he thinks they don't need), he will retreat into silence: "I usually just ignore the question. She knows when I ignore it, that means no. Rather than just come out and say no, or argue about it, I just smile and don't say anything." To say something, apparently, is to go at it toe-to-toe, and this is tantamount to once again putting up for grabs one's hard-won power. The weaker Peter, then,

Family-Centered Connection • 197

cannot play with Barbara as an equal companion for fear of being once more overpowered and outdone by her, nor can he act on the "selfish" urge to go off and play by himself in some third-corner, for that indulgence would weaken his authority to claim the ultimate power that the Bible awards to those who are upright.

By contrast, if Alec and Janet Murray can play a bit more freely in their partnership-corner, perhaps it has to do with Alec's inner self being less cluttered by conflicts about personal power. He seems to find it easy enough to tell Janet anything, at least whatever in his private drama he himself has access to. The result is a more comfortable and equal partnership which can more readily support independent third-corners such as Alec's flying and Janet's horses, both of which seem to result in more settled and centered inner selves, who can thus bond better. The spiral effect can work in either direction.

There are limits, however, to the Murrays' marital connection. Like many men who are eager to move upward from their working-class origins, Alec's marriage agenda was in part an Economic Calling. Especially when Janet became pregnant right away, Alec revved himself up to engage his provider role at full throttle.

> When I was younger I really didn't give a damn about much of anything. I drank, I raised ructions. I was probably on the road to ruin. When we had our son it became important for me to have a decent job. I felt more responsibility. I just felt that "Geez, Al, now you've done it, you've got a son. Now you've really got to buckle down and do a decent job."

Unfortunately, Alec has sometimes fallen into the tendencies of a workaholic, and because so much of his private drama often focusses on his job, his inner self is sometimes cluttered with all his responsibilities. As mentioned, he does his best to open up this part of himself to Janet, but there are times when he is so muddled up with these third-corner concerns that he finds it too difficult to make the transition back to his partnership-corner. Then the marital connection suffers, as summarized rather neatly by Janet:

> When he's uptight, I tend to be uptight. Sometimes he doesn't express himself as to why he's feeling the way he is. In fact, I don't even know if *he* knows why he is. A lot of times of stress are not marriage-related, but it is reflected into the marriage, because he won't tell me what's bothering him. He's got it all inside him—like trying to get this guy to work better with that guy. If he'd spit it out, I don't mind listening to it. But I don't know what it is that's in there. And I don't know if he knows that he's being so introverted at times.

Janet herself may likewise create some obstacles to a fuller marital connection. With such a negative marital paradigm modeled by her parents, and an unsatisfactory relationship with both of these critical people, she has few

198 • *Three Corners*

reliable images to help her translate feelings of closeness and warmth for Alec into actual expressions. In her parents' home,

> Sex was not talked about; it was a dirty word. We didn't see affection in the family. I didn't know how to accept it. I didn't know how to give it. And I think this has probably been one of the hardest things for Alec to put up with, to get me through this whole learning to be affectionate, subduing my thoughts and fears, and just going ahead.

For Janet, the area of emotional expression is still a growing edge. She knows several friends who have benefited from a weekend Marriage Encounter, and she would like to go to one herself. Says Janet, "Communication, that's the one thing they stress. It's probably a weak spot as far as I'm concerned, and maybe even Alec. Sometimes I don't express how I feel and maybe I should. I think there's times when I should be more demonstrative, and I'm not." Like Alec, Janet's inner impulses cannot always flow easily into her partnership-corner, even though she would like them to. When an inner self contains fears, ambivalence, and self-doubts, it may not always be easy to rise up out of one's own interiority to playfully meet someone else. At such times the richness of the marital connection falters.

Notes

1. To compare the Millers' approach to familism, see pp. 150–155.
2. Ibid.
3. This aspect of Janet's personal history is presented in pp. 78–80.

11
Loose Connection

If marriage is like a dance, marital separateness is an arrangement requiring two different choreographies: both dancers may have complex and exciting routines, but they rarely if ever dance together and they attend little to each other's music and movements. Likewise, the approaches to marital connection described within part III are dance-like arrangements. However, each of these connected dances requires just a single choreography; the dancers may at times move in their own spaces, but they remain carefully synchronized with each other, and their individual orbits bring them together at regular intervals.

Couple-centered partners do their most intricate dancing closely intertwined, remaining within reach as much as they can. Family-centered partners often pull apart to include their children; the whole family moves together, although the twosome periodically dances alone to practice its own routines. Partners with a balanced connection like the Hills have more expansive routines and require more space. They may often step to their own respective music, but unlike separate couples they remain closely attuned to each other, and their repertoire includes an impressive array of joint routines. They seem equally adept whether dancing alone, together, or in the company of others.

The last dance to be considered here may be called *loose connection*. Both partners require an enormous amount of separate space. Because they lean toward their separate third-corners, their own connection may look rather thin, especially when compared to couple-centered partners. Nevertheless, they continue to enjoy dancing together at whatever brief intervals they reconnect, and they can do so with a flair and flourish that quickly distinguishes them from separate dancers who lack or have lost the art of moving together. In triangle terms, each of their inner-corners stands closer to some cherished third-corner than to anything else; yet, the pathway from each spouse's inner-corner to the partnership-corner remains open and unobstructed, and both choose to travel it periodically. Figure 9 provides a graphic illustration.

In my data, two-career couples are the most common representatives of loose connection, although many career-centered couples drift into a thor-

200 • *Three Corners*

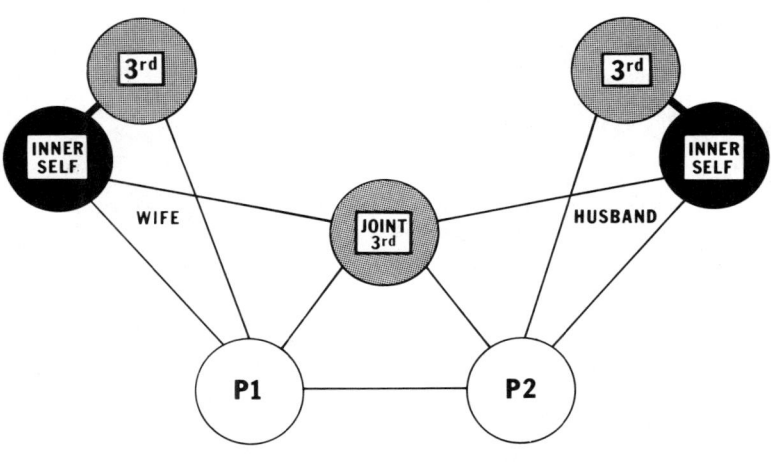

Figure 9. Loose Connection

oughgoing separateness. In certain respects, loosely connected partners both wind up adopting the traditional middle-class male devotion to career. Both are eager to distinguish themselves in some separate sphere of activity, even if that means the couple relationship will frequently be put on hold. Both tend to see partnership as a Safe Haven for career achievement, a marriage agenda described in chapter 3. Men often structure their priorities in this fashion, but because women more typically put their relational needs first, their readiness to reverse these priorities in loose connection deserves comment. Essentially, the answer lies in their familiar paradigm, as we shall see in the two cases that provide us concrete reference.

The Jordans

Gail Jordan is one woman whose childhood home was spared any example of a wife subordinating her own endeavors to a husband's. Gail's mother was widowed when Gail was just one, and she never remarried. She maintained the traditional breadwinner role, while Gail's strongwilled paternal grandmother lived with them and maintained the domestic front. Gail's familiar paradigm thus contained more concrete imagery of adult females functioning without a partnership bond, both outside and inside the home. A powerhouse of energy, Gail entered marriage as an inveterate doer. She had five children over fifteen years and has always been the more active parent. She has usually surrounded herself with a barnyard full of animals whose care is hers. She has somehow found the time to get herself an M.A. and recently a Ph.D., and she has held challenging and absorbing full-time positions whenever possible. With all of these demanding third-corners, it is not surprising

that her partnership-corner has rarely provided Gail's most consuming angle of vision. "My concerns about being married had to do with how free I'd be, whether I'd have someone who'd tell me what I could and couldn't do." Throughout her interview, Gail provided a detailed chronicle of her considerable individual achievements, which at one point included coaching a college sports team to a national championship competition.

As mentioned,[1] Brian Jordan's mother had been both subordinate and subservient to his father, a situation which created a heated paradigm conflict between Brian and Gail early in their marriage. The conflict predictably focussed on the limits of a wife's freedom. Through the years it has largely resolved itself in Gail's favor, partly because Brian's ideological commitments favored female equality in principle, and perhaps also because Brian's own issues with his father made it easier to renounce his father's lording approach to marriage. With nineteen years of marriage behind them, Brian is now convinced that Gail's independence redounds to his own advantage.

> At times I feel it would be nice if she were like my slave, at my beck and call, but really it would be very destructive to both of us. It's just a childlike wish, to have someone wait on me, but in reality I wouldn't want her to be that way. If she just stayed around and cleaned the house, I wouldn't be excited by her or happy with her. I've seen her at times when she didn't have anything outside the home, and she was nothing like the same person she is today. She runs herself into the ground, and I wish she'd slow down a little. But I'd never ask her to quit her job, because she wouldn't be the same person I find so attractive and stimulating.

Both Brian and Gail seem to lean more toward their professional third-corners than toward their own partnership. Brian told me that his work is his greatest satisfaction in life: "I really haven't put as much time in on the family as I have on the job. Learning to temper my life and take more time off for recreation is something I'd like to do better. But I get such a charge out of my work. I never find it boring." Gail has become no less career-oriented. When Brian entered a Ph.D. program in clinical psychology and became deeply immersed in his program, it was not because she had less of his attention that Gail felt uneasy:

> I was jealous of his having the opportunity and my not having the opportunity. The only thing that I could say to myself was, "This too shall pass and you're going to have your turn next." We'd agreed on that. And so that was okay. I could live with it because my chance would come. And I was happy for him because he was happy.

Gail did get her turn before long, earned her Ph.D., and soon became the top administrator for a federally funded program, just after Brian himself

202 • *Three Corners*

had gotten established in a career tailored to his own Ph.D. Once again, Gail's and Brian's occupational third-corners were in symmetry, only at a much higher level of responsibility and involvement than ever before. Recently, it has appeared to Brian that Gail's professional third-corner is sometimes even stronger than his own, which causes him some resentment, especially when he finds himself in the more traditionally female position of arriving home first and then waiting for her to return.

> Part of it is my own doing that I've become so intensively involved in my own program. Gail has modeled herself after that. She's always been achievement-oriented, but it seems even more of her time goes into her job now than ever before. She has had a lot of pressures of meetings, flying to different places, meeting regularly with a representative from Washington. This is all new for her, and I'm hoping that as she gets used to it, she'll be less absorbed in her work than she's been. The last two years as program director have given her a feeling of meaningfulness in her working day. And I've been working on a new program and there are a lot of demands on my time too. So we both find ourselves exhausted at the end of the day and have relatively little time for one another. We were having lunch together, but then she started having meetings over the noon hour. About two months ago it was worse, when we were both angry and frustrated about how things were going.

Whereas in family-centered connection all independent third-corners get subordinated to joint activities with the children, in loose connection these priorities may get reversed, and the children will often have to adapt theselves to their parents' outside pursuits. Gail provided an example and then summarized the needs and strains of a two-career couple:

> Trina was going to fly-up in Girl Scouts—no big deal, but to a child, it's important. And it just happened both Brian and I were going to be out of town, and I didn't think the boys would be too fond of going to a Girl Scout fly-up. And Trina was very understanding. She said, "It's okay, Ma, it's not that important." I just mentioned it to the boys, that I thought that it probably was important, and they could do what they wanted to. And when I called up that night, which I did whenever I was away—I'd check in—they were all delighted because the boys had cooked a pot luck dinner and gone down with Trina to her fly-up. They really did come through most of the time; in fact, I think they perhaps were more responsible when I wasn't there than when I was around.
>
> You need support from the entire family, both husband and kids. Like, my kids do all their own wash. They know that that's their responsibility. You really need, I think, to have the support of the kids. And I think you need the support of each other, and I think that there are crisis times that will happen no matter how organized you are, when he's got to go, and I've got to go, and he's under the gun, and so am I.

At this point the reader may be wondering where any connection is in this marriage, loose or otherwise. To be sure, loosely connected couples may periodically endure times of separateness, but the fact is that their partnership-corners remain highly valued, not just in principle but through a history of real and enjoyable interaction. If their respective third-corner leanings give them a certain freedom from each other, the arrangement also offers the possibility of an easier freedom *with* each other. Both Brian and Gail speak of the vibrant sexuality that has remained intrinsic to their marriage from the beginning. Says Brian, "I still love her as intensely as I did at first. I've found her intriguing, fascinating, stimulating. She's a dynamo of energy. She's very genuine and caring. I'd have a hard time envisioning life without her." Gail obviously reciprocates these feelings, pointing to their capacity to renew their connection at those times when it has grown too thin:

> We used to do a lot of recreating, but not in the four or five years we've been in Maine, until this summer. Then it got to a point where I was saying, "Brian, what about us? What about the kids? What about some time alone without the damned university and the job?" And so he just put a note on his door, "I'm not available all summer due to my family's request." And we took four weeks. We knew we had to do that because we were getting to a point of losing some kind of communication, and also we really needed that rest and relaxation. When you see the danger, you do something.

In many respects, loosely-connected couples such as Brian and Gail Jordan are like colleagues to each other. They offer respect, admiration, and esteem in abundance, and when their careers are similar or at least understandable to each other, they often provide invaluable feedback and advice; they become each other's most reliable sounding boards for trying out solutions to career challenges. At different times, either Brian or Gail has stepped up involvement at home in order to allow the other the chance to devote more time and energy to a Ph.D. program. They offered commentary on each other's research designs, and later found ways to involve each other in their ongoing work. They continue to cheer each other on for any and all of their accomplishments.

With all this support it has been easier for them to modify their respective inner-corners to accommodate the full extent of the other's third-corner devotion and independence. For Brian, whose inner-corner was originally laden with impressions of wives existing to serve their husbands, it has become possible to transform that corner by internalizing some new ideas about partnership and what it can be: "I think the major thing Gail has taught me is what it's like to be a woman and feel affection and caring and still have aspirations and desires to achieve and grow. I never thought of my mother as an object, but I thought of other women as objects, and Gail has helped me recognize that women have the same needs as men."

204 • *Three Corners*

The Kings

Another example of a loosely connected couple is the twenty-seven-year marriage of Cynthia and Scott King. Like Gail Jordan, Cynthia has always favored her independent third-corners and has been happy with her marriage, despite how lean and thin it sometimes is. She told me:

> I think probably my work at school is my highest priority right now. And then Scott, and then the kids. It used to be the kids, then school, then Scott. [The children are grown up, and one has already moved out.] We do have very separate lives. I don't depend on Scott for my joy and my purpose in life, and he doesn't on me. I don't know how a housewife can just stay at home and everything's wrapped up in her husband coming home at night and what he says about his job and all this stuff. When I get home I don't want somebody to talk to me all night long, and I don't think he does either. At school I'm answering a thousand questions all day! When you're continually talking to people you need freedom. And so we have our winding down together, but then I want to be left alone some, as he must too.

Again like Gail Jordan, Cynthia's independent stance toward marriage, her apparent freedom from emotional hunger vis-à-vis her partner, and her comfort in making her career primary all have roots in her familiar paradigm and the attendant structuring of her inner-corner. Cynthia's mother taught her to cultivate her own independence:

> When I wanted to get married, my mother was sure I'd get pregnant and never finish college. College was very important to her since she wasn't able to go. All three of us kids have master's degrees. She's a great lady. She didn't give us a hard time about getting married; she just tried to make us realize. She never worked until I went to college, and then she just got a job as a cashier in a department store because she didn't have any training. She's a very smart, capable woman who never did anything with her abilities because during that time you just didn't. I think she wanted us to have an education so we wouldn't have to depend on someone.

From Cynthia's description, we can easily sense the frustration that her mother must have felt in her own life. Cynthia feels that her mother dominated her father. He never argued, but "He always had a bottle of whiskey in the bedroom closet." My hunch is that this strong-willed woman's economic dependency became an intolerable burden to her, and she passed on to her daughters a feeling that husbands are plagued by inherent weaknesses and that wives should therefore construct married lives in which they can carve out their major satisfactions independently. Closely identified with her mother, Cynthia learned her lesson well, and she adopted a Hedged Bet agenda for marriage: first education and then career are the hedges that best protect a woman from

the inevitable disappointments that arise from depending exclusively on a husband. If everything proceeds as planned, marriage can then be a Safe Haven from which third-corner creative endeavors can be launched.

When Scott went off by himself to enter a Ph.D. program in the fifth year of their marriage, Cynthia seemed to blossom in a situation that many wives would have found insufferable. "That was the year I got independent. Even though I was pregnant and had a two-year-old, I was still teaching and sending Scott spending money." To manage all this, Cynthia eventually moved to the community where she was teaching, taking her first child with her while her mother tended the newborn. Cynthia would come home on weekends to be with the baby. She still prides herself on the fact that she never missed a day of teaching.

> That made a big change in our marriage. I guess I realized that I could be on my own and make it. That's the thing with women. If they get a job and can make it on their own, they're fine. But people didn't used to do that. As long as I was in school, my folks were still paying for us. This was the first chance I had to find out, "My God, I can make it on my own." It was thrilling! It made me more of an individual, and not just Scott's wife, or my mother's daughter, or my father's daughter.

The next year Cynthia and the children joined Scott in New Jersey. After a year there they moved to Ohio where Scott got his first college teaching job. In the five years in Ohio, Cynthia worked mornings running a nursery school. "I didn't try to teach in public school because the kids were little and I felt I should be home with them most of the time." Unlike the family-centered couples described earlier, the basis of the Kings' connection had little to do with the children, who essentially remained Cynthia's independent third-corner through the years. And although outdoor recreational sports had always been one of Cynthia's particular distinctions, her marriage changed this:

> Scott doesn't even swim. After I met Scott, I didn't do things like that anymore either. But after the kids came along, I was the one who'd go skiing and do those other things with them. Scott and I have never had that life together at all. You think of the father as taking the kids to the ball game and stuff. I was the one who played badminton with them and everything else, and Scott didn't. He'd be in there reading a book.

Scott would have no disagreement with Cynthia's analysis:

> She's been a better mother than I've been a father. I remove myself from that role sometimes. She does it very well. What I tend to do is nonpaternal things: that is, I can do the laundry, clean up, cook, go to the grocery store, watch

206 • *Three Corners*

the children as long as it doesn't take active participation on my part. That's basically the role that I always have played. She got to be much more involved with them personally and with their lives.

As with the children, so it is with religion. Church became one of Cynthia's independent third-corners, while Scott remained indifferent and even hostile to religion. In Ohio the Kings worked out a creative arrangement that enabled each of them to go their separate ways concerning religion with a minimum of conflict. Here is Cynthia's account:

> I would take the kids to church and to Sunday School and drop him off at the laundromat, and he would stay there and read the *New York Times* and do the wash, and then I would pick him up after church. I think he volunteered, because he was just sitting home reading and I didn't have time to go to the laundromat. He just figured he might as well sit there and read because he certainly wasn't going to church with me! The things that he has assumed like that [his not going to church], there hasn't been like a big argument.

Despite an undercurrent of resentment about Scott's avoidance of active parenting, religion, and sports, plus many other areas of fundamental difference and separateness that at times have been exasperating to Cynthia, she has rarely lost her equanimity. Remember the basic structure of Cynthia's inner-corner: she was primed to expect that a husband will be saddled with numerous weaknesses and incompetencies, and she was prepared to defend herself against them not by clamoring that he change but rather by developing competencies independently of him. Her hedge against marriage is her independence, so she not only refrains from complaining but she prides herself on her good restraint: "I've let him alone and let him do his thing, and taken care of the everyday, mundane things of life. I don't want to be a nagger. That's another good thing about me—I don't drive him nuts that way."

What, then, does Cynthia get out of the deal? Where is the loose connection that marks this marriage as something decisively different from separateness? The answer lies in Scott's distinctive gifts and his eagerness to share them—in what he actually does, irrespective of all the things he doesn't do. "I was looking for a marriage that would have a high, continuous intellectual quality," Scott tells me. Along with his own finely honed intellectual brightness, Scott came to marriage with an adventurous, cosmopolitan spirit, one that has flowed vigorously into his intellectual productions, his teaching, his political activities, his social conscience, and his travel. When Cynthia says of Scott, "He grew me up," she means that he always wanted to pull her into this expanded vision of life that he had. "A lot of the things I do now I wouldn't have done if I hadn't married Scott. He's just opened up so many worlds to me, so life isn't a big bore."

Loose Connection • 207

When Cynthia first met Scott in college, he was different from most of the people she had known.

> He'd been a lot of places. He'd been in the navy four years, all over the world. He opened up an entirely new world. Books, for instance: he read everything. We had a literature course together. He would suggest two or three books that I might like to read for the course; I never had anybody do that. He would explain a lot of it. We took another course together where we had to read the *New York Times Magazine*, and he'd explain it to me. We used to go out to eat. I'd never had anyone invite me out to restaurants.

After Cynthia began teaching and Scott was in a master's program, he would often talk to her about the politics of her school. This was before the year when she was alone and "got her independence," and Scott still felt "protective" of her at that time. He describes the "analysis" they both do about their job situations, how he first exposed her to this kind of intellectual process, and how she then developed the knack on her own:

> We still do a lot of talking about our job relationships and the personnel relationships in our jobs. Her relationship with her boss, the committees she's on—it's an analysis. I do the same thing. We bring that home. When that started I was doing an analysis in an effort to understand her own situation. I don't need to do that now; she's very clever at those things. But we continue to do it. Now I'm much less protective. We're probably both able to provide a deeper analysis for the other than we could originally. We're much more equal than we were when we were first married.

Cynthia likewise speaks about how she involves herself in the politics of her school and shares this perspective with Scott: "I don't mean just politics—we're both into that too—but we're both into unionism, in the workings of what we're doing. I'm on the executive board of the union; I'm in umpteen committees in the school department because I want a say in my destiny. Scott is also very much into things like that and we talk about them. We're both doers."

Even in the Ohio period, when the children were still young and Cynthia was giving them the lion's share of her attention, she and Scott seemed to share an active social and political conscience together. Says Scott:

> This was the period '60 to '65. We were active in trying to desegregate some of the theaters, and we were active in the beginnings, really, of the nonviolence movement. Norman Thomas came to the house and stayed overnight. A lot of picket lines to be on. And we always went on them together. I'm more radical than she is on domestic politics; we argue sometimes about that. We certainly shared the black revolution's goals completely. We were McGovern people, and McCarthy people before that in '68.

208 • *Three Corners*

Above all else, the Kings are trusted and respected colleagues to each other, much like the Jordans. Their respective third-corner professional interests flow openly and effortlessly into their partnership-corners, and in this principal territory their connection with each other is vital, active, and real. I asked Scott how he's changed as a result of living with Cynthia over the years.

She's helped me develop my ethical sense. She's made me a better teacher, and I don't mean that in any trivial way. She really has liberated me to be as good a teacher as I can be. She's been extremely significant in providing the kind of liberation from other people's feelings, other people's thoughts, other people's attitudes. When my instinct was to do something, her position has always been, "Yes, go ahead and do it." She has been particularly good in refining my political thought. She makes quite clear that she's in the position, she thinks, of being more realistic than I am.

This has been good for me, because it's forced me to rethink my stuff. And she's been tremendously supportive of me in terms of getting my research done and not being involved in the trivial committee work which one can hide oneself in. She's always very careful to tell me, "Why do you do that? You've got other important things to do."

I take her advice a great many times, especially in situations when it's time for me to move on to something new and leave something I've been doing in someone else's hands. I think I've had the same kind of liberating impact on her. That's one of the reasons I think our marriage has worked so well. I have tried to always be extremely supportive of her, whatever she wanted to do—encourage her to do up to her capacity. I want her to be as fulfilled as it's possible to be. I think she should have been president of the union, and she could have, but she said no. But I was pushing her. One of my roles is to make sure that she does live up to her potential. She feels the same way about me.

To be sure, whatever "liberating impact" Scott had on Cynthia did not liberate her from most of the child-care and other domestic responsibilities when they were younger. Couples whose connection revolves primarily around each other's careers are likely to feel the greatest disturbance at the phase of the family life-cycle when the children are still dependent. "When the kids were home, they were very much my life," Cynthia tells me, adding that Scott was sometimes resentful of this, and he was never really willing to share his time with them:

I'd say, "Children, stop fighting," and I'm talking to Scott and the kids. One would try to come and tell me his side, and then the other. This bothers me. I can understand the kids doing it, but I could never understand Scott doing it. As an adult, why does he have to come to Mama to have me hear his side of it? [She laughs.] But it's better now. And his daughter loves him to death and needs his approval. And he gives it, but he doesn't give enough. She's really into politics, and so is he, and she's always trying to get his approbation.

Fortunately for the Kings, Scott is endowed with many endearing graces. He is fundamentally kindhearted, amiable, filled with good will, and always eager to accommodate Cynthia in any way she needs. For example, after several years back in Maine with the children growing older, Cynthia was teaching full-time and she was arbitrarily denied another position she was seeking. She brought suit against this potential employer on the grounds of sex discrimination around the same time she was feeling that all her domestic responsibilities were beginning to hamper her doing other things. Scott's account, confirmed by Cynthia, shows how he rose to the occasion:

> Winning that suit was very good for her—establishing in a small way that women should be accepted on an equal basis with men. But I think it was also very good for our marriage. What it meant for me was that I really did have to face the question: "Are you all mouth, or are you ever going to do what you say you do?" . . . Around that time I had a leave, so I was home writing another book. What I did was to take over what I had been doing part-time. Before that I had cooked a lot of the meals. I like to cook, and when I cook I do the dishes and plan the menu. During that leave period I began to take it over on a pretty formal basis. Now I do 90 percent of the cooking. That aspect of the house is mine. My teaching load at the university is much less than hers is at high school, so I just did it to relieve her of work in the same ways she's relieved me earlier.

In short, Scott wants Cynthia to be able to excel in her professional third-corner the same way he does in his own. He says, "I think both of us recognize that if you're going to be good at your profession you really have to take advantage of every opportunity." And Scott's inclinations are compatible with a lot of marital connection, because he remains open enough in his partnership-corner to want to participate in Cynthia's career successes and share them with her. Cynthia has always, therefore, felt highly valued in her marriage, and Scott has never wanted to exclude her from his own third-corner adventures. She summarizes:

> He's a lot of fun. He's an interesting person. Life is never boring. I've met a lot of interesting people. We've been to a lot of different places. We've been to Europe twice, and I wouldn't have done that if I hadn't been with Scott. He knows about everything. He's fun to travel with; he knows what to see. He reads about where we're going and remembers everything. The kids had a game of trying to stump father. They think of him as the walking encyclopedia.
>
> He's always encouraging me, pushing me on to do other things. He's trying to push me into something now that I'm not interested in—I can't remember what. He treats me like a student—he's always pushing his students to go on to bigger and better things. I don't mean I feel completely pushed; he just suggests it. He influences me in all the things I do, I suppose—

210 • *Three Corners*

I mean, getting involved in stuff, although they've been my own things. But he's always encouraged me to do everything that I do. Very, very supportive. And he thinks I'm great. He just wants me to continually grow. Now I'm trying to cut down on things, because I'm so busy. . . . I really feel very lucky. And he feels the same way. We really hit it off very well. We've had very few problems, and yet, a fascinating life.

Asymmetry in Marital Connection

The foregoing exploration of marital connection in chapters 8, 9, 10, and 11 has had to gloss over some of the complexities, for the sake of analytical clarity. Specifically, each of the four subtypes has been depicted as a perfectly symmetrical arrangement in which the wife and husband structure their respective triangles in exactly the same way. Empirical reality, however, is rarely this neatly packaged. In loose connection, which we have just considered, typically the husband's inner-corner leans even closer to his independent third-corners than the wife's does to hers. She will strain more to balance her outside third-corners with both her partnership-corner and her parenting third-corner. Cynthia King and Gail Jordan both have almost always remained more deeply involved in parenting than their husbands have, even at those times when these women's career demands have become enormous. And both Scott King and Brian Jordan have generally remained more single-minded in their career leanings for longer periods of time than have their wives.

Similarly, in couple-centered connection it would be unlikely to find both partners' inner selves leaning in the same degree, so to speak, toward their partnership-corners. One partner is typically a little more dependent than the other on the couple bond, with this disparity introducing a bit of asymmetry into the relationship. In family-centered connection, illustrated through the marriage of Jack and Sandy Turner, home-centered familism may be the highest priority for both spouses, but in my data the wife leans her inner-corner even closer to child-centered interests than the husband does. Finally, in balanced connection it rarely happens that both spouses will maintain the identical degree of balance between their partnership-corners, their independent third-corners, and their joint third-corner activity. Often the allure of one or another corner will become especially captivating for at least one of the spouses for a period of time, so here again, a bit of an asymmetry may creep into the partnership.

The reader should notice the legacy of patriarchy lurking within many of these examples. Remember that patriarchy is a culture in which women are responsible for child-care and for upholding the partnership bond so that men can be free to create the "outside world" in public third-corners. The asymmetries just noted are all instances in which husbands—middle-class husbands—have more leeway to pick and choose among their three-corner

leanings than do wives. Husbands have the free choice to relax some of their career devotion and become more family-centered or couple-centered, but in loose connection they also have the freedom to give career a higher priority. In either case, wives are still charged with the lion's share of child-care and other domestic service, so their own three-cornered arrangements reflect a diminished opportunity for the utter flexibility that their husbands have.

To be sure, asymmetry in marital connection is not evil. It lends some dynamic tensions to relationships that might otherwise grow placid and complacent. The point here is that in a world of male and female equity, females would claim as much freedom as males to structure their triangle any way they wish, and then they could just as easily initiate asymmetrical triangling moves as males. Who gets left with any or all of the domestic service would be once more up for grabs, and the results could be very interesting.

Note

1. For some details, see p. 44.

12
Connection Undone

Each of the four subtypes of marital connection provides some inner-corner autonomy as well as a strong bond for both partners. The differences depend on the chosen leaning of the partners' inner-corners, whether they lean toward a joint third-corner, their own partnership-corner, their separate third-corners, or remain balanced among all three corners. Whatever the subtype, connection is not an all-or-none phenomenon; it may become mixed with some separateness, or with some tendencies toward dependency on the part of one spouse and distancing on the part of the other. A lot depends on the particular phase of the family life-cycle that a couple is going through. If and when children come, partners who previously enjoyed a real connection may lose it, unless both can reshape their respective triangles to include their children as a new, joint third-corner. To show these difficult dynamics at work, this chapter will follow a case of connection undone.

The Sampsons

For Kelly Sampson, marriage to Don did not at first change her life-style. As she puts it, "There was just no big jump from one pot to another. Everything we did was still just our own interests. We enjoyed what we did together." Those interests included joint friendships and the sports-oriented activities that had marked their three-year courtship in college. By their own design, their first child arrived during their fifth year of marriage. Kelly speaks of a "new era" beginning at that point. Before then, she and Don had maintained physical education positions at different high schools. To Kelly, this two-career couple arrangement was ideal, as it enabled her to avoid her mother's pattern of marital subservience, the one unwanted element from her familiar paradigm:[1]

> Even though we were working in different school systems, we both knew who the other was involved with. We socialized with both sides; my side was never left out. . . . Both of us being involved in coaching, many times we didn't get to

214 • *Three Corners*

meet one another until about eight at night. We didn't leave our work behind when we came home, either; it was a central and common interest. Without it we'd probably have sat there and gone "Duh" at one another.

Once the baby came, the pattern of third-corner symmetry combined with strong partnership-corners began to break down. Kelly quit her job and did not resume working until just after a second child was born, more than three years later. In that three-year interval Kelly and Don drifted into a pattern of increasing separateness with elements of dependency on Kelly's side and distancing on Don's. At home alone with a child by her own choice, Kelly gave up all her other third-corners, while Don did not seem inclined to actively reshape his triangle to make room for the child as a new third-corner. It is hard to say which partner is responsible for this kind of undoing of marital connection, as both seem to undo it together. Says Kelly, "I think I expected more responsibility and help from him with our child. He was busy with his job and coaching." It would appear from this statement that Don initiated some fateful distancing, but there are indications that Kelly also distanced from her partnership-corner to fuse herself with her baby:

> I lost my own sense of identity, but also in our relationship I lost a lot of attention for Don. And part of the way I was drove him away. When he wanted to do something socially, I might have said, "No, you have to be with your kids." And he does like to socialize a lot, and I think during that era I pushed myself in a hole even farther by saying I couldn't get babysitters.

The crux of the matter was not simply that Don distanced from child-oriented activities with Kelly, but that those activities were not enough to satisfy Kelly either, with or without Don's involvement, despite the fact that she was doing what she thought she should by abandoning all her other third-corners. In desperation, Kelly became more and more dependent on Don's coaching career to keep alive the alienated professional part of her inner self:

> I was involved with my child a lot more than I was with him, but I became interested in what he was doing even more, because I had to depend on that. I was totally going in his direction, and I had no outlet. No intelligent adult conversation, baby talk in the kitchen all day long, that type of thing. I'd trip off to football games; it was the only way I could feel involved, and if I wanted to be with him I had to be involved with his program, but yet I could feel myself lacking my own life and slipping further away from being me. And I think maybe that might go back to my mother. I knew I didn't want to be that way. I didn't want to sit home and lose touch with social relationships and being able to talk professionally. . . .
>
> I think that during that time I didn't realize that I wanted to go back to work either, that that was what was wrong with me. Now I can look back and know that I needed that, but I still couldn't say that at that time I would

have gone back to work; I wanted to be home with them anyway. And I still have that feeling too, reservations when I do go out, guilt feelings I guess.

It is clear that the coming of children made a much bigger impact on Kelly's triangle than on Don's. He still had his professional third-corner, plus a continuing flow of exchange from there into his partnership-corner, especially since Kelly had become so identified with his career. Don's account to me is therefore very different from Kelly's. The main thing he stresses was the drastic decline in their sex life for a period after their second child was born. He mentions nothing about the three years prior to that, the time of greatest difficulty for Kelly, because his own life was not all that different in that period, and Kelly tended to keep her frustrations to herself, uncertain about what they were and why they were there.

In contrast, Kelly's triangle went through a radical upheaval. Like Don, she started marriage with her inner-corner already leaning toward her professional third-corner, and a loose but real connection bloomed in their marriage because both remained eager to tell each other the daily news of their third-corner adventures. Each of their partnership-corners therefore had a reliable source of vitality. When children came, they became Kelly's separate third-corner, as Don was not inclined to triangulate much in their direction. Now Kelly had nothing to bring into her partnership-corner that was valuable to either Don or herself. Remember that the inner-corner is the master organizer and choreographer, the assigner of valuation. Both Kelly and Don certainly valued their children, but both endowed their professional lives with a far more glorified status. Thus Kelly's suspending her career was tantamount to suspending her self, as she no longer held the master key to her own validation. Small wonder that Kelly felt increasingly dependent on Don and his career, and more and more empty within her inner-corner:

I became lost as a mother and housewife, and jealous of his still being able to go out to work and have his professional relationships. I didn't care as much about myself, either. After the first child I was extremely heavy and not pleased with myself—the way I looked or I guess the way I felt either. The only way I can describe it is the loss of identity.

Eventually, Don too came to learn about the turmoil that had been churning within Kelly's inner-corner:

We talked about it, and discovered that a lot of what had been going on had to do with her self-image. Even though staying home was her choice, it had lowered her self-esteem. She said to me, "How can I make love with you and feel good about it when I look in the mirror and can't feel good about myself?"

Simple though it may sound, all Kelly seemed to need was a renewal of her own professional third-corner, and everything quickly got back on track

216 • *Three Corners*

for her. Soon after her second child was born, she took a coaching position that at first required her time for just a few hours in the afternoon, at the same school where Don was working. Once again her third-corner came into symmetry with Don's, at least that professional third-corner that meant the most to both of them. Kelly describes the process to me in some detail:

> My personality had a chance to grow again, and I regained my own self-image and self-importance. I wasn't totally tied to the children. Don and I got back more on even ground. He didn't expect as much at home from me, and he began to realize that he had to share more duties. And I was a more pleasing person to be with because my attentions were not totally tied to the kids. We could again talk about his profession and my profession, and common coaching and common careers, instead of my talking about the kids and his talking about his professional position. When it came to coaching in the afternoon, we actually shared the same facility, same office. We would be able to converse and be with one another in the afternoon that way too. And he was interested in my kids, and I was interested in his kids—mutual again, the way it had been before. We always discussed our jobs at home. When I wasn't working we'd still talk about my ideas about his football team, but it wasn't two-way, it was never about something I was involved in.

Kelly's whole triangle had thus shifted again. She relaxed her dependency on Don and her fusion with the children, no longer being so reluctant to leave the latter with a babysitter. Her inner-corner once more being validated and at peace, she lost weight, presumably in the same measure that her professional confidence grew. She didn't need excess food because she had more of her self, and this meant that she could once again bring some vibrancy into her partnership-corner. Don, in turn, could no longer take for granted the primacy of only his own professional interests, and he was forced to take Kelly's schedule and her other needs more into account, thus focussing more attention on his partnership-corner. Connection seemed to return as effortlessly as it had come undone.

Summary of Part III

Let us now draw a few summary conclusions. We have explored four types of marital connection—balanced, couple-centered, family-centered, and loose—and we have just noted how the connecting links between any two corners of a person's triangle can come undone, with serious consequences for the partnership itself. All four types can be thought of as "intrinsic marriages";[2] there is no single formula for happy or successful marriage, just as there is no one life-pattern that will fulfill the inner urgings of every single self. Family-centered connection is probably the most predictable and homespun of partnerships,

the least given to upheavals and other surprises. Loose connection is more likely to stretch the spouses toward their own respective glories and strain their mutual patience, but if they keep alive the links between their separate and their joint worlds, the arrangement can inject considerable excitement, novelty, and unpredictability into their relationship. Balanced connection is probably the rarest form of connection, just because it is unusual to find spouses who are so even-minded that they can "sacralize" virtually everything in their sphere of life-commitments, including their partnership.[3]

The fact that connection can come undone and then get redone suggests that nothing is indubitably permanent in the field of partnerships. Connection can break down and shift into dependency-distancing or some form of separateness, as we have seen. Loosely connected couples especially run the risk of separateness, since they already lean toward their independent third-corners. Couples whose connection is family-centered may also fall into separateness once their children grow up and leave, insofar as the lines between their respective inner-corners and their partnership-corners are too thin.

In general, couples who do forge some connection in their marriage may find that they shift their leanings from one subtype to another as they go through the family life-cycle. Couple-centered connection is more likely to be prominent early in a marriage, when the frontiers of mutual discovery are still unsettled. If and when children arrive, family-centered connection may then emerge, particularly when the children are old enough to enjoy family outings and too young to find their parents boring. Still later, when job commitments are typically at their peak and children are more involved with their own peers, couples may shift into a looser connection, especially if both spouses have rich, third-corner spaces to capture their respective attention. And finally, active grandparenting can promote a return to family-centered connection, or job retirement may be accompanied by a reappearance of the couple-centered variant.

None of these developments is inevitable, and there is no law specifying that any form of connection will ever appear in a given marriage. A lot depends on the familiar paradigms that converge together in a twosome. A lot depends, too, on the particular processes of exchange that mark a couple's interaction. In part IV we shall consider some of these processes.

Notes

1. For some of Kelly's background, see pp. 45–46.

2. The concept of "intrinsic marriage," a marriage in which the couple bond is deeply important to both spouses, was developed by John Cuber and Peggy Harroff, *Sex and the Significant Americans* (Baltimore: Penguin Books, 1966), pp. 132–145. Unfortunately, these authors seem to reduce intrinsic marriage to what I have called "couple-centered connection", and they must therefore overlook the strong components of vitality in other styles of partnership. See especially p. 144.

218 • *Three Corners*

3. Elsewhere, I describe the implications of forming a system of commitments in which everything one typically does becomes "sacralized." See Stephen R. Marks, "Culture, Human Energy, and Self-Actualization: A Sociological Offering to Humanistic Psychology," *Journal of Humanistic Psychology* 19 (1979):27–42.

Part IV
Processes of Marital Exchange

13
Marital Growth and Its Obstacles

In this chapter I shall be looking at types of marital exchange. How do partners deal with the various tendencies they encounter in one another, particularly with the materials they experience as obtruding their way into their partnership-corners without having been invited? I shall center on specific marital issues and the course they take from the time they arise.

The Appropriation Process

While people may choose to marry on the basis of what they already know and like about their partners, it is doubtful that any growth they proceed to make is on the basis of these already known enjoyments. Growth implies some departure from the known and the timeworn, the unfolding of some new capacity. Two developmental principles collaborate in this process. On one hand the growing self undergoes an internal reorganization or restructuring; on the other hand it becomes sensitized to some new aspect of its external environment, making possible some different and more complex ways of interacting with it.

In a marriage that includes some growth, these developmental principles are very much present. The new capacities that emerge may spring from within the person's own inner-corner urgings, or they may arise through the concerted promptings of the other partner. Regardless, a growing partner is one who has reorganized his or her triangle to allow for some novel, more flexible, or broader interchanges with the other partner.

I shall use the term *to appropriate* (literally, to make something one's own) to summarize this expansion of one's partnership-corner to handle some previously alien aspect of the spouse. We have already seen this process at work among some of the couples in this study. Alec Murray does not simply approve of Janet's passion for horses; he appreciates and facilitates it by hauling hay, putting up fences, and going with her to club meetings, thus appropriating that horse-oriented part of Janet, making it a part of himself by actively

222 • Three Corners

interchanging with it. Similarly, Roger Hill does not simply tolerate Betty's active writing career and the travel away from him that it sometimes requires; he himself mingles enough with that side of her nature to actively support it. At one point he was the one who suggested that she make a several-month trip by herself when he saw that her writing project warranted it.

Examples such as these, however, are not the best ones, because the appropriations they depict were easy. Alec was well attuned to Janet's passion for horses from the very beginning, and as her interest continued to develop, he never struggled to accommodate to anything that seemed alien, unexpected, new, or unwanted. The same was true of Roger and his appropriation of Betty's writing career. The most impressive growth processes occur whenever the thing or quality appropriated feels so initially alien that a major internal reorganization is required to let it into oneself, as shown in the following example.

Carl and Elaine Leonard had been married for twenty years when I interviewed them. For half of those years, Elaine contented herself with homemaking and raising three children. When the last child was in school, Elaine got a part-time job. Says Carl:

> It made so much sense that you couldn't fight against it. I pushed her to look for work. She worked a few hours two or three days a week and was always home at noon when I came home for lunch, and in the afternoon when the kids came home. We'd always said the biggest job people can have is bringing up their kids, and that should take priority over anything else.

Carl speaks of the job of child-care in terms of "*people's* biggest job," but he really means that it is a wife's responsibility, for his daily schedule reveals an occupational third-corner that sharply limits his accessibility to his home and family: "I feel a lot of responsibility for the job. I sometimes have to spend up to four nights a week at work. I try not to leave after dinner before 7:30, and I get home by 10:30 or 11:00."

Plainly, Carl came to marriage with the traditional patriarchal expectation that a woman's place is in the home, thereby enabling a "family man" to vigorously make his way in the outside, public world. When Elaine stepped up her own occupational pursuits, Carl fell into an inner turmoil, despite the fact that it was still only a part-time job. He describes the impact:

> When her present position opened up I had a lot of adjustments to make. This is a five-day-a-week, more responsible job. It was like all of a sudden an official notice that my wife is now a working woman in the United States of America. Her first job started out as a temporary one. But now she was permanent. And she was enjoying it. There's a lot of benefit to all of us from her working, but I still didn't like it. Number one, I felt very threatened, because I viewed the man as breadwinner and head of the family. I still do. That's

his responsibility. Her working made me feel inadequate, as if I couldn't quite make it on my own and needed her help. So the worst thing was how it made me look in my own eyes. I didn't fear she'd become independent and leave. But it was a tough time. It affected everything I did.

Essentially, Carl's inner-corner was overburdened with insecurities about his masculine prowess as a provider. Elaine's working led him to feel less of a man, and though he did not much struggle outwardly with her about it, inwardly he could not at first accept that she had urgings that were utterly independent of him or of domestic service. Appropriating that part of Elaine first required a major overhaul of his inner-corner. He had to transform his familiar paradigm of what husbands and wives are supposed to be, so that who Elaine was becoming as a woman and wife would no longer threaten him at the core of his identity. Once this was accomplished, Carl likewise reorganized and expanded his partnership-corner so that he could actively exchange himself with these new energies that Elaine was developing, rather than merely watch them from a distance. Here, he describes his emerging acceptance and his realization that Elaine's growth redounds to his own benefit:

I realized there would be no turning back, that she had to have a professional life of her own. She had always talked about getting a master's degree some day. . . . Elaine will probably work from now on. I hope she does. It's worked out well. She has her own professional friends. There's Elaine, and then there's us, and then there's me. There's some overlap, but we have our separate professional lives. She now realizes where my time was going with my own work. Her intellectual capacity has been enlarged; she's more interesting to talk to. Mostly it's been positive. She's mentioned that she used to feel very narrow and depend on me to bring the outer world back home. Through the years she's often bugged me about not communicating enough. Now we use each other as sounding boards to talk about things that have happened during the day. In retrospect, I think I became a different person as a result of all this.

As Elaine developed an independent third-corner, her inner self grew more confident. She was able to bring new energy into her partnership-corner, and when Carl became willing to exchange with that energy, the lopsided power relationship that had previously governed the relationship began to equalize. Elaine tells me that she became more aggressive around the time she went to work. Carl describes the same development:

When I hold a view on something I tend to rant and rave. For a long time Elaine wouldn't verbally disagree with me. Now she'll openly disagree with me. This takes me aback at first, but it's good. Now we're better able to lay our cards on the table. I love to argue, so if she didn't, it would bring things to a halt. It's more equal now.

224 • *Three Corners*

In this way Carl has a basis for further reorganizing his triangle. Interacting with some qualities of Elaine's that were originally alien to him, he discovers that there is nothing to fear, not even Elaine's increasing power. Her third-corner independence increases the resources she brings to her partnership-corner, and Carl finds that it is to his advantage to meet this more resourceful Elaine head-to-head.

The Myth of the Perfect Companion

To some, it may seem ridiculous to suggest that Carl's acceptance of Elaine's part-time job is evidence of any growth on his part. A hard line of analysis could well ask, "Is it cause for celebration when the oppressor decides not to oppress?" The issue must revolve around how we define growth—whether we see it as the habitual life-pattern of some perfect species of humans, or simply as a choice that any person can make now and then when confronted with alien or unexpected tendencies in their partner. The literature often encourages a myth of the perfect companion, one who unrelentingly works on his or her relationship. "What is desirable is not that marriage partners have a 50–50-type relationship, but that each partner be willing to go 80 or 90 percent to cope effectively in a difficult situation," Nick Stinnett, James Walters, and Evelyn Kaye write in their recent textbook, *Relationships in Marriage and the Family*.[1] Borrowing from Carl Rogers, these authors add that the joy of marriage is "greatly enhanced when both spouses express positive regard for each other that is unconditional. . . . It means that the husband and wife show appreciation for each other *regardless of their particular behavior at the present moment. . . . Such positive regard does not depend on certain demands and expectations being met. It does not depend on the other person's performance.* The person is simply loved and valued as he or she is."[2] (emphasis added)

Few would quarrel with this unselfish stance toward partnership, but how many live it on more than an occasional basis? To hold up such saintly virtue as the essence of marital vitality is to cast the few who measure up as heroic and to write off the rest as defective. Cuber and Harroff's now classic concept of "vital marriage" promotes just such a heroic notion of intimacy. In a vital relationship, they write, "the presence of the mate is indispensable to the feelings of satisfaction which [any] activity provides. . . . An activity is flat and uninteresting if the spouse is not a part of it. Other valued things are readily sacrificed in order to enhance life within the vital relationship."[3] In other words, a vital spouse is one who lives much more for his or her partner than for anything else, a point Cuber and Harroff drive home with this quote from a male respondent: "I cheerfully passed up two good promotions because one of them would have required some travelling and the other would

Marital Growth and Its Obstacles • 225

have taken evening and weekend time. . . . The hours with [my wife] are what I live for."[4]

Carl Leonard is no such marital hero. He does work evenings and occasional weekends, as we have noted. He would probably not turn down a still more demanding career opportunity if it struck him as an enjoyable challenge. Cuber and Harroff would not, therefore, classify his partnership as a "vital" one, nor his marriage as "intrinsic," because they see marital vitality as an all-or-nothing, either-you-have-it-or-you-don't phenomenon. In contrast, I suggest that we see marital vitality as an episodic process instead of an ongoing state or a separate species of marriage. Abandoning the heroic conception of vitality, we are then free to recognize the less spectacular accommodations of one partner to another that are far more in keeping with the growth that average people actually make. In this way we can bring the matter of vitality back down to earth, where it most certainly belongs.

The Foreclosure Process

Not every accommodation can actually be called an appropriation, which implies that the accommodating partner winds up with more than she or he had before, a richer and more variegated reality vis-à-vis the spouse. In the name of acceptance, some spouses accede to their partner's presumed needs in such a way that they must shrink themselves in order to make the adjustment. This process may be called *foreclosure*—any accommodation to originally alien needs, demands, or tendencies in the other that results in a net loss of capacities for the accommodating partner. As in appropriation, foreclosing spouses must reorganize their entire triangle to enable the alien material to become part of themselves, but the outcome is a reduction rather than an expansion of their own opportunities for expression. Their capacity to make novel interchanges either with their partner or with the rest of their environment becomes narrowed instead of broadened. We shall study this process more closely.

Arthur Reed recalls a certain conversation with his wife Paulette during their five-year courtship: "I remember discussing the monetary role and how that was going to be handled. We decided it was my income that was going to take care of the home. That's what I saw as a child. I just preferred my role to be the one that was going to bring home the paycheck, and this was a situation she apparently was comfortable with." While Arthur went to school in the first year of their marriage, Paulette worked, supporting them both. Says Paulette:

> It bothered Arthur for me to be working and going to school. When we got through school and we discussed my continuing to work, he said, "Absolutely not. No wife of mine is going to be working. I'm going to be the breadwinner and that's it." It bothered me, because I really would have liked to have worked until I had children.

226 • *Three Corners*

In fact, once she quit her job, several years would pass before Paulette had children. In the meantime, her role seemed to be to serve her husband's needs:

> He wanted me home and a meal on the table when he came through the door, and he wanted everything in its place. And he was a very gregarious, very outgoing type person. He wanted to be out partying and with his friends. The first few years of marriage it was me trying to keep up with him. Of course, when I didn't have any children it was no problem. But I'm not the cocktaily type person. I enjoy them, but I don't like doing it night after night. I don't drink. I like more educational, broadening type experiences.

As Paulette's life increasingly felt devoid of any meaningful purpose, Arthur became more eager for her to have children: "Arthur wanted children in the worst way, and he thought this would solve my problem of my not having anything to do. He kept saying, 'What you need is children.'" Once children did arrive, Paulette found that Arthur was often resentful, because they took up so much of her time, and he expected Paulette to keep them quiet and unobtrusive, without himself having much to do with them.

While children of course gave Paulette more to do, the lack of any outside third-corner continued to bother her: "It just finally got to the point where I was tied down completely to the house, and I got very upset about it because I needed to get out." Compounding the problem further, for a long time Arthur was resistant to any child-care relief except from Paulette's mother or his own. Though Paulette finally got her way on this issue, she now looks forward to her children being in junior high school, when she wants to return to work part-time: "I'm hoping that Arthur has mellowed a little bit. His sister is now working full-time, and I think he has realized that at times both people have to work, and just staying home doesn't fit the need." Still, Paulette is prepared to foreclose on this need as she has on others in her thirteen married years: "If he was against it, I would try to convince him. If I couldn't, I wouldn't fight it."

We need to be clear about what, exactly, is being foreclosed here, especially since some other housewives I interviewed turned their daily lives into a series of creative projects that provided them continual stimulation. These women differed from Paulette in two important ways. First, their husbands were far more eager than Arthur for one-to-one companionship with their wives as well as for family-oriented activity. Second, these were women whose inner needs could be satisfied principally through domestic projects and activities.

Paulette forecloses in both respects. On one hand she accommodates to Arthur's apparent indifference to intimate companionship with her:

> He likes to be with the men; I've gotten to accept that. It was a hard adjustment for me because I like more of a companionship type thing. It bothers

me still, but I can take it, whereas before it hurt deeply and I felt more insecure from it. It's less of a struggle, because I understand him more.

On the other hand, Paulette also forecloses on her need for some third-corner independence, accommodating to that side of Arthur whose masculine security is premised upon her virtual domestic confinement. I asked her how, if at all, she thinks marriage has changed her:

> I think I am less independent. Before, I would do my own thing as I wanted to. Now I feel the responsibility of meeting my kids' needs and his needs. I cater to Arthur most of the time; it's made me less free, less independent. I think I'm more quiet, more serious. I think it's a bad change. Before, I was very involved with things and people and doing things, and it's hard for me not to be. I don't think I'm quite as outgoing as I was before.

Essentially, Paulette lacks the room to develop her creative capacities either in her partnership-corner or through independent third-corners. To be sure, any healthy relationship must involve some compromise, some subordinating of one's own inner needs and impulses for the sake of honoring the partner's. But Paulette's honoring of Arthur's needs and demands results in a narrowing rather than a broadening of her world. The crux of the matter is that some of our partner's needs may not deserve to be honored. How, then, can a person distinguish between accommodations that are healthy and those that are stifling, between appropriation and foreclosure?

The difference can only be found by scrutinizing the needs themselves—both our partner's and our own—to see what useful or creative purpose they serve. Needs that are rooted in fear, mistrust, self doubt, hostility, anger, insecurity, or feelings of powerlessness will often turn into the kind of demands that rigidly dictate what the other partner should or should not do. If Arthur fears that he will be less important or less of a man if Paulette brings home a paycheck, and his "need" is therefore for her not to work, Paulette's compliance in no way expands his own opportunities for self-expression, nor does it make his anxieties about himself go away. Arthur's fears belong to Arthur; they reside within his own inner-corner, not within Paulette's third-corner activity. When Paulette narrows down her activity at Arthur's request, she reinforces the illusion that she rather than Arthur is responsible for what Arthur fears. Surely there is no virtue in sparing one's partner the burden of facing the very demons that stand in the way of his further development, particularly when one's own personal growth is also sacrificed in the process.

But if fear and insecurity lead Arthur to make demands that do not deserve to be honored, fear and insecurity lead Paulette to honor them through her compliance. Some demons must surely lurk within her own inner-corner too, perhaps demons having to do with losing her father as a girl. He was the one person in her family to whom she felt really close. His death seemed to

228 • *Three Corners*

leave her devoid of any nurturing figures. Does she fear that to forsake Arthur's demand is to isolate her once more from the support she so dearly craves? Or perhaps her readiness to foreclose on her own creative expression dates back to messages she received from her mother, who believed so strongly that a woman's place is in the home that she tried to get Paulette's college advisor to switch her from business into a home economics major. In any case, while Arthur may look like the heavy in this drama, foreclosing partners are themselves responsible for their foreclosure, and we shall now see that there are alternatives for transacting with demands and urgings that simply weaken one's own life expression.

The Challenge Process

When one partner does not wish to accommodate to the other partner's need, there is always the option of challenging that need. In *challenge*, I withhold my accommodation to the alien material presented to me, insisting that my partner change his or her ways so that this alien material is no longer felt as a need or expressed as a tendency. When Paulette discussed continuing working after Arthur finished school, and Arthur insisted that "No wife of mine is going to be working," he effectively challenged an element of Paulette's world that appeared alien to him, and Paulette then reorganized her three corners so as to eliminate this element from her life expression. But the fact is that for Paulette, the need for some outside third-corner was central to the exercise of her creative capacities, and Arthur's need for her not to work was thus alien to her. Instead of complying with Arthur's challenge and thereby foreclosing on her own need, she might have responded with a counterchallenge, exhorting Arthur to give up this need that serves him no useful or creative purpose nor affects the exercise of his own essential capacities.

This is precisely what Millie Robinson did in a similar situation. Like Paulette Reed, Millie married a man whose familiar paradigm left him ill-equipped to accept a wife working. "You go back to your mother," Ron Robinson told me. "She was always home, you know. My mother never worked outside the house." Perhaps the difference is that unlike Arthur, Ron did not turn his need into a demand. Though Ron was "quite a lot resistant" to her working, according to Millie, he was not as resolute as Arthur about it. Millie did stop working for a while, knowing that it caused Ron some discomfort, but when she found that she felt depressed and incomplete, she challenged Ron's need simply by reasserting her own:

I love working. I like to be out with people. It's just a whole part of my life. So I discussed it with him and tried to explain my feelings: "I'm not happy being penned up in the house all day." And I don't know if I got through to him

that time, but anyway I went back to work part-time. I told him before we were married, "It is necessary for me to work." When you've had a good day on the job, you come home a different person. And I've tried to explain to him so many times that it doesn't mean I love him any less because I need this, but it's just a part of me too.

Millie was clear enough about the requirements of her own inner-corner to know the limits of her flexibility. She could not give in to Ron's discomfort without surrendering too large a piece of the self that was most dear to both Ron and herself: "If I stayed home, in a matter of time I just wouldn't have the same outlook on life, and I don't think I would be as enjoyable a person to be with."

Gender and Marital Exchange

Throughout this book I have shown that females and males bring different stances to intimate partnership. There is no iron law at work, but females typically bring a greater focus on their second-corners and the needs of their family; males bring more concern for their third-corners and the world outside the nuclear family. These tendencies are not inherently natural; they arise from particular sociocultural arrangements that lead us to feel that herein lies the surest path to our power and comfort as males and females, as Dinnerstein and Chodorow have argued.

I see nothing necessarily crippling or even limiting about this division of interest as a platform for females and males to embark on as they move into their adult life. What cripples is to remain stuck within the same old tendencies one began with, and so I have defined growth in a marriage as any interaction with qualities of our spouse that are (or were) originally alien to us. Seen from this angle, the fact that females are so attuned to bonding and males to individuating within third-corners potentially exposes each spouse to an alien life-pattern in the other, and hence to a growing edge. If husbands can then move to appropriate some of their wives' bonding aptitude, and wives to appropriate some of their husbands' third-corner vigor in the public world, both will emerge far richer than they began. This mutual appropriation is only possible, however, when each partner is fully attuned and attracted to the other partner's world, a feat that is far easier said than done. We shall first look at the marriage of Tony and Maude Singer, who did make remarkable strides toward such mutual appropriation. Then we shall consider some common obstacles that couples must somehow stumble over, in order to take these kind of strides.

Like most males, Tony Singer learned early on that the fun things in life are to be found in outside third-corners. Growing up an only child with his

230 • *Three Corners*

mother and aunt, he did not seem to find much space within his home to elaborate his own inner-corner strivings:

> I was frequently dealt with in a fairly rigid way. I always had lots of friends around, but I had to go to their houses. More than anything else, I was required to be mature. I was required to have the reflexes and attitudes of an adult long before I even knew what they were. But I did all the things that children did back in the early 1940s, and I did it with my friends. And when I came into the house, I lived in an adult world where I was expected to deal intellectually with adult things. I remember when Franklin Roosevelt defeated Wendell Wilkie, my mother came in and picked me up, in tears, and I was sure that the end of the world had arrived. I can still hear her say, "He lost. Isn't that tragic?" And I was eight years old. I was expected to be able to deal with those kinds of things, and never isolated from them. I had the advantages of two worlds, and in each of them I had a competence. The only thing was, I really couldn't seem to bring that childhood world into the house; I was not expected to act as a child. I could go down in the cellar and play with my chemistry set, but I was expected to leave my chemistry set looking like the dinner table after I was through. And nobody could come down and play with it with me.

Not long after Tony's marriage to Maude, shortly before he finished his clerical training at the seminary, his established pattern of third-corner zeal began to clash with Maude's second-corner cravings. Tony recalls:

> It was more of a pressure for Maude. She was shut up in a horrible apartment with a new baby, and I was the shiny new minister who went out and did all these important things. I was proving how really lovable and necessary I was, and she was stuck with all the crap—including me, and my imperiousness. Over the next fourteen years I had to deal with that, essentially the same kinds of issues that all professional people have—doctors, dentists, clergy—the Messianic complex, that you and you alone are doing the great things and the wife is really the ill-paid employee who keeps the shirts clean, and sits with the babies, and keeps them out of the way, and shines with beauty and dignity when you want to trot her out for professional appearances. It would be some time before we would really come to grips with that, or before I would.

Maude's account focusses on the same clash of alien worlds—his investment in his outside third-corner, hers in her home-centered second-corner:

> I was kind of a romantic, and that meant that he was going to be around a lot. So when I had the baby and Tony was gone a lot in the day and in the evening, that was a real stress for me, and I almost said, "I can't stand this. This is just too much!" And at that point he had never been used to really talking to anybody in depth, and we had never really talked about things.

He had never had anybody to talk to except his aunt—his mother was gone all the time—so he didn't know how! He couldn't share himself. He could share other people's lives and help them, but sharing his own self was something else again. He always kept things in.

Instead of foreclosing on her second-corner needs, Maude somehow found the courage to challenge Tony's lopsided third-corner focus:

I said, "You're not ever telling me anything. You never tell me what you're doing every day. I'm sharing that life with you. I want to know; I'm interested. I love you, and because I love you, I want to know what's happening in your life, and I want to be able to do the same thing." It certainly wasn't intentional; he just never had been able to share with anybody. It really took a long time to work it through. It was kind of frightening to me, and I didn't really know how. He never got angry over the process. And he said he could understand what I was driving at, and that I was right. It was not just in my mind. And we began to talk not just about his job, but our dreams, our fears, our life. It didn't happen all at once, it just evolved. Nothing that I beat up on him to hurry up and do.

Fortunately for Maude, she was free enough of self-doubts and other inner-corner clutter to continue to challenge Tony's world so that her own needs could be met. Tony recalled an incident in which Maude's challenge to his distancing tendencies felt like a turning point:

We did not have much money. We finally came to a point when we had thirteen days until payday, no food in the house to speak of, and I had ninety-six cents to my name. I told Maude to go home to her parents until payday, and I'd keep the ninety-six cents and make it somehow on my own. She said, "No way. You're my husband; this is my home." We sat around and talked about it, and I really tried to convince her that I was right. My eyes still get teary when I think about what that meant in terms of who we were. There was a room in the church where people had been leaving bottles they were too lazy to return. I hauled out every bottle and took them to the store and got about five or six dollars for them, and went out that evening through every alley, and I pulled bottles out of every trash can. I was willing to set aside my pomposity for her, and she would by no means cut out and run and leave me to hang tough alone. We ate very little, but we got by and fed the baby. That incident was really the one that I think put the whole thing together for us. In trying to sort of plunge through, I stopped being the only decision-maker, because my decision had not been a good decision, and she was by no means going to abide by it. That was something that I will thank her for until the day I die. I got down off my high horse and put my family before my profession, and didn't even question it. And that's something that I needed to do.

232 • *Three Corners*

In my data, men who tend to fuse themselves with their careers become especially anxious following a move, and then they are even more likely than usual to shelve their second-corners, worried as they are about proving themseves in their new job setting. Tony was no exception, and at such times the issue of his inaccessibility to Maude and their children would again surface. Over the long term in this twenty-five-year marriage, however, Tony has reshaped his three corners to create more balance. With the help of Maude's urgings and challenges, he has appropriated more and more of her "female" second-corner focus, not only regarding his readiness to communicate more intimately with her about his professional life but also in his eagerness to be with her and to connect with their children.

In turn, Maude came to appropriate more and more of Tony's alien "male" world not just by hearing and talking about his third-corner skills but by cultivating some of her own. This time it was Tony's challenges that prodded Maude to move into what, for her, had been alien territory. Here is Tony's description of this development:

> Maude got her own job, largely at my insistence. It was not that we needed the money. It was much more that everywhere she went, she was Tony Singer's wife. And very shy and retiring. And finally we had this thing where the kids were calling up, one one day and one the next, saying they had stomach aches and had to come home from school. And I said, "There isn't a thing the matter with them. You get out of the house. If you're not here, they won't call." So she dragged around for a while, and finally she saw this. She got the job she has now, part-time at first.
>
> Now there's a world where I'm known as Maude Singer's husband. And I love it! The things we fight about now are the things that she used to accuse me of. We fight about it sometimes and laugh about it sometimes. Like, I used to come home late. I'd say, "I'll be in at five," and I'd show up at 6:30. And I'd commandeer the conversation, talking about all the problems I'd had at work that day, until she was ready to throw up. But she thought it was her dutiful thing to listen to me. And now she's through at four, she'll get home at six. We'll talk for an hour and a half about some kid that's come in there with all kinds of strange difficulties.
>
> The roles are reversed. I take it about as long as I feel like it. Once a month we might have a fight and I'll tell her I'm sick of hearing about this particular subject. Or I'll say, "When I come home, I would very much like to be able to find you here, and I get pissed off when you're not." Well, she says, "I can't always do it." It's just my way of telling her that that's important to me, as it used to be her way of telling me that it was important that I be home. . . .
>
> It's been delightful to watch the things that she takes joy in, and to know that in a sense I've been able to awaken her to a lot of that, and to enjoy her professional relationships, because she handles them well. And to be freer and freer from having to express and affirm just how competent I am. It's

much easier for me now to admit flaws, of which I have a substantial number, because she doesn't hide under the umbrella of my competence; she stands in her own light. I'm not having to prove to everybody what neat people we are.

Maude's account squares closely with Tony's:

I'm just much more free than I was. And he's helped me be who I am. I never would have been, I don't think. Especially getting out, and in my own job. I have a fair amount of responsibility, and I thought I couldn't handle that, but I do it and I do it well. And I'm proud of that. And he's proud of me for that, and he reinforces that feeling. He's very supportive of what I do outside the home, and he's been so understanding about my using the talent that I have. He said, "I told you, I know you can do these things; I see these things in you, and you don't have confidence in yourself." It was that way when I went back to work. He knew that I could do that, but I had to go do it to prove it to myself. I was very shy, and I needed a lot of encouragement. I wouldn't give him all the credit, but he's enabled me, by being who he is, to let me be who I am.

The Singers' marriage illustrates how initially alien gender orientations can be appropriated by each other, particularly when spouses are prepared to challenge each other's insularity. First Maude pulls Tony into her tender world of emotional bonding, companionship, and familism. Then Tony pushes Maude out into the public world of career competence, wider responsibility, and individual striving. Both develop a better working knowledge of how to be in *and* out of the nest of marriage and family life. Through direct experience, both learn more about what it feels like to be their partner, and thus they become more flexible. If androgyny is an equal balance of "masculine" and "feminine" traits, then both of these partners become more androgynous, expanding their inner-corners to embrace a wider variety of experience, and reshaping their second- and third-corners into vehicles more fully equipped to carry a rich outpouring of human purpose.

The Impact of Patriarchy on Marital Exchange

Our patriarchal heritage does not make it easy for couples to accomplish the level of mutual appropriation that the Singers did. When a culture heaps its greatest honors and rewards on public third-corner achievements, when men are expected to be the keepers and guardians of these third-corners, and women are supposed to confine their interests to serving their families and being well provided for, spouses will then find it difficult to exchange their best energies with each other. Under patriarchy, a female is groomed to make

234 • *Three Corners*

other people happy, to identify her own needs in terms of pleasing and serving others. A male is groomed to be a decisive, self-contained bastion of strength whose third-corner prowess not only provides for his dependents but also reflects on his masculinity.[5]

Under these conditions, males and females will structure their respective three corners in seriously flawed ways. Wives' inner-corners tend to lack a clear sense of their own independent needs and urgings as if they have to wait for their husbands' needs to be registered in order to find their own. This insufficient clarity within female inner-corners is often compounded by a poor development of their third-corners as well, and indeed, the one deficiency calls forth the other. Inner urgings require active third-corner outlets to expand, evolve, and become more highly differentiated and clearly defined, but third-corners attain some vigor only when they are nurtured by a decisive, self-aware inner-corner. Women are not to blame for these deficiencies. Patriarchy is a culture that trains women for self-sacrifice rather than for self-clarity, and it reduces their third-corner opportunities to child-care alone, which is often a further venture in self-sacrifice, important and meaningful though it might be.

Husband's inner-corners tend to be overly insistent, driven by a concern to prove their mastery, and filled with longings for individual distinction. The lack of clarity within females' first-corners is matched by an overcertainty within males', a situation which Tony Singer called attention to when he found that Maude's increasing awareness of her job competence freed him of the burden of having to present himself as the competent one for both of them. Husbands' second-corners tend to be unyielding, overly primed for unquestioned support from their partners, and poorly equipped for intimacy, all difficulties that relate to their inner-corner issues. The emphasis on male decisiveness, strength, and mastery does not lend itself to egalitarian companionship or to the disclosure of vulnerability, conditions on which second-corner intimacy most thrives. Husbands' third-corners are certainly vigorous enough, allowing ample opportunity to outwardly sharpen their inner strivings and capacities, but these strivings are too often narrowly focussed on job-related concerns and on other vehicles through which masculine prowess can be demonstrated.[6]

To be sure, not all husbands and wives structure their respective triangles in this fashion, and we have seen how individual personal histories may inspire marital paradigms in which the patriarchal legacy is set aside. Patriarchy dies a slow death, however, and it is exceptionally rare to find spouses who do not bend themselves into the triangular shapes just described, at least in some respects. The point is that to the extent that we do assume these shapes, the capacity of each spouse to appropriate the kind of being that the other is becomes seriously diminished.

For example, when male and female inner-corners are structured in this way, it is hard for spouses to avoid patterns of exchange in which the husband

Marital Growth and Its Obstacles • 235

decisively challenges anything he sees as alien to his needs, and the wife fore-closes on any counterneeds she has in order to meet his. Usually, however, no challenge from his side will even be necessary; she will make sure that he gets what he thinks he needs. A husband says, "If you have to work at a marriage, Meredith must be doing the work, because I'm not doing anything special. Maybe she does it so well I don't even know it." She does! Meredith has this to say: "I was overidealistic when I first got married to really make it work, and maybe went overboard in giving in. As I got older I found out how far I could put myself forth and explain what I wanted."

Meredith makes it clear that she is delighted with her twenty-four-year marriage, and she does not see herself as ever having had to give in on any-thing that was really important to her. She explains, "When I'm with various types of peple I can do what they're doing and enjoy it." Such adaptability may be commendable from one point of view, but it also bespeaks an inner-corner that may have had too little practice defining and recognizing what her own needs and strivings are. She then finds it all too easy to uncritically adopt her husband's needs as what she really wants.

Another wife, Kay Fisher, recalls the way her grandmother similarly used to go along with her grandfather. She then describes how she often does the same in her own marriage:

> Whatever he enjoyed, she enjoyed; whenever he said, "You do this, Girl," she'd do it, and no opposition. I can see her point of view. I feel that way lots of times. It doesn't mean that much to me what we do or where we go. I'm happy to go along. Maybe once in a while I might think I'd like to do so and so, but if I suggest it to him and he doesn't feel like it, it doesn't bother me. I don't think, "The heck with him, he doesn't want to do what I want to do." I've never felt that way about anything. What I want to do isn't that impor-tant; I just enjoy going along with what somebody else likes to do. I see a lot of people who get very upset if they can't do what they want to do. They've made the remark, "I always have to do what he or she wants to do." And I've always thought to myself, "What's the big issue? Maybe you'll get to do what you want later on."

Like Meredith, Kay Fisher is truly enthralled about her marriage. She emotes with teary-eyed joy when talking about her husband, a man I too found extraordinarily charming. She means what she says about not really caring what they do, and perhaps under these circumstances, when the sparks of feeling still radiate after thirty-six years of marriage, it is foolish to dwell on some abstract abuses of patriarchy. Nevertheless, the point deserves to be reiterated and then further explored: Under patriarchy, a female's adapta-bility becomes overdeveloped; her partnership-corner lacks the clear signals from her inner-corner that would enable her to discriminate between what is worthy of her accommodation and what is not. Now since, in Kay Fisher's

236 • *Three Corners*

case, she does not foreclose on anything she wants to do or to be, and her husband Dennis does not challenge her in any way that is exceptionable to her, and since both spouses are genuinely delighted with their arrangement, what is possibly wrong with it?

An important clue is found in Dennis's own account:

> I know she always puts me first. I think anything I say, she would go along with—most anything.

Does she bend too much?

> Maybe sometimes. I think sometimes I'm not that sensitive, and maybe I take advantage. I feel that I wouldn't want to do anything in the world to hurt her, but I feel a lot of times I do. Say we have friends that I know she's not particularly fond of. They would invite us to go somewhere, and I'll say "Well, I know you don't want to go, but I think we should," so we'll go. I know I should say, "I know you don't feel like going so we'll just stay home." She never seems to resent it that much. If she said she did, then I would say, "No, we'll stay home."

Should Dennis take responsibility not only for knowing how Kay feels but also for making the decisions that will serve her unspoken needs? Here Kay would say it doesn't matter that they go; she is happy doing what Dennis wants to do. Having fused her inner-corner with her partnership-corner, she must remain fuzzy about what needs she has that are indepedent of his needs. Necessarily, then, Dennis can be the only initiator in this relationship, the only one whose inner urgings are defined enough to clamor for attention. And Kay, so eager to support whatever he initiates, will do her best to appropriate it, to stretch her boundaries to make it part of herself, no matter how alien or uncomfortable.

Such an arrangement may work to everyone's satisfaction, but it can only promote a one-sided appropriation. Small wonder that Dennis tells me, when I ask if being married to Kay has changed him very much, "I don't think she's been demanding enough on me to make me change." A self can only grow by breaking out of its own insularity, and the alien worlds of partners are tailor-made for such breakthroughs. But Kay seldom presents anything alien to Dennis. Her inner-corner has little content that is independent of him—no strivings that are hungry to find some third-corner outlet, no emergent capacities that demand the space to unfold themselves, nothing to shake up Dennis's existing boundaries. Dennis is the only initiator, and therefore the Fishers' couple reality becomes an elaboration of his inner resources alone. The outcome is paradoxical. Dennis has only limited opportunities for growth in his marriage precisely because Kay wants to go along with anything he already wants.

In this chapter we have explored three processes of marital exchange—appropriation, foreclosure, and challenge. Mutual appropriation (the joint growth process) is no simple matter, demanding much self-awareness, courage, and strength in both partners. To walk the line between appropriation and foreclosure, to sense the broadening impact on oneself of the newly emerging energies from one's partner, and to distinguish these tendencies from those that can only stifle one's own best energies—this requires considerable inner awareness. And to draw the line short of collaboration in the latter instances of would-be foreclosure, and to challenge one's partner's wrongheadedness—this takes courage. And finally, to hold the line on one's own emerging energies, and to challenge one's partner on behalf of these energies—this requires more than a modicum of strength. In the final chapter, we shall briefly consider some aspects of the feminist challenge that are promoting a more even distribution of these qualities among wives and husbands.

Notes

1. Nick Stinnett, James Walters, and Evelyn Kaye, *Relationships in Marriage and the Family*, 2d ed. (New York: Macmillan, 1984), p. 57.
2. Ibid., p. 106.
3. John Cuber and Peggy Harroff, *Sex and the Significant Americans* (Baltimore: Penguin Books, 1966), pp. 55–56.
4. Ibid., p. 56.
5. For a superb treatment of men as providers, see Jessie Bernard, "The Good-Provider Role: Its Rise and Fall," *American Psychologist* 36 (1981):1–12.
6. I use the word "prowess" here in the spirit of Thorstein Veblen. To my knowledge, his *Theory of the Leisure Class* (New York: Modern Library, 1934) is the first systematic treatment of the links between aggressiveness, masculine identity, male economic control, and female domesticity. The unique and original feminist thrust of Veblen's work, first published in 1899, has yet to be explored.

14
The Feminist Challenge to Patriarchy

Over the past decade or so, the feminist project has been transforming our patriarchal underpinnings, enlisting the aid of numerous and diverse resources from our culture. Academic curricula, the legal structure, the mental health professions, the workplace, and other institutional resources are supplying the tools to shape a new epoch of cultural history. The changes so far have not often been flashy, considering that nowadays change seems to require a dressing up in full media regalia in order to be recognized as "visible." The days when feminism could be associated with bra-burnings are long gone, although the association strangely persists in much of the public mind.

"I'm no women's libber," many female respondents exclaimed, perhaps wishing to assure me (and themselves) that they mean to upset no one's applecart by what they are doing in their lives. Most of them had long since formed their marital paradigms by the time that modern efforts for women's equality were rekindled in the late 1960s, and they have never thought of themselves as feminists. Still, many of these women have not only been affected by the accomplishments of feminism, but in their own way they are unknowingly carrying out a number of its goals, as shown throughout this study. What these goals are in terms of marriage and the self can now be summarized.

The undoing of patriarchy within marriage implies changes in all three corners of a woman's triangle, with consequent changes implied for a man's. In the inner-corner the principal project is, as Dorothy Dinnerstein has so well taught us, to reclaim the unique and solid subjectivity that wives so often sacrifice for the sake of pleasing their husbands.[1] Women must overcome the tendency to fuse, and thereby come to differentiate their own center and the needs that flow out of it from those of their partner. To accomplish this, women bonding with other women in consciousness-raising groups, friendships, kinship relations, and workplaces has provided invaluable third-corner leverage. A woman told me:

240 • *Three Corners*

I formed a very close friendship with another person who works with me, a female, and I know my husband's been envious, or jealous, not understanding of my feelings for her. We got to know each other professionally, and we have the same concerns. And we see the issue of working mothers from the same vantage point. I probably do share thoughts or feelings with her that I don't share or find difficult to share with him.

The main second-corner project is for women to directly challenge their husbands. As male needs come up against female counterneeds from time to time, husbands must sometimes get pulled into serving certain of their wives' needs that may be alien to them, or at least alien at first. Self-assured challenge is probably the only way for women to accomplish this task. Female foreclosure has always oiled the domestic wheels of the patriarchal machine, enabling male needs and interests alone to be the ones talked about and jointly acted upon in the relationship.[2] Female needs have, of course, been attended to, when awareness of them has remained alive, but this has often been confined to spaces in which husbands are not present. The issue here is the content of the marriage *relationship*—what comes into it, what gets jointly attended to and elaborated, and what flows out of it. When husbands struggle more to appropriate their wives' worlds, then female interests will comprise a larger share of couple reality, and couple history will come to reflect both spouses' interests instead of husbands' alone.

As for the third-corner, a main thrust of the feminist project has recently centered on the job opportunities that women find to harness their creative capacities. There is little reason to expect this focus to shift, although a number of respondents have managed to turn homemaking into a virtual art form, and some find abundant third-corner satisfaction in spiritual pursuits or various hobbies. Community volunteer work has always provided another third-corner outlet, but women increasingly find that there is no substitute for the sense of greater accomplishment, independence, and pride that an income-paying job affords. Moreover, the public world is shaped primarily in the occupational arena, and to effectively challenge patriarchy is surely to bring more female sensibilities into that arena as well. In turn, the capacities that women cultivate there can vitalize a marriage relationship, insofar as husbands stand ready (or are challenged) to appropriate these new qualities that wives bring home as smarter, more skillful, more aware, and more vibrant women.

I have focussed here almost exclusively on the structure of the self and on the little microworld of marriage. Obviously, there is a larger cultural setting that impinges on marriage and is implicated in any transformation it might undergo. To change the selves who structure a marriage is not impossible without transforming that larger cultural setting, since many of my respondents have accomplished just that. Nevertheless, it is difficult and fraught

with all manner of external obstacles, as if the internal obstacles were not enough. To make things easier for spouses intent on challenging the patriarchal basis of marriage, it would help immeasurably if full-time jobs were redefined as twenty- or twenty-five-hour per week responsibilities, if women were as involved in occupational third-corners as men, and if men were as involved in primary child-care as women. Exploring these changes is beyond the scope of this study, although several points are worth stating. To the extent that partners clean up some of the self-destructive and partner-destructive clutter in their respective inner-corners, they can put their own houses in order. We shall then find that as soon as these two selves come out of their interiority in their day-to-day round of existence, they cannot help but construct third-corner vehicles that carry their wealth of capacities. Since these third-corners of the self are the bridge to the public world, that world will have to restructure itself to accommodate the new energies that flow into it. Evolving selves are public change agents whether they know it or not.

Notes

1. Dorothy Dinnerstein, *The Mermaid and the Minotaur* (New York: Harper and Row, 1976), especially pp. 106–114.

2. For a masterful study of how, among intimate heterosexual partners, male interests are the ones that get developed in informal conversations, see Pam Fishman, "Interaction: The Work Women Do," *Social Problems* 25 (1978):397–406.

Appendix
The Respondents, the Interviews, and the History of the Project

This study is based on interviews with 114 married people (fifty-seven couples) and fifteen recently divorced persons. All couples had been married at least ten years, as I wanted enough marital experience not only for the earliest blush of romance to have faded but also for a variety of issues to have emerged, whether dealt with or not. Table 1 summarizes the couple sample by the length of their marriages.

The vast majority of respondents were in their first marriage, since fewer potential respondents who were ever divorced had had enough years of remarriage to meet the ten-year requirement for being interviewed. Nevertheless, twelve of the 114 long-term marrieds (10 percent) were working on their second marriages, and from these respondents I got data about both of their marriages.

The majority of respondents were Protestants, outnumbering Catholics by more than two to one. Protestants also outnumbered those who claimed to have no religion or to be spiritual but without any particular affiliation by about five to two. More than 20 percent of the sample claimed that religious priorities were extremely high in their life. The impact of religion on marriage is covered in chapter 3.

All but two respondents were currently living in Maine and were interviewed there. The vast majority (87 percent) had either lived in Maine throughout their married life or at least during most of it. More than half of the total sample said they grew up principally in Maine, and another quarter somewhere else in the Northeast. Four respondents grew up in the South, seven in the Midwest, and two in the West. In view of the large proportion of the sample whose marital and living experience has centered predominantly in Maine, an underpopulated state with a small population density, the reader should certainly wonder about the generalizability of findings drawn from such a nonrepresentative population. I shall address this issue shortly.

The educational experience of the sample was considerably more varied. As table 2 shows, the sample as a whole is rather well-educated, although it does include a substantial minority (35 percent) with no college experience at all.

Table 1
Length of Marriage of Couples in Study

Length of Marriage	Percentage of Couples	Number of Couples
10–19 years	48%	27
20–29 years	33	19
30 years or longer	19	11

Concerning employment, all of the men worked full-time except one divorced man who was unemployed and three retired senior citizens. The men's jobs ranged from handyman, bus driver, and garage mechanic to salesman, lawyer, businessman, and college professor. The "higher"-level jobs were overrepresented in the sample, however. Using the manual/nonmanual labor distinction as an indicator of social class, the husband's job was a working-class position in only about 20 percent of the married couples. If we include as working class those jobs that were nonmanual but low-paying and low-skilled, such as store clerks, the ratio rises to about 25 percent. In no case did a husband ever have the principal responsibilities for child-care, except as a short-term, temporary arrangement.

Of the women, about half the sample currently had a full time job, with the other half evenly split between those who had part-time jobs and those who had none, thus bringing the total ratio of wives in the labor force to approximately 75 percent. This percentage is larger than the 56 percent which is the national average, but remember that the sample includes only couples married ten years or longer, with a full 52 percent having been married at least twenty years. The sample thus overrepresents couples whose children had already grown up or moved out. In fact, many of the women in the labor force did not enter or reenter it until their youngest child was well into his or her teen years, and these women had devoted much of their married years to

Table 2
Educational Level of Respondents

	Number of Respondents	Percentage of Respondents
Did not graduate from high school	7	6%
High school graduate	26	21
Vocational training beyond high school	10	8
Some college, but did not graduate	20	16
College graduate	28	23
Master's or equivalent degree	21	17
Ph.D. or law degree	10	8
	N = 122	99

Note: Seven respondents did not supply educational information.

Appendix • 245

homemaking activities. As for the type of job, the women's employment ranged from babysitting at home and stitchworking at a factory to store clerking, teaching school, nursing, and college teaching.

On the whole, the people in the sample are predictably more "modern" than their parents, and they are rather upwardly mobile from their point of origin. More than a few (about 15 percent) grew up on small farms or out in the country, with poorly educated parents. Many of the parents toiled at mills and factories, with their children (my respondents) escaping from rural or small town poverty by dint of a higher education. They make more money than their parents ever did, and they hold more prestigious jobs.

Many working women in the study often come from families where the mother did not work outside the home. While a number of these respondents remained at home until their own children were older, a substantial minority have always been actively employed, even when their children were quite young. Significantly, the number of men who now find themselves with a working and career-committed wife is far larger than the number who had grown up with a working and career-committed mother.

The sample of fifty-seven married couples actually consists of two evenly divided subsamples. My addition of a second subsample reflects a midstream change in research strategy prompted by a radical shift in my understanding of what I was doing and what I needed to be looking for. Originally I had wanted to focus only on couples with extremely vital relationships, on partners whom Cuber and Harroff had described as having "intrinsic" marriages—marriages in which the couple bond itself is given the highest priority. But I was troubled by those authors treating intrinsic marriage as if it involves no real development. I assumed that marital vitality must be the ongoing outcome of a growth *process,* whereas Cuber and Harroff seemed to see it as some final fait accompli, even from the very beginning. "Devitalized" relationships (those which lose their earlier vitality) may go through some significant shifts and turns in their analysis, but those that remain vital are presented as somehow exempt from any relational history except that which simply restates whatever the relationship already is.[1]

Another source of my interest in vital marriages was my previous theoretical work on human energy. I had concluded that contrary to the popular imagination, human energy is not inherently scarce but is flexible and expansible: we run out of it not when our biological supply gets "drained" or "spent" but when our commitment to an activity is less than enthusiastic if not downright disinterested or hostile.[2] Vital marriages, I reasoned, would provide a fertile ground for exploring this supposition empirically. Cuber and Harroff had already provided a head start, since their "intrinsically married" respondents seemed to have ample energy not only to vigorously pursue their demanding careers but also to be engaged, responsive, and devoted spouses. In order to

learn more about how such people approach their lives, however, I would need to follow the unfolding history of particular marriages far more closely than Cuber and Harroff had done.

The next task was to find a sample of vitally married couples. I did not want to depend upon a volunteer system, as I had little confidence in the perceptions that might incline married people to offer themselves up to social science. I knew that when survey researchers ask people to rate their own marriages on a five-point scale from "very happy" to "very unhappy," the vast majority come out either "very happy" or "happy." Belief in a happy marriage is apparently a widespread necessity for the ego, but I doubted that the belief and the actual reality had a very close correspondence with each other. A *Life* survey of 62,000 readers added some additional perspective when it found that although nearly half of the sample rated their own marriages as "very happy," only 12 percent thought that other marriages with which they were familiar were "very happy."[3] I concluded that if people are more scrutinizing observers of other people's marriages than their own, perhaps I could harness this critical faculty in generating a sample of vitally married spouses.

My next step was to send letters appealing for referrals. Using the University of Maine, Orono, mail system, I sent over 2,000 letters to professors, administrators, and personnel. Since this population includes professionals and managerial types as well as secretaries, janitors, groundskeepers, carpenters, cooks, and mechanics, I hoped that a wide variety of backgrounds and perceptions would come to bear on their suggestions of particular couples I might interview. I also assumed, correctly as it turned out, that as my "referees" mentally surveyed the couples they knew, many would suggest couples in which neither partner had an association with the University, so that my actual sample would not be confined to that particular employment community. My letter mentioned that I was doing a study of long-term marriages, and asked for the names of any familiar couples whom the person thought had an especially "close, caring, intimate and vital relationship, even after at least ten years of marriage had gone by." Purposely, I did not specify definitions of these terms, as I wanted the "referees" to use their own definitions. The resulting range of interpretations would hopefully maximize my chances of discovering a variety of types of vitality, if any such variety existed.

Approximately 220 people responded to my request for referrals, some writing that they knew of no such couples, some mentioning the names of one or two, several mentioning as many as seven. I kept a record of how many times a given name was mentioned, adopting the working principle that a couple referred at least twice would be eligible to participate in the study. Using the resulting list of 270 names, I called up the referrals, starting with the couples who had been referred the most number of times. I talked to each spouse, explaining what I was doing and how I had gotten their name. If they agreed to be interviewed, I then made some general remarks about the interview procedure,

the tape recorder, and the rather personal nature of the questions I would be asking. I also explained that I would need to interview each partner of the couple separately, that if one partner declined I would not interview the other one either, and that I would not reveal anything that either of them might tell me to the other. I knew that separate interviews would allow me the best chance of avoiding the tendency of respondents to tell me only what they are willing to let the other partner hear. In this way I sought to heed Jessie Bernard's warning that every marriage is really two marriages—his marriage and her marriage—and that the two marriages are often quite different from each other.[4]

Twenty-nine couples (fifty-eight persons) were interviewed as a result of this procedure. (In the process of generating this sample, twenty-two other couples refused permission to be interviewed, although often one partner was willing or even eager to be interviewed, but the other partner was not. As the interviews proceeded, I discovered that several of my assumptions had been ill-founded. A moderate-sized institution such as the University of Maine, Orono, may contain people from many social strata among its personnel, but most of my referred sample turned out to be white-collar professionals and managerial types. Many more white-collar than blue-collar people responded to my appeal for referrals, and presumably they referred me to couples like themselves. In four of the couples I contacted, the husband did have a blue-collar job, but three of these couples declined to be interviewed.

A second problem concerned my assumption that people might be better judges of other people's marital vitality than of their own. I now suspect that people who can be deluded about the vitality of their own marriages are no better equipped to recognize such vitality in others; if they really could know it when they see it, they would know how to live it themselves. The fact is that many of the couples who had been referred to me at least twice had unsatisfying marriages by their own criteria if not by mine. I later learned that a number of referred couples whom I did not interview went through a divorce in the several years following my appeal for referrals. As for the twenty-nine couples I did interview, two have since split up, while in four more at least one partner told me of some deep, long-standing dissatisfactions with the overall relationship. Another three couples lived largely separate lives, avoiding any tangible connection with each other, although for the most part they were satisfied with the situation as it was. Of the remaining twenty, only thirteen couples truly impressed me by their obvious devotion to each other, their intricacy of knowledge about one another, their eagerness to share themselves, and their genuine readiness to do anything they possibly could to serve the other's needs and concerns. The other seven couples all had some ongoing points of important contact, and they were satisfied with how things were going, but it was clear that there were also huge areas of their respective inner dramas that remained unspoken, hidden, and guarded from disclosure,

248 • *Three Corners*

as if it was simply too dangerous to risk the predictability and safety of the partnership for the sake of addressing issues that could rock the boat.

In summary, my referral technique for securing a sample of vital marriages was partially successful. Thirteen truly impressive couples out of twenty-nine was not, after all, so bad a ratio, and I learned a great deal from them about the dynamics of marital connection. On the other hand I was also successful, despite my intent to the contrary, at producing a sample that covered the entire spectrum of possibilities, ranging from marriages that were just plain awful by their own criteria to those that were "fair-to-middlin'," all the way to those that seemed inspired by a stroke of enchantment. In the meantime, something new had begun to emerge as this collection of interviews unfolded. I noticed that while some respondents recalled dramatic shifts, turns, and changes in their marriages, many others could not recount a single new development in all their years together even though they went through the same family life-cycle progression as most couples. They accommodated their partnerships to the arrival of children, to job changes, to residential moves, to children growing up and leaving home, and so forth. Nevertheless, when the dust settled after each such episode, neither partner could lay claim to anything new between them *as a couple.* Different things to talk about do not necessarily lead to different ways of talking, listening, and responding, nor do they even insure that people will begin to talk at all if they were never in the habit of doing so.

Marital reality was now becoming far more complicated. Some marriages seem to change and take new turns, others do not. And of the marriages that most impressed me (and that most gratify those who live them), only some underwent these twists and turns, while others stayed relatively unchanged. In general, some marriages struck me as having needed to change and, appropriately, having done so. Others that probably needed to change managed nevertheless to keep things as they were. Some marriages seemed so comfortable and satisfying that they neither needed nor experienced any significant change. And some marriages that were just as comfortable seemed to go through profound changes and upheavals anyway. It was clear that my preconceptions were wrong: marital vitality is *not* necessarily a unilinear development; it does *not* always begin with two naive partners who are ill-equipped to accommodate each other; and it does *not* always end with these partners having expanded their boundaries to more fully handle each other's personal worlds. If some marriages go through this kind of development, many do not, including some that would be the envy of virtually anyone.

It took one other stroke of insight to set me on a new track. I discovered that the more I talked to my respondents about the most significant facets of their premarital biographies, the more understandable their entire pattern of marriage became. As a working principle, I now believe that *all marriages make perfect sense,* exactly as they are. This does not mean, of course, that marriages are equally good, vital, or happy, nor that the attempt to change

them is futile or undesirable. What it does mean is that any marriage gets superimposed upon two wider, biographical contexts. From out of those unique contexts arise marital tendencies, issues, and urgencies. Whatever we see as marital behavior or belief will thus become rational and intelligible as soon as we know enough about the larger context that inspires it.

These considerations led me to shift my thinking about vitality in a partnership. If marital tendencies are relative to their wider biographical contexts, then feelings of marital vitality must likewise take shape within the same parameters of possibility that those unique contexts map out. At this point in the research, the whole question of marital vitality became subordinated to two more fundamental questions. First, how might I talk concretely about marriage as a convergence of two already unfolding life-histories? I began to think of this as the question of the *statics* of marriage. And second, regardless of whether a given convergence can be described as a "vital" one, what are the dynamics that give rise to, maintain, or rule out further historical developments of the convergence itself, of the process that we popularly think of as "a relationship."

The impact of these broader questions prompted me to interview a second subsample of long-term married couples and a separate subsample of recently divorced persons. As I was now focussing on the whole process of marital development, it no longer made sense to confine myself to a referred sample of couples presumed to be vitally married. The task at hand was to maximize the diversity within the new subsamples, so that my resulting theory of marital statics and dynamics could be serviceable for the study of any population, vitally married or not.

A random sampling strategy was one way of achieving this end, and this sample proved simple to obtain. Around this time in 1980, the University's Social Science Research Institute (SSRI) was conducting a pre-election telephone poll of the Maine electorate, using standard random sampling techniques. It was easy enough to select some areas in central Maine and to have SSRI screen the polled respondents from these areas for marital status and, if married, for length of marriage. Those married ten years or longer were informed of my project and were asked if I could call them to solicit their participation. In this manner I secured a sample of twenty-eight couples about whom I knew nothing except that they had been married at least ten years. In addition, a subsample of fifteen recently divorced persons was secured through randomly sampling newspaper listings of divorces occurring over an eighteen-month period. The ensuing interviews proceeded in the same fashion as in the "referred" subsample, with questions added to the divorced group's interviews to uncover important postdivorce developments in their stance toward partnership.

The random sampling device was effective in producing the intended diversity of respondents. Despite the fact that for the twenty-eight couples who

agreed to be interviewed, another forty couples declined, I am hard put to identify any pattern of selective bias that could mark the participants as a different population of married people than the refusers, aside from a greater tendency of people age fifty-five or older to decline. The sample includes a much broader range of backgrounds and socioeconomic circumstances than does the referred sample. It includes people who were deeply satisfied with their marriages (though a smaller percentage than that in the referred group) as well as people who were profoundly dissatisfied, people who were talkative and people who were so taciturn that I could not imagine why they agreed to participate, people who had walked a straight and narrow path through their marriages and people who had taken many side trips.

The interview procedure averaged about two to three hours per respondent. Most interviews were done in the respondents' homes. The interviews were focussed but open-ended, and there were always many more unscheduled questions asked than scheduled ones. Interviews began with some standard demographic data, moved on to significant recollections of childhood and to perceptions of the parents' marriage, then to expectations and hopes for the respondent's own marriage, to courtship experiences, and to recollections of the first year or so of marriage. Most of the remainder of the interview focussed on the ensuing marital career, probing any potential conflicts, transitions and turning points, changes in feeling and perception, and important events.

In general, respondents were given the freedom to direct the interview into the areas that were most salient in the development of their marriage and of their overall feelings about it. Most respondents spoke at length about children and their impact, jobs and job changes, sex, and recreation. Quite a few respondents spoke candidly about one or more extramarital intimacies they had had, with a few letting me know how privileged that information was and that I was not to reveal it to anyone, especially their partner. The resulting collection of marital histories is richer, more varied, and more detailed than I had anticipated in my fondest hopes for the project. Like other researchers who have conducted these kind of in-depth interviews, I was continually amazed and gratified by the level of honesty, forthrightness, and candor with which my respondents approached the interview.

In the analysis of marriage that is offered in the rest of this book, I make no reference to the particular subsamples from which the case materials are drawn, because I quickly came to the conclusion that the respondents are not essentially different from one subsample to the other. The divorced respondents dealt with the same kinds of issues and were moved by the same kinds of dynamics as the ones who stayed married, only at certain junctures these dynamics may have locked both partners into an unbridgeable impasse. The final outcome may have been different, but the process leading up to it was not.

Once more, then, we come to the question of the generalizability of these findings. Here I shall make the strongest disclaimer that I possibly can: the findings of this study cannot be generalized to any known population on any scientific grounds. Even the random sample of couples cannot be generalized to the population of central Maine from which they were drawn, because there were too many refusers in proportion to the couples who agreed to participate. In any case, the inductive, qualitative, exploratory purpose of this book makes the question of generalizability irrelevant. Exploratory studies are designed to show how a process or pattern of development works, not to indicate its frequency in a given population. The aim is to clarify and illuminate phenomena about which too little is known. So far as I know, Three Corners is the first attempt to document marriage as a long-term development that is superimposed upon two separate life-histories. It is the first study of marital development to explore phases, turning points, and immobility that does not impose a priori conceptions of the phases that "should," logically, be important in a marriage. That is, by allowing a varied sample of respondents to tell their own histories and developments, we emerge with a theory of marital dynamics that is informed by the data, instead of forcing the analysis of marital development into preconceived molds.

Finally, the ultimate test of an exploratory theory is just how readily it can be put to work in a variety of settings. In the case of a theory of marriage, this test is a tall order, because so many different people are married, often in seemingly strange ways. Readers of Three Corners will have to see for themselves whether it helps them to illuminate and map out their own unfolding marriage. Obviously, I am prejudiced that it will, without destroying the richness of anyone's particular experience. The trick of theory has always been to spread an elegant umbrella over phenomena, without squeezing them together so much that their variety becomes invisible.

Notes

1. John Cuber and Peggy Harroff, Sex and the Significant Americans (Baltimore: Penguin Books, 1966), especially chapter 7.

2. Stephen R. Marks, "Multiple Roles and Role Strain: Some Notes on Human Energy, Time and Commitment," American Sociological Review 42 (1977):921–936.

3. Reprinted in J. Gipson Wells, Current Issues in Marriage and the Family, 2nd ed. (New York: Macmillan, 1979), pp. 21–26.

4. Jessie Bernard, The Future of Marriage (New York: Bantam Books, 1972).

Bibliography

Aldous, Joan. *Family Careers: Developmental Change in Families*. New York: Wiley, 1978.

Bernard, Jessie. *The Future of Marriage*. New York: Bantam Books, 1972.

———. "The Good-Provider Role: Its Rise and Fall." *American Psychologist* 36 (1981):1–12.

Blood, R., and D. Wolfe. *Husbands and Wives*. New York: Free Press, 1960.

Blumstein, Philip, and Pepper Schwartz. *American Couples*. New York: William Morrow, 1983.

Bott, Elizabeth. *Family and Social Network*, 2d ed. New York: Free Press, 1971.

Bowen, M. "Theory in the Practice of Psychotherapy." In *Family Therapy*, ed. P. Guerin. New York: Gardner Press, 1976.

———. "Toward the Differentiation of Self in One's Family of Origin." In *Family Interaction: A Dialogue between Family Researchers and Family Therapists*, ed. J. Framo. New York: Springer, 1972.

Chodorow, Nancy. *The Reproduction of Mothering*. Berkeley: University of California Press, 1978.

Cuber, John, and Peggy Harroff. *Sex and the Significant Americans*. Baltimore: Penguin Books, 1966.

Dinnerstein, Dorothy. *The Mermaid and the Minotaur*. New York: Harper and Row, 1976.

Duvall, Evelyn, and Brent Miller. *Marriage and Family Development*, 6th ed. New York: Harper and Row, 1985.

Fishman, Pam. "Interaction: The Work Women Do." *Social Problems* 25 (1978): 397–406.

Goodman, Marvin. "Expressed Self-Acceptance and Interpersonal Needs." In *Family Roles and Interaction: An Anthology*, ed. J. Heiss. Chicago: Rand McNally, 1968.

Gove, Walter, and Jeanette Tudor. "Adult Sex Roles and Mental Illness." *American Journal of Sociology* 78 (1973):812–835.

Holahan, C., and C. Gilbert. "Conflict between Major Life Roles: The Women and Men in Dual-Career Couples." *Human Relations* 32 (1979): 451–467.

Kuhn, Thomas. *The Structure of Scientific Revolutions*. Chicago: University of Chicago Press, 1962.

254 • *Three Corners*

Marks, Stephen R. "Culture, Human Energy, and Self-Actualization: A Sociological Offering to Humanistic Psychology." *Journal of Humanistic Psychology* 19 (1979):27–42.

——— . "Multiple Roles and Role Strain: Some Notes on Human Energy, Time and Commitment." *American Sociological Review* 42 (1977):921–936.

Maslow, Abraham. *Motivation and Personality*, 2d ed. New York: Harper and Row, 1970.

Pearce, J. *The Magical Child*. New York: E.P. Dutton, 1977.

Rubin, Lillian. *Worlds of Pain*. New York: Harper and Row, 1976.

Scanzoni, John. *Sexual Bargaining*, 2d ed. Chicago: University of Chicago Press, 1982.

——— . "Social Processes and Power in Families." In *Contemporary Theories about the Family*, Vol. 1, ed. W. Burr et al. New York: Free Press, 1979.

Slater, Philip. "On Social Regression." *American Sociological Review* 28 (1963): 339–364.

Stinnett, Nick, James Walters, and Evelyn Kaye. *Relationships in Marriage and the Family*, 2d ed. New York: Macmillan, 1984.

Veblen, Thorstein. *The Theory of the Leisure Class*. New York: Modern Library, 1934.

Waller, Willard, and Reuben Hill. *The Family: A Dynamic Interpretation*. New York: Holt, Rinehart and Winston, 1951.

Wells, J. Gipson. *Current Issues in Marriage and the Family*, 2d ed. New York: Macmillan, 1979.

Index

Abandonment, 105, 114–115, 171; fear of, 22–23, 29–30, 36, 51, 148, 227–228

Accessibility, 37, 106, 175; of husbands, 38, 65, 93, 96–97, 113, 127, 222, 230, 232; of parents, 22–23, 41; of wives, 35, 93, 232

Affection, 96, 175, 198; of parents, 23

Agenda. *See* Marriage agendas

Agenda clash, 95–98, 147, 171

Alcohol, 56; and Avoiding the Demon, 50–51; and respondent's parents, 25, 27, 42, 51, 71, 79

Appropriation, process of, 221–225, 227, 229, 232ff, 236–237, 240; defined, 221

Assertiveness, 85, 104, 111, 123

Asymmetry: of triangulation, 106, 113–114, 145. *See also* Triangling moves

Attachment, 22–23

Autonomy, 115, 117, 119–120, 139, 155, 179, 183–184, 191, 194; of females, 32, 35, 44, 47, 132–133; lack of, 138, 187; in marital connection, 166, 177, 213

Bernard, Jessie, 237, 247, 253

Bonding, 5–6, 115–118, 121, 139, 153, 194, 197, 229; and wives, 110, 112–113, 117, 143

Bott, Elizabeth, 55, 88, 253

Boundary confusion, 117, 120

Bowen, Murray, 2–4, 7, 130, 133–134, 155, 253

Career, 70–77; as central third-corner, 40–42, 199–201, 203–204, 213–214, 230

Challenge, process of, 93, 104, 116, 146, 228–229, 233–237, 240; defined, 228

Child care, 116, 120

Child rearing: as central purpose of marriage, 65–70, 81, 140–141, 148, 150, 152–153, 191, 202

Children, 69–70, 148, 202; as companions for lonely wives, 68, 112, 117, 126–127; desire for having, 65, 140, 144; as third-corners, 35, 113, 129, 177, 185, 190, 205, 213

Chodorow, Nancy, 4–5, 7, 30, 32, 48, 105, 116–117, 120–121, 128, 139, 142, 155, 229, 253

Communication, 52, 142, 176, 178, 181, 198, 203, 223, 231–232

Conflict, 17, 32, 97, 134, 143, 147–148; arising from partner's third-corner, 35ff, 44–45, 96, 115; avoidance of, 25, 52–53, 72; in courtship, 44, 81, 96, 124; images of parents', 16, 25, 52, 71–72; lack of, between parents, 24, 27, 122; willingness to engage in, 25, 53, 122. *See also* Paradigm conflict

Connection (marital), 7, 98–99, 135, 169, 192, 195, 197–198, 248; balanced, 7, 159–167, 199, 210, 216–217; couple-centered, 7, 169–181, 185, 210, 216; family-centered, 7, 183–199, 202, 205, 210, 216–217;

256 • *Three Corners*

Connection (marital), *(continued)*
loose, 7, 199–211,, 215–217; as
undone, 213–217
Courtship, 11, 20, 34, 79, 86, 96,
123, 191; and conflict avoidance,
25, 124; and marriage agendas, 51,
54, 61–62
Cuber, John, 217, 224–225, 237,
245–246, 253

Decision making, 26–35, 37
Dependency, 111, 133, 144, 166, 210,
216
Dependency-distancing, 7, 106–131,
135–136, 144, 169, 172, 180, 187,
213–214, 217; defined, 111
Dinnerstein, Dorothy, 4–5, 7, 30–31,
106, 229, 239, 241, 253
Distancing, 111, 113, 116–118, 127,
147, 163, 166, 214, 231
Divorce: of respondent, 20, 52, 57,
117, 119, 243, 247, 249; respondent's attitude about, 20, 22, 25,
51, 59, 148, 171; of respondent's
parents, 19, 22, 42, 51, 77–78, 80,
114, 171, 174
Dysfunction, personal, 133–134; as
depression, 114, 131; as nervous
symptoms, 126–127, 134, 154

Extramarital relationships, 36, 104,
250; fantasies of, 12–13, 132; of
parents, 51, 59–60; of respondent's
partner, 104, 118

Familiar paradigm. *See* Marital paradigms
Family-centeredness, 184, 187; as a
duty, 187–191. *See also* Connection
(marital)
Family, extended, 55–58, 70–73, 81,
146
Family life-cycle, 67–68, 208, 213,
217
Fathers, 124, 126; accessibility to
respondent as a child, 22, 40–41,
66, 73–74, 96, 120–121; as critical
of children, 72, 142; as model of
third-corner independence, 30, 32,
38ff; and seductiveness in daughters, 32, 45. *See also* Marital
paradigms

Females, 33–34; and bonding, 115,
139, 143, 229; fusion with partnership-corner, 103, 116; gender
development of, 4–5, 31, 38, 42,
105, 116–117; and independent
third-corners, 42ff. *See also* Wives
Feminism, 7, 237, 239–241
First-corner, 3, 104; issues in, 17–21.
See also Inner-corner; Inner self
Foreclosure process, 225–228, 235–
237, 240; defined, 225
Friends, 3–4, 35, 131, 146, 152, 162,
239–240
Fusion, 98, 111, 120, 129, 139, 155,
236; with children, 127, 129, 154,
184, 187, 190, 216; defined, 116;
with partnership-corner, 103, 132–
133; of wife with husband, 117–
120, 127, 144, 187, 236

Gender, 5, 42, 116, 189; and marital
exchange, 229–233; and person-
ality, 5–6, 30–31. *See also* Females;
Males
Goodman, Marvin, 50, 87, 253
Growth, in marriage, 1–2. *See also*
Appropriation, process of

Homemaking, 113, 131, 139, 144–
145, 185, 204, 222, 226, 240,
244–245
Housework, 104, 166
Husbands: as accessible to family,
184, 192, 194, 226, 233; as career-
oriented, 75, 113, 145, 149, 173,
187, 197, 201ff, 210–211, 215,
222, 232, 234; and distancing,
115–118; as dominant decision-
makers, 27, 31, 125, 134, 137,
163, 196, 225, 231, 234–235; encouragement of wives' third-corners,
162, 185, 192–193, 201, 203,
208–210, 216, 221–222, 232–233;
as leaders and definers of wives,
33–34, 118, 125, 206–207, 234;
and rules governing third-corners,
93, 110, 132, 225; and separative
triangling moves, 109–110, 114–
115, 117, 126, 129, 143, 150, 187;
third-corner independence of, 38ff,
68, 98, 103–104, 106, 111–113,
135, 143, 154, 193–194, 209,

229–230; willingness to share power, 30, 134, 163, 223–224. *See also* Males

Independence, 5, 191; female, 39, 44, 93, 117, 119–120, 134–135, 200, 227, 240; male, from females, 30–32, 38–39, 93, 96, 105–106; and power, 36, 45; third-corner, 32, 36ff, 44–48, 81, 193–195, 200. *See also* Triangulation
Individuation, 6, 115–117, 119, 121, 127, 129, 138, 142–143, 163, 179, 229
Initiative, 45, 115, 118, 123–124, 132, 135, 177, 184, 236
Inner-corner, 3, 6, 26, 86, 98, 135, 153–155, 164, 166, 190, 206, 210, 213, 215, 234; awareness of, 176, 197, 234–236, 239–240; clutter in, 87, 163, 197–198, 227–228, 231, 240, 247; complexity of, 45, 162–164, 195; conflicts in, 195ff; connection with partnership-corner, 180, 185, 191, 195ff, 199, 206, 210, 216–217, 223; defined, 3, 179; and need for third-corner outlets, 45, 163–164, 179, 194–195, 214, 216, 226–229, 234, 236; reshaping of, 165, 195, 203, 221–223, 233, 239; as storehouse of marital imagery, 86–87, 181. *See also* First-corner; Inner self; Self
Inner self, 3, 5, 131–132, 134, 155, 162, 177, 184, 191, 195, 214; defined, 3; in romantic fusion, 101–102, 129. *See also* First-corner; Self

Jealousy, 36, 40, 110–111, 126, 132–133, 196, 201, 215, 226

Kinship network. *See* Family, extended

Leisure. *See* Recreation
Love, 79–81, 117, 120, 124, 175, 177, 203, 224

Males: and approaches to domestic power, 30–31; as definers of couple, 103, 240; gender development of, 5, 30–31, 38, 105–106, 116; and independent third-corners, 39ff,

103, 229; and individuation, 5, 105–106, 115–116, 139, 143, 150. *See also* Husbands
Marital comfort, 139, 143–144, 147, 197; as joint triangulation, 150, 152; and separateness, 139, 144
Marital consensus, 147–152
Marital development, 7, 13, 155, 248–250; absence of, 91, 136–138, 146, 150, 152–153, 184, 245, 248; factors in, 149. *See also* Marital history
Marital disturbances, 111–115, 133, 144, 147–149, 208; origin of, 105–107
Marital dynamics, 3–4, 7, 87, 107, 111, 113, 132, 249, 251; defined, 91–92; and triangulation, 36, 150, 153, 175; varieties of, 98–99
Marital history, 146, 149, 240, 249–250; absence of, 91, 143, 152, 154–155, 245, 248; as joint third-corner history, 150
Marital paradigms, 48–49, 82, 86–87, 97, 112, 151, 169, 174, 191, 217; and abandonment, 22–23; and affection, 23–24; and conflict, 24–25, 52–53, 111, 113–114, 151; defined, 13–17; and dependency of wife, 39, 44–45; embracing the, 27, 55, 59, 83, 139; falling into the, 15–17, 21, 23, 29, 35, 41, 43, 54, 73–74, 83, 96–97, 110, 115, 135; and female independence, 44–45, 200, 204, 213, 228; as negative, 33, 77–78, 80, 197–198; and power and decision making, 26–35, 201; rejecting the, 15, 22, 25–26, 50, 59, 66, 213; and religion, 59, 159, 188; and shifts of emphasis, 98; and third-corner management, 37–38, 44; transforming the, 15, 159, 172, 223; and triangulation, 106–107, 114–115, 132, 154, 230
Marital socialization, 11–13
Marital statics, 6, 9–88, 91, 249
Marks, Stephen, 7, 218, 254
Marriage: as a dance, 117, 199; as metaphoric concept, 86
Marriage agendas, 6, 49–86; Avoiding the Demon, 50–55, 59, 62, 77, 148; For the Children, 65–70, 86,

258 • *Three Corners*

Marriage agendas *(continued)*
98, 140, 148, 150–155; defined,
49; Economic Calling, 61–65, 71,
86, 138, 197; Hedged Bet, 76–82,
86, 191, 193, 204, 206; Open, 82–
86, 150–151, 153, 159; Religious
Calling, 58–61, 86, 94, 150, 187–
188; Safe Haven, 70–76, 86, 138,
174, 200, 205; Safe Return Home,
55–58, 60, 70, 86, 138, 140, 144
Marriage Encounter, 61, 133, 135–
136, 147, 175, 198; ideology of,
135, 178–179; and marital dynamics, 178–181
Masculinity, 30, 124, 127, 142, 223,
227, 237; as economic prowess,
138, 234; as rejection of femininity
and female control, 30–31, 33, 38
Maslow, Abraham, 50, 87, 254
Mothers, 113, 120–121; attachment
to daughters, 120, 139–140; craving for nurturance, 38–39; criticism
of daughters, 20–21, 32–33, 122;
daughters' fusion with, 116, 120–
121, 124, 126, 136, 138, 140;
dependence on their husbands,
29–30, 95, 172; as financially
dependent, 78, 204; as housewives,
110; as modeling service to a husband, 31, 44, 74–75; as modeling
third-corner independence, 44,
172–174; and sons' differentiation,
116, 142; as third-corners of married daughters, 42–43, 139, 143

Needs, 3, 20, 49, 92, 97, 104, 117,
119, 123, 226–227, 231, 234–236,
240; deficiency, 50, 54, 58, 62, 82;
growth, 50, 54

Paradigm. *See* Marital paradigms
Paradigm complementation, 138; defined, 92
Paradigm conflict, 94, 114–115, 145,
147, 170, 201; defined, 92; in
patriarchy, 93
Paradigm consensus, 144, 149; defined, 92
Paradigm source, 14; change in,
171–173
Parents: as models for marriage, 11,
13, 15, 27, 57, 59, 77, 82, 95,
110, 170. *See also* Fathers; Mothers

Partnership-corner, 6, 86, 98, 118,
154–155, 162–163, 195ff, 201,
203, 215, 221, 227; in dependency-
distancing, 118; expansion of, 164–
165, 176, 195, 206, 209, 221–
223, 233, 236; imagery of affection
in, 23–24; imagery of belonging in,
22–23; imagery of conflict in, 24–
26; imagery of power and decision
making, 26–35; movement toward,
175, 191; in romantic fusion, 101.
See also Second-corner
Passivity, 81–97
Patriarchy, 31, 43–44, 93, 233–236,
239–241; and dominance of fathers,
27; and economic independence, 37;
female accessibility in, 38, 210–211;
female adequacy in, 21, 233–235;
and female third-corners, 42–43,
210–211, 222, 234–236; and paradigm conflicts, 93. *See also* Females;
Males
Pearce, Joseph, 1–2, 7, 254
Power, 45, 152, 154, 175, 197, 223,
229; as central second-corner issue,
26–35; of husband, 103, 124, 138,
196; and third-corner independence,
36–37, 45
Principle of less interest, 36, 175
Providers, husbands as, 61–63, 73,
144–145, 223

Recreation, 40, 75, 161, 165, 201,
203, 250; as third-corner, 4, 35,
106, 150, 177, 186–187, 205, 240
Religion, 35, 58–61, 67, 81, 136,
160, 175, 178, 191, 243; as independent third-corner, 146–149,
206; as joint third-corner, 188, 190
Resources: from jobs, 36–37; from
third-corners, 45
Romantic fusion, 7, 101–107, 111,
129; defined, 101
Rubin, Lillian, 56, 88, 254

Second-corner, 3, 155, 230–234; defined, 3; issues in, 21–35. *See also*
Partnership-corner
Self, the, 3, 86, 116, 120, 124, 240;
as defective, 34, 80–81, 112, 180;
as differentiated, 117, 119–120,
123; -esteem, 131, 145; as a triangle, 3–4, 14, 98–99. *See also*
Inner-corner; Inner self

Separateness, marital, 7, 129–155, 166, 170–171, 192, 199–200, 203, 206, 213–214, 217, 247; as comfortable arrangement, 139, 143, 169, 172, 180; defined, 130–131; and third-corner symmetry, 136, 144, 169, 172, 180

Sex, 198; in courtship, 59, 79; in marriage, 149, 151, 175, 203, 215, 250

Social class, 71–73, 210, 246–247, 250

Stability, marital, 143–144, 153–154; as balance between comfort and disturbance, 147–150

Symmetry: of spouses' third-corners, 53, 131–132, 143–144, 150, 202, 210, 214, 216; as stabilizing factor in marriage, 38, 53, 112, 131–132, 144, 146–147, 155, 216; of triangles, 102, 110, 112–114, 129–130, 210–211, 214–215

Third-corner, 4, 6, 86, 98, 143, 161, 175, 226–227, 233, 240; defined, 4, 35; issues concerning, 35–48; lovers as, 36, 104; in marital connection, 178, 186, 194–195, 197, 199, 207–208; as refuge, 79; in romantic fusion, 101. See also Independence; Individuation

Triangles: balance within, 191, 194–195, 210–211, 213, 215–216, 232; in dependency-distancing, 111; in marital connection, 166, 177, 185–186, 199, 208, 210–211, 213–214, 216, 221, 223–224; in patriarchy, 234–235, 239; in romantic fusion, 101; in separateness, 130–131; theory of, 2–4

Triangling moves, 4, 106–107, 143, 211; husbands and, 106, 109, 154; separative, 106, 111–112, 114–116; wives and, 132–133, 144, 146. See also Separateness, marital; Third-corner; Triangulation

Triangulation, 4, 113; defined, 4; of husbands, 106, 110, 115; and marital comfort, 147; as mover and shaker of marital dynamics, 4, 36, 132, 149–150; of wives, 106, 110. See also Triangling moves

Triangulation, joint, 36, 166; as marital connection, 185; as marital separateness, 150–155, 190

Waller, Willard, 36, 38, 48, 254

Wives: accessibility to husbands, 38, 93; dependence on children for companionship, 68, 129, 143, 149, 208; dependence on husbands, 30, 93, 117, 119, 131, 138, 143, 214, 236; encouragement of husbands' third-corners, 208; as lacking separate identity, 103, 105, 118–120, 214, 234; and pleasing husbands, 31–32, 35, 109, 119, 235–236; responsibility for child care, 38, 166, 208, 210–211, 214–215, 222, 226, 234; as submissive to husbands' authority, 27, 34, 74, 125, 226; and third-corner independence, 43–48, 93, 133, 136, 162, 171–172, 174, 180, 193–194, 200–201, 204–206, 210–211, 223, 227; third-corners of, 42–48, 134, 186, 214, 234; and wanting more attention, 97, 113, 132, 189, 230; and working, 75–76, 127, 137, 151, 159, 169, 185, 201–205, 214–216, 222–223, 225–229, 232–233, 240, 245. See also Females

Work, 113, 120–121; as male third-corner, 106. See also Career

Working class, 192, 197; fathers of respondents, 28; and mother–daughter bond, 139; and Safe Haven, 71–72; and Safe Return Home, 56, 71–73. See also Social class

About the Author

Stephen R. Marks is an associate professor of sociology at the University of Maine, Orono, where he has taught since 1972. He earned his Ph.D. at Boston University, and has published articles in *American Journal of Sociology, American Sociological Review*, and *Journal of Humanistic Psychology*. His ongoing interests center on cultural patterns and their impact on the qualities of the person.